Advance praise for *On the Brink*

"A history that's as illuminating for the policymaker as it is for the informed citizen. If you want to know how close the world came to nuclear war in 2017—and how to avoid it in the future—this is a must-read."

"Van Jackson has written an insightful, detailed, and frightening history of the Korean nuclear crisis. It is like a thriller with the sequel yet to be written. Readers will understand both how deeply dangerous the past few years have been and how many nuclear dangers remain lurking just over the horizon."

"*On the Brink* is a smart, readable explanation of the nuclear crisis of 2017—one that explains how Washington and Pyongyang found themselves on a collision course, and one that offers sage advice about managing the risk of nuclear war in the future."

"*On the Brink* is a timely, serious, and substantive treatment of a perennial national security problem for the United States. Jackson successfully weaves theory, history, and policy into a book that makes every reader smarter on North Korea. Recommended reading not just for experts, but for general audiences."

"With a deep sense of history, Van Jackson has given us a vital record of a near-disaster. Vigorous, wise, and highly informed, *On the Brink* decodes the theatrics and leaves the lessons inescapably clear for future generations."

"Van Jackson provides an excellent scholar-practitioner's guide to the history of US-North Korean misunderstanding and mutual hostility. He provides a clarion call regarding the scope and magnitude of the danger that surrounded the Trump administration's efforts to grapple for the first time with vulnerability to North Korean nuclear capabilities."

Scott Snyder, author of *South Korea at the Crossroads*

"A terrific and terrifying story of bumbling into a nuclear crisis because of unrealistic goals and a failure to understand North Korea. Van Jackson, a fine scholar of Korean affairs, has written a remarkable history that anyone wishing to avoid nuclear war—or make sense of North Korea—should read."

Robert Edwin Kelly, Pusan National University

On the Brink

In 2017 the world watched as President Donald Trump and North Korean leader Kim Jong Un traded personal insults and escalating threats of nuclear war amid unprecedented shows of military force. Former Pentagon insider and Korean security expert, Van Jackson, traces the origins of the first American nuclear crisis in the post-Cold War era, and explains the fragile, highly unpredictable way that it ended. Jackson analyzes the US response to North Korea's increasing nuclear threat in the context of Trump's aggressive rhetoric, prior US policy failures, the geopolitics of East Asia, and North Korean strategy, including the acceleration of its nuclear program under Kim Jong Un. He argues that the Trump administration's policy of "maximum pressure" brought the world much closer to nuclear war than many realize—and charts a course for the prevention of future conflicts.

Dr Van Jackson is Senior Lecturer in International Relations at Victoria University of Wellington, Global Fellow at the Woodrow Wilson International Center for Scholars in Washington, and the Defence & Strategy Fellow at the Centre for Strategic Studies. He served in the Obama administration as a policy adviser and strategist in the Office of the Secretary of Defense, participating in nuclear negotiations with North Korea and formulating deterrence policies with South Korea.

On the Brink

Trump, Kim, and the Threat of Nuclear War

Van Jackson
Victoria University of Wellington

 CAMBRIDGE
UNIVERSITY PRESS

CAMBRIDGE
UNIVERSITY PRESS

University Printing House, Cambridge CB2 8BS, United Kingdom

One Liberty Plaza, 20th Floor, New York, NY 10006, USA

477 Williamstown Road, Port Melbourne, VIC 3207, Australia

314–321, 3rd Floor, Plot 3, Splendor Forum, Jasola District Centre, New Delhi – 110025, India

79 Anson Road, #06–04/06, Singapore 079906

Cambridge University Press is part of the University of Cambridge.

It furthers the University's mission by disseminating knowledge in the pursuit of education, learning, and research at the highest international levels of excellence.

www.cambridge.org
Information on this title: www.cambridge.org/9781108473484
DOI: 10.1017/9781108562225

First published 2019

Printed in the United States of America by Sheridan Books, Inc.

A catalogue record for this publication is available from the British Library.

ISBN 978-1-108-47348-4 Hardback

CONTENTS

ACKNOWLEDGMENTS

My work on Korea started at 17 years old in Monterey, California, when the US Air Force sent me to train as a Korean linguist at the Defense Language Institute. I've continued working on Korea issues one way or another—as an analyst, policy official, pundit, and scholar—ever since. When I entered my language classroom for the first time as a know-nothing teenager (back in the year 2000), the first inter-Korean Summit had just taken place. One of my instructors at the time told me there was no more North Korean nuclear problem. I never imagined that, 18 years later, not only would the nuclear issue still be unresolved; North Korea would be a de facto nuclear weapons state. In some ways, it makes this book feel like something I was always meant to write—the culmination of 18 years working at the intersection of the Korean Peninsula, deterrence, and US foreign policy. It's history, it's policy, it's international relations, and yet on some level it's also deeply personal. This is by no means a memoir, but I've either chronicled or directly participated in many of the events depicted here.

It's common for book-writing to incur lots of debts, and that's very much the case with this one. National security mogul Ryan Evans deserves a lot of credit, as friend, enabler, and network broker. Ryan also played a unique role in making this book happen, by encouraging me to write the *Nuke Your Darlings* series that he published on War on the Rocks. It was a bit strange at first to chronicle every day's writing progress and let thousands of strangers see it, but it kept me accountable to a strict writing regimen, helping me write this manuscript in record time.

Victor Cha has been an informal mentor for as long as I've been writing about Korea, even though on the substance we occasionally disagree. His impact on me has been much greater than vice versa—perhaps the nature of mentoring. But I've been grateful for his career advice at every stage, as well as for the opportunities he's helped connect me with along the way. This research was supported by the Laboratory Program for Korean Studies through the Ministry of Education of the Republic of Korea and Korean Studies Promotion Service of the Academy of Korean Studies (AKS-2016-LAB-2250001). Without Victor, I probably wouldn't have had that research support.

I'm also grateful to my colleagues at the Centre for Strategic Studies and Victoria University of Wellington. Rob Ayson, David Capie, Manjeet Pardesi, and Rob Rabel endured more expletive-laced conversations about Korea than they ever imagined, often from a colleague who showed up in the morning bleary-eyed and unshaven after writing the book long into the night. New Zealand has been an amazing home base for writing this book, and gave me just the right amount of detachment from the churn of Washington to do it.

The historical narrative I present in this book is constructed from openly available sources, but I've made judicious use of dozens of interviews with current and former officials to make sure that narrative is as correct as possible. I owe special thanks to a large number of people, many of whom shared their insights on the condition of anonymity. But among those I can name, Patrick McEachern, Terence Roehrig, Abraham Denmark, Keith Luse, Scott Sagan, Ryan Hass, Zach Hosford, Kevin Kim, Mason Richey, Vipin Narang, Adam Mount, Frank Aum, Christopher Green, Dan Pinkston, Mike Urena, Rob York, Ryan Jacobs, Hans Schattle, Youngwuk Kim, Michael Schiffer, Drew Winner, David Straub, Mira Rapp-Hooper, Steve Denney, David Santoro, Andrew O'Neil, Matt Squeri, Jennifer Hendrixson-White, Jake Stokes, Yoon Young-kwan, and Robert Kelly were all generous to me in some way relating to this book. Some of these great folks read parts of my manuscript, provided critiques, or sent me useful source material. Others offered counsel along the way that helped me shape the manuscript. Some even allowed me to interview them, or introduced me to US officials who became valuable interview subjects.

I must confess I never would have pulled the trigger on this book if my Cambridge editor, Lucy Rhymer, hadn't seen a strategic opportunity for it. Without her active encouragement, I'm not sure I would have polished off that book proposal and put my other research on hold. And while any errors in the book are on me, Lucy was terrific at shaping the manuscript as I wrote it to make it resonate with the broadest possible audience.

The most crucial enabler of this book is, of course, Kristin Chambers. She knew how time-consuming this project would be, and she pushed me to do it when I hesitated at first. She makes everything possible, and that's no exaggeration. Aside from being my daily dialogue partner and the first place I go to test my narratives, she also took on a disproportionate burden to keep our daily routines going. I literally wouldn't have had the windows of time to write this book without her support, and for that I'm extremely grateful. I only hope that the book proves worthy of the investment we've both made to make it happen.

While parts of this book have the advantage of deep historical perspective, the more recent chapters—on the Trump years—represent merely a first cut at history. More time is needed to determine if my interpretations here are correct, and if I've even seized on the right themes. I've been sensitive to what Daniel Nexon calls "analytical normalization" of the highly abnormal Trump presidency, while also avoiding polemical broadsides aimed at Trump. Again, time will tell if I've struck the right note. One thing I can assure the reader of: in this book I have rendered the most forthright, evidence-based, and unjaundiced explanation of the US–North Korea nuclear crisis (and its end) that I can. Whatever its flaws, I hope it serves as a useful touchstone for future desk officers, diplomats, soldiers, and scholars.

MAPS

Map 1 The Korean Peninsula in 2018. Reproduced with permission of Scott LaFoy/
Andrew Facini

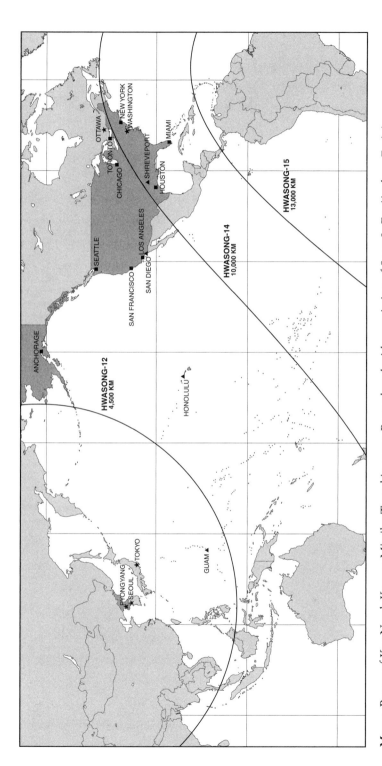

Map 2 Range of Key North Korean Missiles Tested in 2017. Reproduced with permission of Scott LaFoy/Andrew Facini

INTRODUCTION

In 2017, for the first time since the Cold War, a US president found himself explicitly, publicly, and repeatedly threatening war against a nuclear-armed adversary. On August 8, 2017, the *Washington Post* published part of a leaked Defense Intelligence Agency assessment with an alarming conclusion: North Korea could now arm ballistic missiles capable of reaching the United States with nuclear warheads. Later that day, President Donald Trump faced a gaggle of reporters and bellowed, "North Korea best not make any more threats to the United States. They will be met with fire and fury like the world has never seen." North Korea fired back that it was considering a missile strike against Guam, a US territory that was home to a nuclear bomber base, as a "warning signal to the US." Addressing the UN General Assembly a month later, Trump declared he "would totally destroy North Korea" if it attacked the United States or its allies.

In response to Trump's fiery UN speech, North Korean leader Kim Jong Un issued a rare statement that derided Trump as "mentally deranged," vowing he would make Trump "pay dearly for his speech calling for totally destroying the DPRK." North Korea's Foreign Minister subsequently claimed Trump had declared war on North Korea, giving them the right to shoot down the US bomber aircraft that had recently become a frequent presence in the South. Months prior to the crisis, it had already become routine for US officials to ruminate publicly on "military options" for dealing with the North.

Shortly after Trump's UN speech, and amid the escalating war of words, rumors of an impending evacuation operation to remove American civilians from the Korean Peninsula—a classic prelude to war—made front-page national news in South Korea. US Navy surface ships operating within striking range of North Korea were then given "warning orders" to program North Korean targets into their guidance systems and prepare for a strike operation.[1] This was followed by disavowed reports of US nuclear-capable bombers being put on 24-hour alert—something not done since the darkest days of the Cold War. On October 8, Senator Bob Corker, Chairman of the Senate Foreign Relations Committee and a member of the Republican Party, warned that Trump "doesn't realize we could be headed toward World War III with the kind of comments he's making."[2] By that time, as one administration source claimed, "Everyone wants a 'preemptive war' now except [Secretary of Defense] Mattis."[3] North Korea's state media subsequently lamented that war with the United States had become "an established fact ... The remaining question now is: when will the war break out?"[4]

Only six months later though, on June 12, 2018, Trump met with Kim Jong Un in Singapore. It was the culmination of a six-month global charm offensive from Kim Jong Un that included an April 27, 2018 inter-Korean summit. Kim and South Korea's President Moon Jae In came out of that summit (the first meeting of Korean leaders in more than a decade) issuing the "Panmunjom Declaration," a joint statement committing both Koreas to reconciliation and peaceful unification. The Singapore meeting between Trump and Kim had the rhythm of Kim's summit with Moon. Trump and Kim displayed bonhomie, shared a meal, shook hands in front of the camera, and signed a short joint communiqué in which Trump offered unspecified "security guarantees" and North Korea committed to the similarly unspecific "complete denuclearization of the Korean Peninsula," using even vaguer commitment language than in some of its past nuclear agreements with the United States. Nevertheless, Trump lavished praise on Kim Jong Un, and the next day, he tweeted, "There is No Longer a Nuclear Threat from North Korea." Yet nothing about the quantity, quality, or operationality of North Korea's nuclear warheads and missiles had changed. In symbolism, if not in substance, the Trump–Kim summit of June 2018 signaled a radical departure from the confrontation of the year prior, even though the underlying nuclear conflict remained the same. Given the immense stakes involved, the rapid swing from war footing to a mood of détente, despite continuity in North Korea's nuclear arsenal, cries out for an explanation. What happened, and why?

Specifically, why did the Trump administration in 2017 claim to reach such a starkly different conclusion than prior US presidential administrations about the need for military force against the world's newest nuclear state, only to reverse course the following year? What role did Trump and the US policy of imposing "maximum pressure" on North Korea play in either causing or resolving the nuclear crisis that emerged? What motivated Kim Jong Un's diplomatic outreach to South Korea and the United States in 2018? And to what extent is the nuclear standoff with North Korea a harbinger of future crises in what scholars now call the Second Nuclear Age? In short, what are the origins and implications of the first American nuclear crisis in the post-Cold War era? Addressing these questions reveals just how close the world came to nuclear war during the early Trump presidency. It also provides an informed basis for advising how best to avoid that near-tragedy from reappearing, in Korea or elsewhere.

The most obvious answers to these questions about the 2017–18 nuclear standoff—North Korea's hostility or Donald Trump's tough talk—are only part of the story. North Korea has long been a belligerent and politically isolated state, whose colorful threat-making toward the United States and South Korea was as vivid in 2017 as it had been in the 1960s. It was also on a decades-long journey to become a nuclear weapons state capable of threatening the United States. But some of the most significant accelerations in North Korea's nuclear and missile capabilities (miniaturizing nuclear warheads to fit on missiles that could reach US territory in the Pacific) actually predated Trump by several years, and therefore cannot be described as the "cause" of the crisis, important factor though it was. What is more, Korea experts inside and outside government viewed North Korea's behavior as largely predictable; North Korea was, after all, building a nuclear arsenal that it frequently admitted was aimed at rectifying an imbalance of power with the United States and guaranteeing regime survival. It is illogical to single out predictable events as the cause of a crisis, given that the very definition of crisis involves unexpected events and high-stakes decisions.[5]

Similarly, Trump critics and many foreign policy elites in Washington were quick to finger Trump's indiscipline as the cause of crisis in Korea. In this view, Trump's irresponsible Twitter habit and his own incendiary rhetoric toward Kim Jong Un brought on the crisis. But this explanation, while not wrong, does not explain everything. At various points during his presidency, Trump has threatened numerous other countries, from Afghanistan to Iran to Syria, and even Venezuela, including with the possibility of military action, without triggering anything like the crisis on the Korean Peninsula. Trump's words and leadership style proved problematic for US foreign policy, but *how* it created problems and fueled a crisis depended greatly on the surrounding circumstances he inherited.

Even if Trump had never existed, the situation in Korea was growing increasingly dire. And as I argue later in the book, a Hillary Clinton presidency would have found itself sleepwalking into a crisis with North Korea at some point, even if a shorter, less explosive, and more manageable one than that which occurred during Trump's tenure. Any thoughtful portrayal of the origins of the crisis in Korea must account not only for Trump's leadership style on the issue or North Korea's strategic trajectory, but also the conditions that made some kind of confrontation with North Korea plausible even under a Clinton presidency.

The way the crisis ended similarly eludes the most obvious explanation. The Trump administration was quick to take credit for Kim Jong Un's decision to pursue crisis-ending diplomacy with the outside world in 2018, claiming it was due to its policy of imposing maximum pressure on the North. In this view, military confrontation, tough talk, and tougher economic sanctions brought Kim to heel. As Trump lawyer Rudy Giuliani boasted, Kim Jong Un "got back on his hands and knees and begged" to meet Trump.[6] But that narrative ignores the role maximum pressure played in causing the crisis of 2017 in the first place, and that in the past North Korea had almost always responded to pressure with pressure in kind. It was why US threats over the years repeatedly begat counter-threats, missile launches, and nuclear tests. Capitulation to threats or bullying was simply antithetical to North Korean strategic culture. What is more, North Korea weathered threats of war and economic strangulation for decades as it pursued the bomb. The idea that, in 2018, merely intensifying these same elements of pressure would suddenly induce North Korea to abandon its own strategy under duress defies both common sense and a long historical record that suggests the contrary.

Origins of a Nuclear Crisis

This book shows how the nuclear crisis that arose in 2017 was the result of several forces converging in time: a gradual narrowing and hardening of US policy toward North Korea; Kim Jong Un's resolve to secure a viable nuclear deterrent against the United States no matter the cost; and a US president with a penchant for personalized insults and extemporaneous threat-making. These overlapping forces created multiple realistic pathways to the unthinkable: nuclear war with North Korea. There would have been no foreseeable off-ramp from conflict if not for a different set of fortunate convergences: North Korea demonstrating the technical ability to fire missiles able to reach anywhere in the United States in late 2017; Kim Jong Un's willingness to prioritize economic development after securing a minimally viable nuclear deterrent; South Korea's hosting of the Winter Olympics in March 2018; the snap election of a dovish progressive president in South Korea as the crisis brewed; and Trump's fondness for the pomp and circumstance of meetings with foreign heads of state, combined with his unique amenability to requests from South Korea and China for restraint and diplomacy.

North Korea's Path

The nuclear crisis Trump faced during his first year in office was not solely a function of US decision-making past and present; it was the convergence of that decision-making lineage with North Korea's own. For nearly all of its history, North Korea has treated the United States as a threat to its existence, in propaganda and in practice. In the North Korean version of history, it was not the North, but rather the United States and South Korea that launched an invasion in June 1950. It is the United States that has always stood in the way of unifying the Peninsula under the communist North. And for more than 60 years, it was the United States that rendered South Koreans into mere puppets while threatening to invade the North at any moment. By any reasonable measure, North Korea has generally hated and feared the United States.

North Korea's popular antipathy toward the United States has some basis in fact, as we shall see, but was nevertheless manufactured in Pyongyang. North Korea's ruling family—starting with its founder,

Kim Il Sung (1948–94), his son, Kim Jong Il (1994–2011), and his grandson, Kim Jong Un (2011–present)—deliberately seared a history of victimization at the hands of American power into the fiber of North Korea's being. Three generations of the family-run Kim regime have benefited from an external enemy as a basis for unity and a rationale for decades of large-scale human misery within its borders. Something had to bind a people who, in the 1990s, suffered a famine so severe that it killed between 800,000 and 1.5 million people.[7] Orwellian propaganda vilifying the United States has partly served that unifying purpose, in conjunction with a number of other tools of political and social control.

When Kim Jong Il, who had formally ruled North Korea since 1994, died in 2011, dynastic succession passed to his youngest son, Kim Jong Un.[8] The eldest, Kim Jong Nam, was seen as possibly too keen on opening North Korea to the outside world and embarrassed the family when he was caught at Narita International Airport in Tokyo in 2001, traveling on a fake passport in hopes of visiting Tokyo Disneyland. The middle son, Kim Jong Chol, was seen as effeminate and unlikely to have the wherewithal to rule. He was also rumored to be a fan of the musician Eric Clapton (not that there is anything wrong with that). In contrast with his father and grand-father, Kim Jong Un grew up surrounded by luxury and endowed with privilege. The universe bent for him. Though Jong Un was young, his precise age is unknown (thought to be 33 at the time of the nuclear crisis). He was educated in Switzerland, and was a bright enough but unremarkable student. In governing style and public persona, Kim Jong Un has chosen to emulate his grandfather, a gregarious politico who exercised centralized rule, rather than his father, who was insu-lar, insecure, and relied on state institutions to stay in power. After coming to power in 2011, he has frequently given public speeches, and has been portrayed in state media as being comfortable out and about among common folk. He and his wife, Ri Sol Ju, go out of their way to try and create a Kennedy-esque image of youth, stylishness, and vigor.

Many expected Kim Jong Un's reign would be short-lived because he was an inexperienced millennial and the youngest of his father's children. Yet Kim Jong Un set about immediately killing and purging large numbers of senior North Korean officials (more than 300 as of 2017[9]) and replacing them with loyalists and trusted family members. From the outside he appeared to be proactively silencing any whiff of internal opposition to his rule.

But girding himself against internal dissent was only one necessary step in seeking regime security. His country was also geopolitically isolated. China, with whom it shares a large, porous border, was technically its only ally, yet the regime's relationship with China was marked by mutual antipathy. North Korea had long been famously defiant of Chinese preferences, and in turn it could not count on China for its security. Kim Jong Un refused to even meet with China's Xi Jinping until 2018, when he turned to global diplomacy as a way to dampen the nuclear crisis. Because Kim could not rely on outside powers for his security, he sought a viable nuclear deterrent to guard against external threats. The decision to pursue a reliable nuclear strike capability was one that built on what Kim Jong Un inherited from his father and grandfather: a regime with a functional nuclear device and a nuclear industry with two successful nuclear tests. But Kim not only continued the nuclear pursuit of his father and grandfather; he did it with a gusto all his own, conducting four nuclear tests and 86 missile tests in only six years. His Swiss education initially gave some hope that he would be a reformer who would open the North to the world, but any prospect of opening took a backseat to nuclear survival in the initial years of his rule. Kim's pace of testing nuclear and missile devices made good on the nation's long-stated intention to achieve a secure deterrent, which it believed was the only means of rectifying a dangerous imbalance of power with the United States. Under Kim Jong Un, as with his forebears, North Korea sought nothing short of guaranteeing a nuclear attack against regional military bases and American cities if the United States invaded or sought regime change.

In order to secure that ability, North Korea needed to diversify the types of missiles it developed, disperse the locations from which missiles could fire, increase its overall missile inventory, and miniaturize nuclear warheads so they could be fitted on missile delivery systems. Kim Jong Un made significant advancements on all these fronts through accelerated testing, and by making military-technical nuclear progress the regime's top priority in 2013, alongside economic development (these twin goals referred to as the "*byungjin* line").

Because of its nuclear and missile progress, North Korea made the greatest strides toward regime security during Kim Jong Un's early years in power. From the US perspective, however, it was in those early

Kim years that it saw North Korea evolve from a local security threat, limited largely to the Korean Peninsula and its surrounds, to a long-range threat with the potential to attack strategic US positions in the region, and even the US homeland itself. Kim's accelerated pursuit of nuclear weapons vexed US policymakers and North Korea's neighbors. The American public gradually became more alarmed as the traditional image of North Korea—a Cold War outpost, with aging and poorly maintained Soviet-era conventional military equipment, run by an eccentric dictator—gave way to an image of a global twenty-first-century threat, with an advanced offensive cyber capability, a large stock of chemical weapons, and a survivable nuclear-armed missile arsenal.

Kim Jong Un's commitment to nuclear weapons made him no less responsible for the 2017 nuclear crisis than Trump. Yet the confrontational decisions of Kim and Trump were extensions of what each inherited. Kim's strategy built on, rather than jettisoned, the legacy of his father and grandfather. That strategy, aimed at girding himself against internal challengers, demonstrating a viable nuclear deterrent, improving people's standard of living, and elevating North Korea's international standing, gave fuel to the nuclear crisis, but also played a unique, decisive role in bringing the crisis to an end. Once North Korea demonstrated the technical ability for one of its missiles to reach anywhere in the United States (which it did with the November 28, 2017 test of the Hwasong-15 intercontinental ballistic missile), Kim sought to mute Washington's talk of giving him a "bloody nose" by pursuing an ambitious agenda of international diplomacy, aimed at sanctions relief and the normalization of North Korea as a de facto nuclear state. In essence, the crisis came to a close only because Kim had gotten far enough along the nuclear path to feel secure against external bombing or invasion.

America's Path

The United States was already drifting toward an acute military confrontation with the North when Trump ascended to the presidency. Under President Obama, the United States persisted with the policy goal it maintained since the end of the Cold War: denuclearization through the complete, verifiable, and irreversible dismantlement (CVID) of

North Korea's weapons and nuclear program. It also continued with war planning and a military posture toward Pyongyang that was specifically configured to achieve regime change and Korean unification in the event of a conflict. But those aims were relics of the Cold War, when North Korea did not have nuclear weapons capable of striking the United States and its allies. The North's unprecedented leaps in nuclear capability, starting in 2012, were rendering those goals obsolete, and deceptively dangerous, unless the United States was willing to entertain a nuclear war. In prior decades, North Korea not only lacked nuclear weapons and reliable missile systems to deliver them; many thought it to be on the verge of collapse and focused primarily on regime survival. Under these conditions, US coercive diplomacy may have been of questionable value, but it was not particularly risky.

The great danger became that America's historically preferred approach to North Korea (coercive diplomacy) was laden with heightened risks against a newly emboldened nuclear weapons state run by a young and inexperienced dictator. Military deployments, exercises, and veiled rhetorical threats could be calamitous if North Korea interpreted them the wrong way. Despite the shift in strategic circumstances, North Korea policy and planning under Obama proved remarkably consistent with all of his post-Cold War predecessors: combining deterrence, pressure, and intermittent diplomacy in pursuit of the maximalist objective of CVID, even though that objective grew further out of reach with time.

As it became evident that Kim Jong Un was intent on pursuing a nuclear strike capability no matter the price, Obama's policy rigidified, but never quite took on a sense of visible urgency. Consequently, all manner of pressure on North Korea was at its historical peak when Trump came to office, and military solutions were being publicly ruminated on for the first time in years. Trump officials believed that the Obama approach had failed to contain the North Korea threat, and saw a departure from it as essential, but America's path was already largely fixed on what Trump's team would eventually dub "maximum pressure," which primarily differed from Obama's North Korea policy only in tone. In addition, Trump gave foreign policy hawks much greater prominence in his administration—especially at the National Security Council (NSC)—and oversaw the interagency and external marginalization of the State Department, reducing the role for diplomatic options. As I discuss later in the book, Trump himself blunted State Department diplomacy with North Korea on multiple occasions in 2017. As a result, the Trump administration disproportionately emphasized the one part of US foreign policy (the military and rhetorical threats) that most directly drove North Korean paranoia, insecurity, and justification for both its nuclear weapons and its constant war footing. Trump's national security team was ideologically predisposed to a hawkish approach; the conditions they inherited from Obama played to their bias. Adding Trump's extreme rhetoric to this volatile mix simply accelerated the collision of America's path with that of Kim Jong Un.

South Korea's Shift

Although the nuclear crisis of 2017 was primarily between the United States and North Korea, there is no way to understand it without an appreciation for South Korea's important role in US–North Korea relations. South Korea's perspective on North Korea was embedded in its domestic politics. For decades, South Korean progressives saw the North as a wayward sibling, advocating policies favoring diplomacy, reconciliation, and economic inducements. South Korean conservatives, by contrast, have long viewed North Korea as an existential and political threat, advocating militaristic solutions of deterrence, containment, and even regime change. For the decade prior to the nuclear crisis of 2017, conservatives ran the South Korean government, pursuing an increasingly hard-line policy toward the North that leaned heavily on military threats and its alliance with the United States.

South Korea's conservative approach in these years decisively impacted US policy. The ability of the United States to ponder alternative approaches to North Korea was constrained by the imperatives of keeping allies reassured of US commitments. In the years before the crisis, South Korean governments under Presidents Lee Myung-bak (2007–13) and Park Geun-hye (2013–17) respectively were always in the background, encouraging the United States to seek nothing short of comprehensive denuclearization, in tandem with the isolation of the North. Early in the 2017 crisis, however, South Korea underwent a sudden and dramatic shift in government that removed the conservatives from power and

brought to the presidency Moon Jae In, a progressive who promised a reconciliatory approach to North Korea.

Before President Moon came to office, South Koreans popular-
ized a term that described their marginal role through much of the
nuclear crisis: "Korea passing." It connoted that big decisions affecting
them were being made over their collective heads, without due consideration to their interests. As Trump blustered toward crisis and settled
on a maximum pressure approach, South Korea was an afterthought.
Even after Moon became president in May 2017, the South Koreans
remained on the periphery of the looming question of whether war
would occur. But everything seemed to change after Kim Jong
Un's January 1, 2018 New Year's speech inviting reconciliation with
the South, which became President Moon's moment to reassert the
South Korean role, brokering diplomacy and shifting the narrative
away from notions of preventive war and toward peace. Whatever the
long-term consequences of Moon's diplomatic gambit, it coincided with
Kim Jong Un's strategy to bring an end to the imminent threat of nuclear
war the year prior.

Why the Crisis Matters

This book has multiple purposes. First, in the most straightforward sense, it provides an informed perspective on the origins and
end of a defining nuclear crisis: how Washington and Pyongyang
ended up on a nuclear collision course, and the felicitous, idiosyn-
cratic way that all sides avoided catastrophe. It explains how the
United States ended up in a situation where, for the first time since
the end of the Cold War, inadvertent nuclear war became plausible,
and American anxieties about nuclear war reached a fever pitch
not experienced in decades. The history presented here reinforces
a hard-learned lesson from Cold War studies of coercion that
contemporary nuclear scholars and practitioners too often ignore:
coercion is difficult and risky, and nuclear coercion even more so.
Believing otherwise encourages dangerously irresponsible policies.
Processes of communicating threats to adversaries—the "diplomacy
of violence," to borrow from Thomas Schelling—involve orchestrat-
ing complex military and diplomatic organizations.[10] Orders are
frequently implemented in ways other than how leaders intend.
The receiver of a threatening message may interpret it in a manner

other than what the sender intended. The sender of a threatening message, in turn, can misunderstand what the receiver of the message will actually respond to, or how they might respond. And the precise timing (or context) of the issuance of a threat can cause an adversary to either jump to radical conclusions, ignore it altogether, or fail to recognize the threatening communication for what it is. In short, as I show throughout this book, opportunities for bad judgment and catastrophic misperception are as common today as when earlier generations of scholars first warned of their prevalence in world politics.

Second, the book illustrates how leadership in foreign policy amplifies, and gets constrained by, ongoing historical processes. Important as Trump and Kim Jong Un were to the telling of this story, remembering these events as nothing more than something *they* caused and resolved ignores how the legacies they inherited from their predecessors defined what was possible in the circumstances each faced, as well as the crucial role that other external factors played in forestalling nuclear war. Kim, Moon, and Trump mattered at crucial moments but understanding how and to what extent they made a difference requires situating them in time.

Accumulated history conditioned the threat perceptions of US and Korean officials. History also exercised a kind of "lock-in" effect on the goals of both sides, making it harder to compromise established policy positions as events ensued. Kim was exercising a more robust version of what his father and grandfather had pursued. For the United States, recasting what it saw as US interests in Korea felt impossible to those involved in the decisions. And history narrowed the choice of strategies available to either side. For Trump, a departure from Obama's risk-averse North Korea strategy fed his troubled, risk-prone North Korea strategy.

The way the crisis ended—indeed that the crisis ended at all without war—followed a similar dynamic. Everything that helped resolve the crisis in 2018 (Kim's charm offensive, Trump's attitudinal pivot from confrontation to diplomacy, and Moon's ceaseless efforts to establish better relations with the North) looked superficially like the decisions of bold leaders taking history in their hands. But their initiatives were only unlocked because North Korea attained its goal of demonstrating a viable nuclear deterrent at the end of 2017. Without North Korea realizing the first principle of its security strategy when it did, and without South Korea just so happening to host the Winter Olympics immediately after North Korea's nuclear milestone, Trump would have had little choice but to succumb to the arguments of preventive war advocates; Moon's outreach would have continued to go nowhere, as it had for most of the crisis; and Kim's crisis-blunting charm offensive never would have happened when it did.

Finally, my rendition of events here has real-world implications for practitioners of foreign policy. In the final analysis, maximum pressure played a central role in bringing about the nuclear crisis and, at best, a background role in resolving it. If policymakers come to believe that maximum pressure was a virtue rather than a gratuitous risk, future crises will be inevitable, on the Korean Peninsula and elsewhere. Maximum pressure against small nuclear-armed states engenders a distinct set of dangers about which policymakers should be fully witting before entertaining them.

In making the case for preventive war against North Korea, Senator Lindsay Graham explained in December 2017 that "North Korea is the ultimate outlier in world order ... I don't know how to put North Korea into a historical context."[11] He believed the extreme option of a preventive war against North Korea was justified by what he saw as the extreme, historically unprecedented nature of the threat it posed to America. This book aims do precisely what Graham could not: put North Korea and decisions about it in a comprehensible historical context. It may be the world's best chance at avoiding nuclear war.

1 THE INHERITANCE OF DONALD TRUMP AND KIM JONG UN IN KOREA

The initial division of the Korean Peninsula indirectly resulted from the breakdown of the Soviet-British-US tripartite "alliance" in World War II. In discussions among Franklin Roosevelt, Winston Churchill, and Joseph Stalin prior to the end of the war, one of the few points of consensus was their view of Korea. The three great powers issued the Cairo Declaration in 1943, stating that "mindful of the enslavement of the people of Korea [under Japanese colonial rule since 1905], [we] are determined that in due course Korea shall become free and independent."[1] It acknowledged the Korean people's will to self-determination, but it also implied that Korea should gain independence only when the great powers deemed it ready. Korean civilization was thousands of years old, but the Western perception at the time was that Korea had often been a supplicant to either China or Japan. In the twentieth century, collective Korean opposition to Japanese occupation was a unifying and emotive force. Japanese imperialism before and during World War II made a fiery imprint on contemporary Korean nationalism.

By the end of World War II, the Soviet Union and the United States were emerging as rivals. Despite having found common cause against Nazi Germany in wartime, US differences with the Soviets, and in particular with its totalitarian leader, Joseph Stalin, were too great to sustain their cooperative relationship after victory. In the closing months of the war in the Pacific, when the Soviet Union finally agreed to join the fight against Japan, its forces began moving into Manchuria and the northernmost part of the Korean Peninsula.

The United States saw a potential threat to post-war Japan and its interests in the Pacific if the Soviet Union took hold of the Korean Peninsula, yet it appeared the Soviets could not be stopped from occupation. So rather than abandon Korea or fight a new war to preserve it as a geographic buffer, two mid-ranking US military officers pulled out a map of the Korean Peninsula and drew an arbitrary line at the rough midpoint of the Peninsula, which the United States ultimately proposed to the Soviets as a way to create distinct zones of responsibility for temporarily administering Korea.[2]

In the years following the end of World War II in 1945 and before the Korean War in 1950, it appeared that communism was on the march in Asia. Communist movements had sprung up across Southeast Asia, and the Chinese communists under Mao Zedong overran the mainland in its civil war for control of modern China, forcing Chiang Kai Shek's nationalist forces to regroup in Taiwan. In the communist-held northern part of Korea, the Soviet Union installed Kim Il Sung—a young Korean known for waging guerilla warfare against the Japanese in Manchuria during the war—and all but withdrew Soviet forces. Facing what appeared to be a communist wave, the United States backed the anti-communist, authoritarian, and Western-educated Syngman Rhee to lead the South, maintaining only a token military presence prior to the outbreak of the Korean War. The leaders of both Koreas, Kim and Rhee, were each hell-bent on unification of the Peninsula. In June 1950, Kim would get his chance.

The Outbreak of the Korean War—and Chinese Intervention

Kim Il Sung implored Stalin to back him in a bid to retake the Korean Peninsula on several occasions prior to June 1950. Kim tried to convince Stalin he could invade and occupy the whole of South Korea before the Americans could mobilize a response.[3] The Americans, Kim thought, would see North Korean occupation as a foregone conclusion and be dissuaded from launching a counter-invasion. Stalin rebuffed Kim's requests initially, but changed his mind in 1950, as long as Kim first won China's buy-in for an invasion,[4] which Kim secured that May. Stalin likely felt more comfortable with Kim's proposition after the Soviet Union successfully tested a nuclear device the year prior. He may also have been convinced that America would not intervene in a Korean Peninsula war because of a recent public statement by US Secretary of State Dean Acheson. On January 12, 1950, Acheson gave remarks at the National Press Club in Washington about the Soviet threat and US strategy in the Pacific, defining a US containment "defense perimeter" that arced from the Aleutian Islands down to Japan in Northeast Asia and through the Philippines in Southeast Asia. The perimeter explicitly left out the Korean Peninsula and Taiwan, but Acheson had not necessarily intended to signal that the defense perimeter somehow made Korea "available" for communist encroachment.[5] US policy toward Asia at the time was filtered through the American grand strategy of containment. Policymakers saw the potential spread of Soviet communism as a threat and sought to oppose it wherever it emerged: a strategy that eventually necessitated a series of US alliances across Asia, including with South Korea and Japan.

Whatever Stalin's reasoning, the decision to indulge Kim's request led to North Korea launching a rapid southern invasion on June 25, 1950, overrunning most of South Korea in a matter of weeks. The Truman administration decided immediately that it needed to intervene. Domestically, it could not hazard the political appearance of losing still more ground to the communists; it was already smarting from Mao Zedong's unification of the Chinese mainland under communist control. Strategically, Truman justified intervention to Congress this way: "If we let Korea down the Soviet will keep right on going and swallow up one piece of Asia after another. We had to make a stand sometime or let all of Asia go by the board."[6]

Only two days after North Korea's invasion, the Truman administration obtained a resolution from the newly established United Nations demanding North Korean forces withdraw from South Korean territory and return to the northern side of the 38th parallel.[7] The United Nations' imprimatur of the US-led intervention in Korea was an act of two-way legitimation: the United Nations answered a hard test of its relevance soon after its birth, and the Truman administration gained international authorization for what would be framed in the United States as a "police action" rather than a war. The United States also benefited from UN backing in an operational military sense, gaining access to an international coalition of military support from 16 troop-contributing nations. Crucially, the only reason the United States was able to secure UN authorization for Korea was because the Soviet Union had been boycotting its own seat on the UN Security Council. The Soviets wielded a veto that could have prevented UN action in Korea, but from January 1950 abstained from voting as a protest of the nationalist Chiang Kai-Shek holding China's seat (as leader of the Republic of China/Taiwan) on the Security Council at the time.

US intervention in Korea had an immediate impact. The United States bombed North Korea's overextended forward troops, forced a gradual retreat of North Korean ground forces, and in September launched the famous "Incheon Landing," a US amphibious invasion on Korea's west coast that cut off North Korean troops from supply lines. But these tactical victories bred hubris in an already overconfident General Douglas MacArthur, a hero of World War II who was now leading the war in Korea.[8] MacArthur decided that pushing North Korean forces back to the 38th parallel was not enough. After retaking Seoul in September, he ordered UN forces to push past the 38th parallel in October, triggering massive Chinese intervention on behalf of a beleaguered North Korea.

Circumstances conspired to ensure the Korean War had neither winners nor a decisive end. China's decision to join North Korea in fighting UN forces prevented MacArthur from unifying the Peninsula under the South, but only in conjunction with other US incentives to fight in a self-constrained way. Even during the Korean War, defense of Western Europe remained the centerpiece of US strategy. America's conventional forces in Europe were aimed at deterring a Soviet invasion, but were already thin relative to the Soviets, who had vastly superior numbers and firepower. The Truman and Eisenhower administrations, therefore, could not rob Europe to pay Asia. If military resources came to a direct tradeoff between regions, Europe would be the priority. Politically, too, the United States was constrained in how it fought North Korea and China. Despite Eisenhower's presidential campaign threat to resort to nuclear bombings to bring the Korean War to a close, US officials were aware of the abhorrence of nuclear use and the emerging nuclear taboo. And because the United States intervened in Korea under the auspices of the United Nations, the war was fought not as an unrestricted campaign with a formal congressional declaration, but as a "police action" under the pre-existing powers of the presidency. That framing meant that war had its limits; a scorched-earth, win-at-all-costs approach, as had occurred in World War II, was not viable.[9]

By 1951 it was clear the conflict would be a stalemate, so the United States, under the auspices of the United Nations Command, began negotiating a ceasefire with China and North Korea, which it finally secured two long years later. Everybody wanted to stop the bleeding of the war, but everybody also wanted favorable terms for doing so. North Korea proved the most intransigent and unrelenting, despite having suffered the greatest magnitude of casualties and economic destruction. Technically, South Korea was not a formal signatory of the Armistice Agreement that indefinitely suspended the war. It is tragic and ironic that the Armistice Agreement would see both sides agree to divide the Peninsula roughly along the same geographic and political lines as before Kim Il Sung's 1950 invasion. The United States "dropped 635,000 tons of bombs" during the war, a staggering figure that excluded 32,557 tons of napalm.[10] General Curtis Lemay, former Commander of Strategic Air Command, gave an interview in which he ballparked that "we killed off—what—twenty percent of the population of Korea as direct casualties of war, or from starvation and exposure?"[11] Of that, North Korea's population, which numbered less than ten million at the beginning of the war, fell by an estimated 1.3 million by its end. Yet, through three and half years of fighting, little had changed politically or territorially.

The Conflict Between North and South Korea

In the decades that followed the suspension of the Korean War, a peace treaty never replaced the Armistice Agreement, meaning the Peninsula technically remained in a state of suspended war. The reason was simple: no party to the Armistice Agreement had been willing to pursue peace on terms that would be acceptable to the others. China wanted a non-adversarial geographic buffer. North Korea wanted the withdrawal of US forces and the unification of the Peninsula under the leadership of the North. South Korea also wanted unification, but under its leadership, not the North's. And the United States wanted to maintain the independence and security of South Korea, among other longer-term strategic interests, such as protection of Japan as it rebuilt its economy and society after World War II. It is thus misleading to view the Armistice Agreement per se as an impediment to peace. It is more accurately a byproduct of historically irreducible conflicts of interest between North Korea and the US–South Korea alliance.

In the initial decade after the Korean War, North and South Korea—run by dictators Kim Il Sung and Syngman Rhee respectively—mobilized national resources and their relationships with foreign patrons to rebuild their economies and their militaries for another conflict. Kim and Rhee each sought to finish the Korean War in their favor, which, for a time, necessarily meant invading and deposing the other. In the ensuing decade, Kim fought off internal challengers to his rule, including a coup attempt in 1956.[12] For Kim, surviving would-be usurpers "brought him an unprecedented measure of autonomy, which he employed to eliminate his political rivals and firmly establish his despotic rule in North Korea."[13] From a position of much greater internal security, Kim "prevented North Korean society from enjoying the benefits of de-Stalinization,"[14] and began developing a cult of personality that linked the fate of the nation to his own. Notwithstanding attempts to unseat him from power entirely, from Kim's perspective, the United States was the only thing really stopping him from taking the South and unifying the Korean nation once his military was rebuilt. In the South, the anti-communist Rhee was also looking to unify the Peninsula by force, but the United States took active steps to bridle his ambitions. Neither the Americans nor the Soviets wished to reopen the Korean War. Consequently, North and South settled into mutual antagonism. The practical inability to start war again made its suspension in 1953 effectively the beginning of an entrenched rivalry.

Juche and North Korean Strategic Culture

As North–South rivalry rigidified, separate ways of living and thinking emerged in each Korea. The South would remain a dictatorship until popular elections in 1987, but as early as the 1950s its economy was open to the West and its neighbors. In the North, an attitude of unfettered independence manifested in its foreign policy, even when, in practice, North Korea relied heavily on Russia and China as external benefactors, especially in the decade after the Korean War. Scholars disagree about the meaning and significance of the Korean concept of *Juche*, often translated as "self-reliance," for understanding North Korea. For some it is little more than ideological window-dressing that only the naive observer takes seriously.[15] For others, *Juche* represents a crucial political institution that reveals something about North Korean identity.[16] For still others, *Juche* runs much deeper, permeating most aspects of North Korean life, as a pseudo-humanist philosophy, a slogan for foreign policy, and the basis for a "unique" kind of nationalism.[17]

The precise extent of *Juche*'s relevance is less important than the fact that reference to *Juche* is pervasive in North Korean propaganda aimed at foreign audiences,[18] and is reflected in the attitude underlying North Korea's strategic and foreign policy decisions, even if not because of the prevalence of the term itself. For practical purposes, *Juche* amounts to "anti-great powerism," meaning the self-reliance that North Korea has always striven to project had to do with the country determining its own fate rather than deferring to the interests of its larger and more powerful neighbors.[19]

North Korea (and Kim Il Sung in particular) was insecure about the fact of heavy reliance on Soviet patronage from the time that Kim took control of the North in 1946. Kim had been a Soviet military officer. The Soviet Union effectively maintained North Korea as a trusteeship that it bequeathed to Kim. North Korea, especially in its early years, relied totally on Soviet trade, development assistance, and military capacity. And Kim could not launch the Korean War until Stalin gave his blessing. Even worse, the factions who launched the 1956 coup attempt against Kim Il Sung had received support from China and the Soviet Union to unseat him, sewing seeds of permanent distrust. The coup's failure thus facilitated Kim's uniquely independent position relative to his great-power patrons.[20] Kim was successful in steering an independent policy path, but South Korea deliberately stigmatized Kim's heavy reliance on the Soviets to make the superior claim to being the legitimate Korea, seizing "the nationalist high ground by opposing trusteeship, portraying Kim and his fellow communists as tools of Moscow."[21]

The combination of North Korea's pre-World War II history of colonial subjugation to imperial Japan, its near total reliance on the Soviet Union in Kim Il Sung's early years, the failed coup, and the zero-sum identity competition between North and South Korea all fueled a strong desire for Kim to avoid becoming a puppet of great powers, which is how North Korean propaganda has always portrayed the South. In the 1960s, a still-enduring style of North Korean foreign policy emerged that emphasized its independence from China and the

Soviet Union, even when it continued to extract assistance and investment from them. No matter how much it depended on external
patrons, North Korea always tried to prevent dependence from
becoming control. A blanket error of US policymakers since the
1960s has been the incorrect assumption that the Chinese or the
Soviets might control North Korea, when the reality was always that
no outside power could.

The "Second Korean War"

Korea experts sometimes refer to the late 1960s as the "second
Korean War" because of the level of violence experienced during that
time. After recovering from the ravages of war and, to a great extent,
consolidating his control of North Korea, Kim Il Sung began a renewed
push toward his primary political goal: Korean unification under his
leadership. Rather than invade and occupy as it did in 1950, Kim settled
on a more nuanced, but still aggressive strategy that had two major
components. One was stimulating pro-North revolution in the South.
The other was fracturing South Korea's alliance with the United States.
Violence, appropriately calibrated, served both parts of Kim's political
strategy, in concept at least.

During this period, North Korea relied on limited guerilla warfare and deliberate, isolated acts of violence to generate friction with
both South Korea and the United States. It engaged in hundreds of small
firefights along the Demilitarized Zone (DMZ), including during a
presidential visit by Lyndon Johnson in 1966. It forced down multiple
US aircraft: a US Army helicopter, an RB-47 reconnaissance aircraft,
and an EC-121 reconnaissance aircraft.[22] It bombed two US infantry
barracks in South Korea in 1967.[23] It famously seized the USS *Pueblo* in
1968, a naval intelligence ship with more than 80 American sailors on
board, holding its crew hostage until the United States apologized for
violating its sovereignty.[24] And only two days prior to the *Pueblo* crisis,
North Korea staged what became known as the "Blue House Raid,"
involving a team of commandos who came within a couple hundred
yards of assassinating South Korea's President Park Chung-hee.[25]

These acts of "adventurism," as the CIA described them at the
time,[26] arose from mixed motives. They simultaneously functioned as a
probe of US resolve, a way to erode South Korean confidence in the
reliability of the US defense commitment, and a way to undermine Park

Chung-hee politically. In the minds of North Korean officials, the cumulative weight of these acts of friction also conveyed North Korean resolve to the United States, which they believed forestalled a US invasion of the North.[27] Politically, Kim Il Sung hoped that pairing military friction with subversive propaganda efforts in South Korea would generate demand from within South Korea to end its alliance with the United States and throw off Park's dictatorship in favor of unification with the North.

The Second Korean War era was a trying time for the United States and South Korea because, on more than one occasion, North Korean violence triggered a crisis in which the United States seriously considered retaliation that would have brought on war again, though policymakers at the time were uncertain about the consequences of retaliation. Paradoxically, the repeated US decision not to retaliate was both a means of crisis management and a moral hazard: it was why none of the crises during this period erupted into a renewed war, but it also convinced Kim Il Sung that the United States would not retaliate if the attacks against it (or South Korea) were appropriately limited. North Korea was fully prepared to automatically respond to pressure with pressure in kind—including violence for violence—and if the US response escalated the situation, the Korean People's Army (KPA) intended to go to war.

In the early 1970s, North Korea abandoned its strategy of limited violence and revolution, partly in response to the region's shifting geopolitics. President Richard Nixon announced the "Nixon Doctrine" during a speech in Guam in 1969, calling on Asian allies to do more for their own defense, which ultimately justified withdrawing 20,000 troops from South Korea, as well as the gradual "Vietnamization" of the unpopular Vietnam conflict. Then, in a bold strategic move, Nixon and Mao Zedong pursued a rapprochement that culminated in the China–US Shanghai Communiqué in 1972. Amid the prevailing "mood of détente," and with little other than deterrence to show for years of aggressive probing and adventurism, Kim Il Sung decided to try a more accommodating approach to the United States and South Korea, and the South's Park Chung-hee did the same.

Through the Nixon, Ford, and Carter administrations, North Korean foreign policy vacillated between peaceful overtures and reversion to outright hostility and violence, but without returning to the level of violence seen during the 1960s, or the strategy that necessitated it.

The Origins and Evolution of the North Korean Nuclear Problem

North Korea's interest in nuclear weapons dates as far back as the 1950s, when it repeatedly sought nuclear technology from the Soviet Union, Soviet clients, China, and eventually Pakistan.[28] It succeeded in obtaining a small research reactor from the Soviet Union, and sometime in the early 1960s, it began construction on the nuclear reactor at Yongbyon, which, by June 1984, led intelligence analysts to judge increasingly that the site was indeed for the purpose of developing an atomic bomb.[29] By 1986, the Yongbyon reactor was capable of producing as much as one plutonium-based nuclear device per year.[30]

The Reagan administration took notice of North Korea's nuclear development, but it would not draw any government-wide conclusions about North Korea's intentions; neither did it make North Korean nuclear activity any kind of policy priority. The George H. W. Bush administration, by contrast, would reach a near unanimous conclusion that North Korea was pursuing a nuclear weapons program. That conclusion led President Bush to issue National Security Review 28 (NSR-28) in February 1991, which led the Bush administration to settle on an approach of "comprehensive engagement," a robust deterrence posture combined with diplomatic outreach and negotiation with Pyongyang to arrest the emerging nuclear challenge. Following NSR-28, US policy toward North Korea would differ across successive presidential administrations only in the approach taken, but the imperative of a non-nuclear North Korea became a fixed part of US policy discourse.

Why North Korea Wanted the Bomb

North Korea's drive for nuclear weapons was a symptom of endemic feelings of insecurity, though over time its motives became more layered. In the plainest terms, North Korea's enduring hostile relations with the United States and South Korea, and the unwillingness to simply rely on either China or the Soviet Union for its security, made the ultimate weapon the ultimate guarantee of regime survival. North Korea was a target of recurring US nuclear threats before, during, and after the Korean War.[31] That history of facing unmatchable nuclear threats was part of the calculus behind it showing a strong interest in nuclear weapons.

North Korean officials were also acutely aware of the stakes involved in their various foreign policy gambits, and the precarious military situation that left little room for strategic errors. As a North Korean official commented in 1980, "Below the 38th Parallel a million soldiers have arms turned against us ... If we are not careful, if we do not make the correct moves, we run the risk of being crushed or sold."[32] Myong-do Kang, a defector who was also the son-in-law of a former North Korean prime minister, told a South Korean newspaper in 1995 of "the apprehension the ruling class feels. Their fears started with the August 1976 tree-cutting incident at the Demilitarized Zone. At that moment they were on the verge of war. North Koreans believed they would lose because South Korea had one thousand U.S. nuclear weapons and the North Koreans had none. I think that was when Kim Il-Sung and Kim Jong-il decided they needed to develop nuclear weapons."[33] Nuclear weapons, Kim Il Sung hoped, would put North Korea in a more stable position and help buffer against the downsides of miscalculation or risk-taking.

But it is difficult to segregate North Korea's existential security motivations for nuclear weapons from the larger xenophobic and *juche*-oriented attitude it displayed to the world. The North Korean "style" in foreign policy justified pursuing extreme or unusual options in the name of retaining a sense of control over its own destiny. Kim Il Sung demonstrated a preference over time for policy options that allowed him to deal with outside great powers on equal (or at least not obsequious) terms. And to North Koreans, survival required risk-taking; superior resolve could compensate for inferior size. North Korea's nuclear obsession was not "caused" by a *juche* strategic culture, but the latter enabled the former.

The passage of time has introduced reinforcing incentives for the North to obtain and retain nuclear weapons. For one thing, decades of nuclear negotiations proved the program itself had value as a bargaining chip. Although hardly offsetting the cost of economic sanctions, as a direct result of bargaining with its nuclear program, North Korea has obtained millions of gallons of heavy fuel oil, cash payments and reimbursements amounting to tens of millions of dollars, and thousands of tons of food aid. Its nuclear program had also become a means of generating prestige for the regime, domestically and internationally.[34] Many of its nuclear and missile tests were publicly celebrated in North Korea, and its nuclear weapons were seen as a sign of its technological sophistication. Its nuclear status was such a point of pride that it revised its constitution in 2012 to reflect its hard-won identity as a nuclear power. What is more, global events since North Korea committed itself to the path of nuclear weapons acquisition have only reaffirmed its strategic decision. As longtime North Korea guru Andrei Lankov observed:

> Top North Korean families remember quite well that Muammar Gaddafi was the only strongman in the modern world who agreed to surrender his nuclear weapons program in exchange for promises of economic benefits. The sorry fate of the Libyan dictator and many of his supporters serves as a timely reminder ... The 1994 Budapest Memorandum on Security Assurances (Budapest Protocol) has also served as a warning against excessive belief in so-called security guarantees. The Budapest Protocol provided Ukraine with guarantees of its territorial integrity in exchange for the country ridding itself of the nuclear weapons it inherited from the collapse of the Soviet Union. As we know, these guarantees ... were of no help whatsoever when the Crimean Peninsula was taken by Russia.[35]

Add to the examples of Libya and Ukraine the fate of Saddam Hussein's Iraq in 2003, and you have, from North Korea's perspective, powerful incentives to retain nuclear insurance against regime change, especially considering the contrasting observation: that no nuclear power has ever been invaded. This comports with North Korea's long-held view that "international obligations, treaties, guarantees, and written promises are seldom worth the paper they are written on if not supported by force."[36]

The generations-long time horizon of North Korean nuclear activity suggests not only a deeply entrenched commitment to becoming a nuclear power, but that the North Korean state had an impressive amount of discipline, marshaling resources and cumulative technical knowledge in the pursuit of nuclear weapons, even at the near-term expense of other priorities, like developing its economy or elevating its standing in the international community. This discipline was possible because, under Kim Il Sung and his progeny, North Korea sustained its own distinct theory of national security that assigned disturbingly high importance to obtaining nuclear weapons; there was no point to economic prosperity without security. This matters for US–Korea relations in the twenty-first century if only because North Korea has traveled a long, arduous road to obtain nuclear weapons. It would be unreasonable to think North Korea would turn around and relinquish its hard-earned strategic assets because of economic pressure, diplomatic isolation, or even military threats—all of which it endured for most of its existence anyway.

North Korea So Lonely

The timing of North Korea's nuclear breakout (the early 1990s) was significantly informed by its growing international isolation. By the 1980s, North Korea's general approach to the outside world was having an alienating effect. Its routine willingness to resort to militarized violence and terrorist tactics, and its failure to repay loans to Soviet bloc friends, left North Korea in a category of its own. But even beyond North Korea's alienating behavior, adverse geopolitical circumstances at the end of the Cold War also left North Korea abandoned by old allies. North Korea lost Russian patronage when the latter normalized relations with South Korea in 1990, in conjunction with growing Russo-US cooperation on nuclear arms control and nonproliferation issues. That shift prompted Kim Il Sung to write Moscow, "In such circumstances, the DPRK-Soviet alliance would become meaningless and we would have to prepare countermeasures to produce our own nuclear weapons to replace the weapons we had depended on for our alliance."[37]

Two years later, China too normalized relations with South Korea. At the same time, North Korean officials were dismayed by the failure of communism in Europe, and saw Germany's unification following the collapse of the Berlin Wall in 1989 (which involved East Germany's absorption into the West German government) as a bellwether threat for the Korean Peninsula.[38] Worse, the first Gulf War against Saddam Hussein's Iraq put on display the then-unrivaled capabilities of modern American warfighting, and a corresponding willingness to use it against small dictatorships that lacked a nuclear deterrent. These events collectively reinforced Kim Il Sung's belief that North Korea needed nuclear weapons in the post-Cold War era even more than in the past.

From Concern to Crisis: The Agreed Framework

In contrast with the comparatively low-key treatment of the North Korean nuclear issue during the Reagan and Bush administrations, during the Clinton presidency, North Korea's clandestine nuclear program would become a US national priority and a very public issue of concern. America's emergence from the Cold War as the world's sole superpower meant it lacked the galvanizing threat of the Soviet Union to focus its strategic thinking. In the absence of a singular vivid threat to narrow the gaze of the US national security community, various "military operations other than war"—from counter-narcotics to humanitarian assistance—took on elevated importance. Following the Pentagon's 1993 "Bottom-Up Review" of defense roles, missions, and strategy, preventing the proliferation of nuclear weapons became the top national security obsession for the remainder of the 1990s. North Korea just happened to be the world's most openly defiant state pursuing nuclear weapons at the height of American national security concern about that very issue.

The Clinton administration's overarching foreign policy goal in 1993 and 1994 was to compel the North to verifiably comply with its commitments as a signatory to the Nuclear Nonproliferation Treaty (NPT). That required ensuring International Atomic Energy Agency (IAEA) nuclear inspectors access to known and suspected nuclear facilities to assess North Korean compliance with its nonproliferation obligations. Everything the United States did in the crisis must be judged relative to that larger aim. The Clinton administration had an overwhelming preference from the outset to pressure North Korea. As one US official involved in the negotiations remarked, "Everyone on the American delegation was gung-ho to sock it to these sons-of-bitches."[39] Yet, forced to adapt to the exigencies of the moment, the United States vacillated uneasily between carrots and sticks, diplomacy and threat-making, all in the name of convincing North Korea to abandon its nuclear weapons program and submit to IAEA verification inspections.

But Kim Il Sung had not come to the nuclear decision lightly, and there was no reason to expect him to be easily moved from the path he set for his country. Even so, at that time, North Korea had not yet passed the point of no return; nuclear weapons were a means to an end, and the right incentives and assurances could have potentially substituted for them, especially because it was still years away from having a functional nuclear device. But what combination of inducements and signals would allow the United States to reach its goal?

Figuring out what it would take to convince North Korea to verifiably abandon its nuclear program required painstaking diplomacy, credible shows of good faith or benign intent, and a willingness to compromise. The United States very nearly proved inadequate to the task. In 1993 and 1994, US officials in the Clinton administration were divided about how much compromise was advisable, and whether North Korea would ever seriously give up its nuclear ambitions. They were also split on the crucial question of whether any deal with North Korea should require it to come clean about its past nuclear processing activity or simply focus on the more achievable goal at the time: preventing any further nuclear advances. In the hubristic glow of having "won" the Cold War, many US arms control experts in the State Department wanted the maximum concession from North Korea—for it to grant historical transparency—while deterrence-focused officials at the Pentagon cared primarily about forestalling North Korea's nuclear program going forward.[40] Yet everyone on the US side agreed that, at minimum, North Korea's nuclear efforts had to be stopped, though it was unclear at what cost.

The crisis atmosphere started building in 1993, with both the United States and North Korea making veiled threats toward one another, then escalating to more explicit threats amid military exercises, deployments, and heightened military alert postures. By March 19, 1994, North Korea was threatening: "Seoul is not very far from here. If war breaks out, we will turn Seoul into a sea of fire."[41] This was a credible threat; thousands of pieces of long-range artillery were positioned to strike Seoul on virtually no notice, and with no way to prevent it should North Korea take such an action. The situation became so tense that even the US decision to deploy Patriot missile defense batteries to South Korea (a defensive system, as the name implies, with rather modest capability) was both a deliberate cudgel in US coercive diplomacy and, from Pyongyang's perspective, a possible indicator of a planned US invasion. US and North Korean goals were in direct conflict, and the more the United States brought pressure to bear on North Korea, the more North Korea responded with greater defiance and ever more grandiose threats.

Throughout the 1993–94 crisis, nobody serving in government at the time seriously urged preventive strikes against North Korean nuclear facilities, but the Clinton administration was heading toward that outcome anyway, before Jimmy Carter's fateful intervention in June 1994. General Gary Luck, Commander of US Forces Korea (USFK) and the UN Command, told Clinton that if North Korea responded with a war, the likely cost would be "a million and a trillion"; that is, a million casualties and trillions of dollars in economic devastation.[42] Nobody wanted that. Nevertheless, the preventive attack option was considered, planned for in detail, and presented among other less dramatic but still escalatory options in 1994. The trouble was that even the alternatives to a preventive strike moved the United States down the path toward war, and if North Korea misjudged US actions at any given moment, it might have preempted US coercive efforts with a first strike of its own.

The United States was already working on convincing the UN Security Council to impose economic sanctions—a difficult process because it required buy-in from China and Russia—undeterred by North Korea's recurring warning that it would consider UN sanctions an act of war. The United States had also been deliberately wielding the threat of military exercises as an instrument of pressure to aid its negotiating posture. In June 1994, as it appeared negotiations had reached an impasse at the height of the crisis, Secretary of Defense William Perry prepared three options for President Clinton, each of which involved moving various types of supplemental US forces in and around South Korea.[43] All of the options risked triggering conflict, depending on whether North Korea perceived the moves as part of a pre-war military buildup. Earlier in the crisis, a North Korean official had conveyed that they studied the US way of war in Iraq and "This will not be a situation like the Iraq war. We will not give you time to collect troops around Korea to attack us . . . if it is clear you are going to attack, then we will attack."[44]

But Perry and Chairman of the Joint Chiefs of Staff Shalikashvili both recognized that, facing an intransigent North Korea in spring 1994, significant military reinforcements needed to be available for rapid

reaction if North Korea responded to US pressure with escalating retaliation. Because of the context that preceded it—telegraphing threats of war,
heightened hostility, and a diplomatic impasse—moving forces into the
region might have incentivized North Korea to take preemptive military
action. Perry must have believed that, whatever the possible unintended
consequences in taking necessary defensive measures, they were prefer-
able to leaving US forces in South Korea exposed and poorly positioned
for an escalation of the situation from crisis to conflict.

The United States managed to avoid that potentially war-
triggering military buildup because at the same time that Perry and
Shalikashvili were presenting military options to President Clinton on
June 16, former President Jimmy Carter took an independent (but
heavily coordinated) initiative to visit Pyongyang and meet with Kim
Il Sung. Carter found Kim congenial. Kim reduced the crisis to a
matter of mutual mistrust and North Korean insecurity. The essence
of the Kim–Carter discussion was that if the United States would help
North Korea obtain light-water reactors (LWRs) for nuclear energy
and security assurances against the United States attacking North
Korea with nuclear weapons, then North Korea could allow IAEA
inspections to resume and end its current nuclear program. More
modest reciprocal steps would be necessary in the interim. As lead
US negotiator Robert Gallucci commented, "there wasn't sufficient
trust for one to take a very large step assuming the other would take
the compensatory counter step. There had to be a series of smaller
steps."[45] But both sides were willing to resume negotiations, which
culminated in the Agreed Framework. Though Kim Il Sung would die
the following month, succeeded by his long-groomed son, Kim Jong Il,
the work of Assistant Secretary Gallucci ensured the younger Kim
stayed on board with finalizing negotiations. The Agreed Framework,
signed by the United States and North Korea in Geneva on October
21, 1994, established a roadmap for US–North Korea rapprochement
and the end of North Korea's nuclear program. In exchange for North
Korea allowing the resumption of IAEA inspections and their ability
to continuously monitor a freeze of all activity at North Korean
nuclear facilities, North Korea would be provided the construction
of two LWRs within ten years (via international consortium),
500,000 tons of heavy fuel oil per year (via the United States) until
the LWRs came on board, and a formal US assurance that it would not
threaten or use nuclear weapons against the North. Both sides also

agreed to establish reciprocal diplomatic liaison offices and gradually normalize relations.

America's Nuclear Threat Consensus about North Korea

The Agreed Framework was a way out of an escalating crisis, but it had problems. It paid only lip service to relations between North and South Korea. It did nothing to address North Korea's conventional military threat or its large chemical weapons stockpile. It additionally left unresolved North Korea's missile arsenal, which was a growing problem and would ultimately be the means of delivering nuclear warheads.

From the moment the United States and North Korea concluded the deal, they also struggled to implement it. US intelligence eventually determined North Korea was continuing with a clandestine nuclear program. Neither side ever established diplomatic liaison offices. The United States had multiple delays in the delivery of heavy fuel oil shipments and the provision of the LWRs, which North Korea imputed with the most malign assumptions, just as the United States did over suspicions of North Korean violations of the Agreed Framework. In 1998, North Korea fired a Taepodong-2 rocket over Japan that catalyzed a missile defense crusade in conservative foreign policy circles, which the George W. Bush administration would take up with vigor.[46] And the United States implemented a series of punitive economic sanctions on North Korea during a period that, through implementation of the Agreed Framework, was supposed to be an era of rapprochement.

The Limits of Reciprocity under Clinton

The failure to improve the hostile relationship with North Korea and the gradual collapse of the Agreed Framework are both attributable to the prevailing political context and, relatedly, the inherently fragile way in which the deal itself was structured. Politically, the Clinton administration pursued the Agreed Framework without any kind of buy-in from the Republican-controlled Congress, who had a hawkish policy preference toward North Korea and opposed dealmaking with an untrustworthy adversary. The Clinton administration judged Congress's exclusion as tactically necessary in order to strike an agreement with North Korea, but it also meant the Republican

Congress would share no stake in preserving the deal. Through the remainder of the Clinton administration, Republicans opposed and undermined the Agreed Framework at every opportunity, by imposing new sanctions, continually denouncing North Korea and the Agreed Framework itself, and hindering the provision of US assistance (both in the form of the LWRs and heavy fuel oil shipments).

The structure of the deal's implementation, as tit-for-tat, incrementalist reciprocity, was also tactically necessary, but strategically imprudent. Democrats and Republicans alike viewed North Korea as a threat; they only disagreed about how to mitigate it.[47] But subscribing to a North Korea-as-threat narrative narrowed the options available to the Clinton administration for dealing with it. Conceding that another country is a genuine threat preempts grand gestures or strategies as insensible; the Clinton administration would not want to be seen as vulnerable to attacks of being weak or poor stewards of the nation's security. Senior State Department officials would therefore repeatedly attest at the time that the deal precluded any leaps of faith or trust-building, and would not survive unless North Korea held perfectly faithfully to it. As Secretary of State Warren Christopher noted, "We are under no illusions about North Korea. Implementation of the framework will be based upon verification, not trust."[48]

From 1995 onward, neither side was able to conform to the difficult standard of a tightly synchronized action-for-action arrangement. It makes sense, then, that North Korea would hedge against the deal by secretly cheating, while granting partial IAEA inspector access to its facilities. In hindsight, it was also naive to expect that a half-century of deep hostility and mistrust, coupled with a direct strategic conflict of interest, could be rectified through a modest, legalistic arrangement that fully half of Washington opposed. A survivable deal would have required either magnanimous concessions from the United States or a willingness to accommodate modest cheating and failures of implementation; the situation did not allow for either possibility.

The Schizophrenic Bush Years

When the George W. Bush administration came to office in 2001, it inherited congressional Republicans' skepticism of the Agreed Framework. The Bush approach to foreign policy was initially dubbed

"ABC" (Anything but Clinton) and North Korea policy was a center-piece. Bush's inclusion of North Korea in his famous "Axis of Evil" State of the Union speech in January 2002 presaged a resumption of open US–North Korea hostility. By the end of the year, the United States had confronted North Korea with evidence of cheating by secretly running a uranium enrichment program, in violation of the deal. The accusation exploded into mutual recriminations, North Korean with-drawal from the NPT, and the US suspension of heavy fuel oil shipments and international suspension of the construction of LWRs, effectively killing the Agreed Framework in spirit and substance.

But the following year, as the first phase of the Iraq War was coming to an end, both sides agreed to negotiate a new bargain that would serve the same big-picture purpose as the old one. Through the Six-Party Talks (6PT), launched in August 2003, the United States and North Korea negotiated the terms of an IAEA-verifiable freeze and dismantlement of the North Korean nuclear program. Designed to include North Korea's neighbors, China, Russia, South Korea, and Japan, the 6PT became an unwieldy, multilevel, multipart negotiation process, involving everything remotely connected to North Korean insecurity, ranging from diplomatic normalization and regional govern-ance architectures to economic development, North Korean abductions of Japanese citizens during the Cold War, and, of course, conditions of North Korean denuclearization. It offered a similar set of inducements to Pyongyang as the Agreed Framework had, but packaged it differently and presented it as a regional negotiation rather than a US–North Korea problem per se. Like the Agreed Framework, the 6PT also proceeded on the principle of "action for action."

The 6PT had successes and setbacks. The biggest success was a September 19, 2005 Joint Statement in which North Korea, for the first time, agreed that "it had nuclear weapons, that it would give them up, and that it would end all associated nuclear programs."[49] This was followed by the biggest failure, North Korea conducting its first test of a nuclear device, on October 3, 2006.

Yet North Korea would agree to return to the 6PT less than a month later. In keeping with the spirit of talks that were on-again, off-again, in June 2008, North Korea made the highly cooperative gesture of destroying the highly visible cooling tower at the Yongbyon nuclear complex. The demolition of the cooling tower had no meaningful effect on its ability to produce nuclear weapons, but the symbolism seemed meaningful at the time, and a major reason the Bush administration made the controversial decision to remove North Korea from the equally symbolic State Sponsors of Terrorism list that same year (which the Trump administration would reverse in November 2017). But North Korea would refuse the IAEA's protocols to verify North Korea's nuclear dismantlement as overly intrusive, a rebuff that echoed the shortcomings of Agreed Framework implementation during the Clinton era. North Korea declared the talks "dead" in July 2008, but held one final round of discussions in December, which ended with utter disagreement about verification protocols for nuclear dismantlement.

Because of an abundance of skepticism among US policymakers that North Korea was capable of upholding commitments, as well as a dearth of mutual trust, the seemingly small detail of whether and how to verify North Korean compliance with its nuclear freeze and dismantlement agreements has been a recurring point of failure in efforts to denuclearize the Korean Peninsula and improve relations with the North. By September 2008, North Korea was actively reversing steps toward dismantlement it had previously taken at Yongbyon and accused the United States of not living up to its commitments and of trying to violate North Korean sovereignty (the latter a common claim when North Korea wanted to resist a US request or demand). Once again, the only kind of agreements that could have been sustainable, involving either grand concessions from the United States or allowances for some North Korean nuclear backsliding, were politically implausible to US officials. And as we shall see, these same basic problems would similarly plague nuclear negotiations and North Korea policy during the Obama administration.

2 NORTH KOREAN STRATEGIC THOUGHT

Before turning to the evolution of Obama-era strategy toward North Korea, this chapter offers an essential primer on how North Korea thinks about coercion and its nuclear weapons—to the extent that we know—and the kinds of dangers that arise therefrom.[1] Some of what we know about North Korean strategic thinking and its intentions comes from defector testimonies after fleeing to China or South Korea, though we often cannot take their claims at face value. Some of it comes by fiat, from public statements by government officials privy to intelligence reports that the public never gets to see. If enough policymakers say the same thing enough times across enough presidential administrations, then there must be something to it. But much of what we know comes from inferences drawn either deductively, from the structure of the situation, or inductively, from "Pyongyangology," that is, parsing North Korean words and deeds for hidden meaning. Either approach involves a certain amount of educated guessing. When it comes to claiming anything meaningful about North Korea, therefore, acknowledging a margin of uncertainty is healthy. US officials called on to make choices about Korea are faced with uncertainties and risks at every turn. This has always been the case with North Korea, but nuclear weapons have changed the character of those uncertainties and risks, largely for the worse.

The role of nuclear weapons in North Korean strategic thinking must be distinguished from the motivation that first led them to pursue nuclear weapons. Even recognizing that the foremost purpose of North Korea's arsenal is for security, we need to understand *how* North Korea believes nuclear weapons help it achieve security. After all, anything the United States does regarding the threat or use of force *should* depend on how it expects North Korea to respond, which in turn depends on the strategic beliefs of Kim Jong Un and North Korean military elites. In this chapter, therefore, I take on two tasks. The first is to articulate how North Korea thinks about coercion generally. Whether and how North Korea would use weapons in a crisis or conflict depends to a great extent on its "theory of victory"—a term of art among nuclear scholars that describes beliefs about coercion; how force and the threat of force achieve security goals.[2] Nuclear weapons have to fit within prevailing sensibilities and beliefs that elites share about the relative merits of force. A "theory of victory" tells us what those sensibilities and beliefs are.

The second task of this chapter is to explain how, given its theory of victory, the presence of North Korean nuclear weapons generates risks distinct from those posed by a non-nuclear North Korea. Rather than claim that North Korean nuclear strategy hews to one ideal-type approach over another, I explain the variety of ways North Korean nuclear weapons introduce new and sometimes counterintuitive risks.

North Korea's Theory of Victory: Offensive, Reputational

Koreans have many proverbs and sayings for which they are famous, but one of the most common, especially in military and security circles, is the rather self-explanatory "I die, you die." It is the emotional corollary to North Korea's often used strategy of brinkmanship in threat-making and bargaining; getting what you want by exploiting your willingness to annihilate yourself over principle. It does not mean, however, that North Korean elites or Kim Jong Un are suicidal; they are not. Self-preservation is as important for the Kim regime as it is for anyone. But there are two problems that make North Korean self-preservation manifest differently than for other states.

The first is that the North Korean people have been heavily conditioned over time to expect a future war. As Pak Su-hyon, a North Korean who defected to the South in 1993 and served in Kim Il Sung's personal security service, told journalist Bradley Martin in 1995, "The problem is, people want war. They believe they are living this hard life because there's going to be a war ... They believe they'll die either way, from hunger or war. So the only solution is war."[3] The anecdote was offered at a time that North Korea was suffering an extreme famine, but it is indicative of a more general mindset resolved to the eventuality of war, echoing through time.

That echo was heard even in 2017, when *The New Yorker*'s Evan Osnos visited North Korea and his host from the Foreign Ministry repeated a version of it: "Three million people have volunteered to join the war if necessary ... in terms of dignity we are the most powerful in the world. We will die in order to protect that dignity and sovereignty."[4] Statements like these, as well as much of North Korean history, suggest that the North Koreans would rather accept a war than capitulate—or even be seen as capitulating—to outside pressure on matters that they see as being of existential importance. The practical consequence of this fatalism about a future war at the popular level is that the regime can plausibly lead its people into a conflict without alienating or being deposed by the people. As long as it does not lead to externally imposed regime change, a war could actually play very favorably in the domestic politics of the Kim regime. Thus, whereas political scientists sometimes conceive of popular will as a constraint on the ability of leaders to make war, in North Korea, not only is popular will not a constraint on war, it may actually encourage it under certain circumstances.

The second, more important, problem is that the regime exhibits peculiarly dangerous beliefs about the role of threats and military violence for self-preservation. North Korea under the Kim dynasty has always believed in the *imperative of the offense*: that clear shows of hostility and resolve (i.e., a willingness to take risks and die) are necessary to deter enemy aggression. It also believes that *adversarial reputations* matter a great deal: North Korea expects that adversaries will judge its future resolve based partly on what it does in the present moment; small actions of toughness or weakness can therefore have exaggerated consequences in the future. When you combine these twin beliefs (the merits of offense and importance of reputation) suddenly the history of North Korea's threats and uses of force makes much more sense.

Take, for instance, the private statements of senior North Korean officials to Soviet counterparts in the wake of North Korea's shooting down of the US EC-121 reconnaissance aircraft on April 15, 1969. The attack, which killed all 31 Americans on board, was the most aggressive North Korea had ever launched against the United States outside the Korean War. Heo Dam, North Korea's Deputy Foreign

Minister, told the Soviet Ambassador to Pyongyang, North Korea is "ready to respond to retaliation with retaliation, and total war with total war," and that the Americans "did not draw the proper lesson from the *Pueblo*," referring to North Korea's capture of a US naval intelligence vessel and its crew the year prior.[5] Heo implied that the United States should have learned about North Korea's willingness to take such actions because the seizure of the *Pueblo* demonstrated it. In effect, North Korea was using violence to socialize the United States to expect certain consequences under certain conditions. Soviet Ambassador Sudarikov followed this conversation with a similarly toned exchange with North Korea's Foreign Minister Pak Seong-Cheol. Pak told Sudarikov:

> If the Americans had decided to fight then [when the EC-121 was shot down], we would have fought ... we wage firefights with the Americans in the area of the 38th parallel almost every day. When they shoot, we also shoot ... But no special aggravation arises from this ... we've also shot down American planes before, and similar incidents are possible in the future ... It's good for them to know that we won't sit with folded arms ... If we sit with folded arms when a violator intrudes into our spaces, two planes will appear tomorrow, then four, five, etc. This would lead to an increase of the danger of war. But if a firm rebuff is given, then this will diminish the danger of an outbreak of war. When the Americans understand that there is a weak enemy before them they will start a war right away. If, however, they see that there is a strong partner before them, this delays the beginning of a war.[6]

Notably, these words were shared in private with a Soviet patron who was trying to understand why North Korea would provoke the United States with violence and warning of the danger of doing so. This makes them more credible and more revealing than public statements intended to influence the United States. They also illustrate North Korea's offensive, reputational beliefs about the efficacy of coercion. When Pak states that "if we sit with folded arms ... this would lead to an increase of the danger of war. But if a firm rebuff is given, then this will diminish the danger of an outbreak of war," he is articulating the core theory of North Korean coercion: North Korea believes going on the offensive prevents the United States from invading. In other words, showing strength and resolve prevents war, while showing weakness invites war. Pak's justification of recurring friction along the DMZ conveys similar thinking: to North Korea, the accumulation of sporadic small-scale clashes with the enemy actually prevents war because it ensures that the enemy will judge North Korea as having firm resolve in the future. Small acts of aggression have exaggerated payoffs.

Kim Il Sung communicated a complementary rationale to Romanian dictator Ceauşescu in 1971, explaining North Korea's provocations in terms of the expectation that the United States would not retaliate because it showed an unwillingness to do so in the past: "Americans don't want to continue this fight. The Americans let us know [through their inaction] that it's not their intention to fight the Koreans again."[7] Kim Il Sung judged the United States on its track record, just as he expected the United States to judge North Korea based on *its* track record. North Korea's twin beliefs, in offense and adversary reputation, are the only plausible explanation for the otherwise puzzling historical pattern: why a much weaker North Korea has attacked much stronger US and South Korean adversaries hundreds of times since the 1960s. For a small power to repeatedly attack a larger power without being suicidal, it must expect that the larger power will not exploit its superior power; North Korea made that inference about the United States during the Cold War, based on the latter's track record of restraint.

North Korea's offensive, reputational thinking about threats and violence is not confined to the Cold War. We find the same pattern of thought and action emerging between North Korea and the United States in the 1990s,[8] and in crises as recent as 2010.[9] North Korea repeatedly used small-scale, limited acts of violence for political ends that were much bigger than warranted by the acts themselves, attributing outsized effects (deterrence of America) to their deliberate accumulation of friction: "it's good for them to know that we won't sit with folded arms," as North Korea's foreign minister told the Soviet ambassador. In 2002, North Korea's lead negotiator, Deputy Foreign Minister Kang Sok Ju, expressed the other side of this belief, telling US Assistant Secretary of State James Kelly that "If we disarm ourselves because of US pressure, then we will become like Yugoslavia or Afghanistan's Taliban, to be beaten to death."[10] Showing weakness invites war all the same, but on less favorable terms than if it drew first blood.

Moreover, a rare quantitative study examining North Korea from 1997 to 2006 found that when the United States displayed more aggressive international intentions toward other adversaries, as with the 2003 invasion of Iraq, North Korean vitriolic rhetoric would surge, not diminish.[11] In these instances, North Korea could have gone mute and largely stayed out of view while the United States focused its ire on others. Instead, it opted for a rhetorical posture of effectively warning the United States off of bringing its hawkish propensity to the Korean Peninsula. This is consistent with the prevailing North Korean view that offense is the best defense. When Evan Osnos visited Pyongyang in 2017, one of his hosts, the vice-president of the Institute for American Studies (a regime-run think tank), hinted at the oft-heard origin of such thinking: "Historically, the Korean people have suffered because of weakness. That bitter lesson is kept in our hearts."[12] Kim Jong Il told former President Bill Clinton much the same when the two met in 2009, a meeting I will discuss at length in the next chapter. Kim claimed his "military-first" policy, which involved going on the offensive at times, "had nothing to do with hostility," but rather with deterrence: "The DPRK was a small country surrounded by giants. The Korean nation had suffered Japanese occupation . . . the purpose of the military-first policy was not to attack others but to prevent other countries from attacking the DPRK."[13] Internalized narratives about their own experience lead them to believe that even small projections of resolve help keep enemies at bay.

Over time, then, North Korea has expressed in word and deed that taking calculated risks is how it believes a smaller power survives amid threats from much larger enemies. The risks it decides to take flow from this offensive, reputational understanding about the utility of threats and the "diplomacy of violence," to borrow a phrase from strategic studies pioneer Thomas Schelling. When North Korea's Foreign Ministry stated on December 7, 2017 that war with the Trump administration had become an "established fact . . . The remaining question now is: when will the war break out?" they were expressing a fatalism with roots in their strategic thinking.[14] Virtually everything of consequence that North Korea says and does draws on antecedent narratives and stock beliefs that it has nurtured over time. The way North Korean officials think about coercion in particular makes it highly unlikely that they respond to anything they perceive as unprovoked pressure with anything but pressure in kind, even if such a response triggers war. This does not mean that North Korea is "undeterrable," or that North Korea can never be struck without leading to a war. But unprovoked attacks, attacks that make the regime's leadership appear weak or irresolute, or attacks that appear to the regime as a prelude to a larger military campaign, will generate retaliation and escalation. To North Korea, the failure to respond to pressure with pressure will bring war just as surely as an escalating spiral of retaliation, so they have scarcely any alternative to hitting back if they are hit first. In this context, whatever additional legitimacy or economic benefits nuclear weapons may provide, nothing could be more valuable than a weapon that allows North Korea to make good on its emotional and strategic need to ensure that "I die, you die." This theory of victory matters because it is the context within which North Korea makes decisions about nuclear weapons.

Risks of War, Nuclear and Otherwise

At the time of writing in 2018, North Korea was a de facto nuclear weapons state, and the destructive capacity and survivability of its nuclear arsenal improved every year leading up to the nuclear crisis. Between 2006 and 2017, North Korea conducted six nuclear tests, gradually increasing the yield of the blasts. North Korea claimed its sixth test, on September 3, 2017, was a hydrogen bomb, the nuclear yield (around 100 megatons) of which was several times greater than the bombs dropped on Hiroshima and Nagasaki together in 1945. The blast yield made the claim at least plausible. Through iterations of research, development, and testing, North Korea has improved its ability to deploy ever larger destructive nuclear yields. Crucially, it also improved its ability to miniaturize nuclear devices to fit on delivery vehicles like ballistic and cruise missiles.

One would be forgiven for asking how North Korea's nuclear weapons makes the situation on the Korean Peninsula more dangerous than the ever-present danger of decades past. Even without a nuclear arsenal, North Korea has so much long-range artillery targeting South Korea's capital, Seoul, that it could destroy most of it in a matter of hours. It also has a large chemical weapons stockpile, and has not acknowledged any particular taboo around the use of chemical weapons. North Korean agents used a chemical weapon to assassinate Kim Jong Un's older brother in 2017 at Kuala Lumpur International

Airport. If Kim could use such weapons against his own brother, we should also expect them to be used in the event of open conflict. And North Korea's military, despite being comprised of Soviet era equipment, is the fourth largest in the world and enjoys all the natural advantages that come with fighting in home territory.

But the introduction of nuclear weapons can heighten dangers in new and sometimes counterintuitive ways. Nuclear weapons limit what adversaries wishing to avoid nuclear war can do to North Korea. They increase the upper-end costs of misperception, miscalculation, and worst-case scenarios. They grant North Korea greater optionality in pursuing non-nuclear coercive violence, making North Korean offensives more difficult to predict, defend against, and deter. And they may embolden North Korean officials to adopt more aggressive strategies in the pursuit of political goals.

Guaranteed Nuclear Conflict

Before North Korea had nuclear weapons, the United States and South Korea could have prevailed in a war to eliminate the Kim regime, but doing so would have come at a high cost in blood and treasure. A nuclear North Korea has the ability to guarantee that the price of eliminating the regime will not just be blood and treasure, but the world's first nuclear war between nuclear states. Since the United States dropped atomic bombs on Japan in 1945, conflicts between nuclear powers have happened on occasion, but both sides always kept the conflict limited and localized. In those conflicts, nobody attempted to impose regime change on the other side, or invade the capital of their adversary. With North Korea though, the United States and South Korea have a long track record of planning and expressing a willingness to pursue regime change or forced unification of the Peninsula, which would effectively erase North Korea as we know it.

In theory, the United States could locate all of North Korea's nuclear-armed missiles and launch a disabling first strike that wipes them out before they could be launched. But by diversifying the systems it uses to deliver nuclear payloads, which include traditional fixed garrison missile sites, road-mobile launchers, and roving submarines, North Korea makes its nuclear weapons harder for its adversaries to detect and destroy. North Korea has also begun using solid fuel (as opposed to only liquid fuel) to prepare missiles, making launches much harder to detect beforehand and reducing the amount of time it takes for repeated launches. Thus, a first-wave US attack to eliminate North Korea's nuclear arsenal is not only fraught, even under the best of circumstances; it gradually becomes impossible as the North's nuclear and missile inventory grows, it relies more on mobile missile launchers, and it disperses its nuclear and missile forces to a wider range of locations.

When its nuclear arsenal is sufficiently large and diverse that it proves impossible for the United States to destroy with a preventive attack, North Korea will at that point possess an assured retaliatory or "secure second-strike" capability.[15] The accelerated pace of North Korean missile testing in 2015 through 2017 was aimed at achieving an "assured retaliation" capability as quickly as possible. Any nuclear capability short of that threshold creates perverse incentives for North Korea to resort to nuclear first use, for reasons discussed below. A survivable nuclear arsenal, by contrast, guarantees that North Korea can turn any war, invasion, or attempt at regime change into a nuclear conflict. If the regime realizes its days are numbered, there is no incentive for them to refrain from going nuclear. And because of how North Korea thinks about the political value of using force, it has not only the ability but also the willingness to resort to nuclear use; the only uncertainty is the conditions that would lead it to doing so.

Nuclear Escalation (First-Use Instability)

Nuclear weapons create the unique risk that North Korea engages in nuclear first use, even though the US–South Korea alliance does not intend to pursue regime change or invade Pyongyang. North Korea has sought and arguably has a secure second-strike retaliatory capability, but it nevertheless has incentives to use nuclear weapons in a first-strike (preemption/prevention) capacity anyway. In either case, we know that there are certain situations where Kim Jong Un would feel pressure to resort to nuclear use regardless of precooked doctrine, not only because of an "I die, you die" mentality, but because anyone in North Korea's position would have similar incentive to go nuclear depending on the situation. This could play out in three different ways, each of which could occur even if the United States refrains from using nuclear weapons itself.

Misperceiving "Use or Lose"

The first way is through inadvertent nuclear escalation out of misplaced desperation. In the fog of crisis or conflict, North Korean generals and national security officials close to Kim Jong Un (or, of course, Kim himself) become incorrectly convinced that the United States is coming to remove the Kim regime. This amounts to nuclear first use for reasons of misperception. It is plausible because of what the KPA needs to do to keep the nation secure—use its strongest weapons while it has them—but also because North Korea knows about the US military playbook. North Korean hackers stole alliance war plans in 2016,[16] making Kim Jong Un fully aware of the alliance's preparations to do what it openly signals: dismantle the Kim regime in the event of war. The US "way of war" also follows a fairly predictable pattern that even North Korean officials have taken notice of, explaining that they would strike first if they believe the United States is preparing for invasion.[17] Many of the actions the United States would take in the lead-up to war, however, it would also take for other reasons having nothing to do with a full-blown war. For instance, US measures intended to protect its bases in the region (such as a military buildup in Japan), or to conduct a limited strike against North Korea (such as attacking North Korean air defenses so that US bombers can attack a North Korean target without getting shot down), are also actions the United States would take as part of executing an invasion of North Korea. How would Kim Jong Un know the difference in advance, and could he afford to be wrong? Even defensive US military actions in or around the Korean Peninsula can be misinterpreted as indicators of a US-led invasion or regime change, forcing Kim Jong Un into a "use or lose" scenario with North Korea's nuclear arsenal.[18]

The Pakistan Model

A second way North Korea might resort to nuclear first use follows the Pakistan example. A small state might be convinced of the need for nuclear weapons when facing a larger adversary, yet believe that mere possession of nuclear weapons is insufficient for it to be secure. If that larger adversary has many more and better nuclear weapons, the nuclear imbalance may force the smaller state with fewer nuclear devices to compensate by using its limited arsenal early in a crisis or conflict, in hopes that escalating the situation would deter the larger adversary from further aggression. This is the basic logic of Pakistan's "asymmetric escalation" nuclear strategy against India: a first-use nuclear doctrine.[19] Because India's conventional military and nuclear forces are much larger, Pakistan has pursued a deliberate strategy of nuclear first use if it finds itself in a conventional conflict with India. Its reasoning: escalate the situation in order to compel India to de-escalate the situation. Applying this logic to the Korea context, North Korea would resort to nuclear first use to scare the United States into believing that the situation can become much costlier than intended, causing US officials to restrain themselves or sue for peace. While we do not know North Korean nuclear strategy, we can see that the structure of the military situation shares important similarities with Pakistan.[20] North Korea also faces an unfavorable conventional military balance; it, too, has only a small number of nuclear weapons, which means it faces the risk, however small, that its adversary could eliminate its nuclear arsenal in a preventive attack; and it, too, faces an adversary that maintains nuclear superiority over it. All else being equal, militarily inferior states with only a handful of nuclear weapons facing off against a larger nuclear adversary will find nuclear first use attractive in the name of "escalate to de-escalate." Because the logic of nuclear escalation through first use in the Pakistan example relies on the fact of having a small, inferior nuclear arsenal, the incentives for such an "asymmetric escalation" strategy change as North Korea develops a larger, diverse, and more survivable nuclear arsenal.

More Offense, More Deterrence

But the motivation for asymmetric escalation does not necessarily derive only from the fact of a small, inferior nuclear arsenal. There is a third, less likely, but still plausible pathway to North Korea launching nuclear weapons in a first-use capacity, regardless of the size or survivability of its arsenal, hewing closely to a general deterrence model of conflict that has been distorted by North Korea's offensive, reputational theory of victory. The distorted deterrence model of limited nuclear first use is straightforward: North Korea could use nuclear weapons as a way of demonstrating superior resolve that would warn off a US invasion or regime change. This is the essential logic of North Korea's offensive, reputational theory of victory; it is the same reasoning that led to a string of North Korean acts of unreciprocated violence in decades past. Using nuclear weapons for this reason would seem utterly reckless and amount to brinkmanship, and would therefore seem utterly implausible. But given how North Korea thinks about the utility of threats and force, it may find itself in a situation where small-scale conventional violence appears to be losing its potency to deter US or South Korean aggression. On such an occasion, carefully delimited nuclear first use would up the ante. Turning up the volume on competitive risk-taking will restore flagging North Korean confidence in its ability to deter alliance aggression. Like the Pakistan model, it reflects a deliberate escalation strategy, but rather than being compelled by an inferior nuclear arsenal, it is compelled by a perceived need to be more offensive than usual to sustain general deterrence. That distinction is important because it means North Korea could resort to nuclear first use even if it secures a large, survivable nuclear arsenal.

It bears mentioning that nuclear first use for any of the above reasons is not a high probability outcome, but given the destructive implications, any increase in risk, and even a marginal total risk, merits policy attention.

More Rungs on the "Escalation Ladder"

A third danger from nuclear weapons in the North Korea context is that they make available military options that North Korea once deemed too risky or options of last resort. Before North Korea was a de facto nuclear state, it threatened war against South Korea and the United States countless times; one of its most famous threats was to turn Seoul into a "sea of fire," which it could do without nuclear weapons. But it was obvious at the time that the North's ability to attack Seoul posed no practical threat except if war broke out anew. Seoul was a ripe target for North Korea's military as a hostage, but once attacked, North Korea would have played out its strongest hand, making an attack on Seoul tantamount to suicide. Possessing nuclear weapons makes once-infeasible options like an artillery barrage on Seoul more thinkable than in the past. It is no longer obvious that an attack on Seoul, especially if carefully circumscribed, would automatically lead to an alliance invasion of Pyongyang because of North Korea's ability to turn it into a nuclear war. To be sure, North Korea would be taking a big gamble if it chose to attack Seoul, and it would suffer costs for doing so. But North Korea's nuclear deterrent against invasion makes, for North Korea, a risk out of what was once a certainty (the regime-change consequences of attacking Seoul). And this does not mean that North Korea could attack Seoul with impunity; only that the ultimate cost (regime change or the total destruction of North Korea) becomes evitable, and some alternative, lesser form of punitive retaliation more likely. This example illustrates how, in theory, nuclear weapons give North Korea the ability to more easily calibrate its use of force, up and down a metaphorical ladder of escalation, because it reduces the risk that any given move it makes will trigger a general war.

Were there such a thing as an "escalation ladder," North Korean nuclear weapons could conceivably reduce the risk of war by calibrating force as needed to achieve what it wants. The problem, of course, is that the ladder is illusory; it is a mental construct that encourages overconfidence in the ability to achieve political goals through careful applications of force and threat-making. Cold War history repeatedly showed that coercion cannot be reliably calibrated, and believing otherwise opens the door to a conflict that spirals out of control.[21] The "escalation ladder" metaphor fell out of favor among scholars by the latter part of the Cold War because it wrongly implied that 1) there exists an objective series of moves or threats that increase or decrease tensions at will, and 2) one can easily manipulate an opponent through carefully calibrated threats. It underestimates the pervasiveness of misperception in world politics.[22] North Korea's offensive, reputational theory of victory primes it to place stock in dangerously illusory escalation ladder thinking. Adding nuclear weapons to this mindset just adds rungs to North Korea's mental escalation ladder. Put differently, nuclear weapons are likely to convince North Korea it has greater freedom of action to go on the offensive in different ways and with different levels of intensity than it did before it had nuclear weapons. This is because of pre-existing beliefs it has about the political efficacy of force.

In addition to freeing up previously off-limits military options, nuclear weapons can also quite literally and directly give North Korea options for using nuclear force that it did not have before. As North Korea refines its ability to make more controllable nuclear devices with smaller destructive yields, it will eventually be able to field "tactical" (sometimes called "non-strategic" or simply "low-yield") nuclear weapons by placing small nuclear devices on rockets, artillery shells, or landmines.[23] Because tactical nuclear weapons have deliberately reduced destructive capacity, they are generally thought to be more usable, and therefore a more credible way of threatening an adversary. North Korea has a well-documented credibility problem,[24] especially with nuclear-armed missiles, but tactical nuclear weapons would actually help them rectify that problem. Threatening nuclear war with missiles might be seen as threatening suicide, which makes it of dubious credibility; but threatening smaller attacks using low-yield nuclear artillery or something similar might be more believable. While tactical weapons themselves do not necessarily make North Korean violence more likely, they provide another option for engaging in violence should they choose to do so. But make no mistake: using tactical nuclear weapons would usher in the first nuclear conflict of what scholars describe as the Second Nuclear Age.

The Emboldenment Question

Closely related to, but analytically distinct from, the escalation ladder problem is the problem of emboldenment. Does the possession of nuclear weapons breed a more confident and aggressive North Korea? Logic suggests it does, but the historical record is unclear. In 1965, political scientist Glenn Snyder posited that US-Soviet competition exhibited a "stability-instability paradox"—that nuclear weapons and the logic of mutually assured destruction prevented both sides from launching a nuclear war, but because both sides were deterred from that worst-case scenario, they were paradoxically freer to pursue lower levels of friction with one another, including through proxy wars for global influence.[25] When international competitors square off, in other words, strategic-level stability begets tactical-level instability. That logic seems to describe the pattern of Cold War competition, as well as the history of the Korean Peninsula since 1953; in the Cold War as in Korea, the world has witnessed tremendous small-scale violence, proxy wars, and international friction, but no unrestricted wars involving the great powers.

Extending this logic to a nuclear North Korea, we should expect that North Korean confidence in the strength of its nuclear deterrent would embolden it to pursue revisionist foreign policy goals, including unification of the Peninsula, and limited violence regardless of the foreign policy goal. Evidence of such a connection, however, is mixed. A growing number of Korea watchers agree that Kim Jong Un has embraced more aggressive foreign policy ambitions, but not necessarily because of its possession of nuclear weapons. Whereas in the 1990s and early 2000s North Korea's foremost concern was the relatively modest, defensive goal of regime survival,[26] scholars and policymakers increasingly converge on the belief that Kim Jong Un seeks to unify the Peninsula under his leadership and force the withdrawal of US forces from South Korea.[27]

That judgment requires nothing more than taking North Korea at its word. These have always been North Korea's goals, but when nationwide famine and natural disasters converged on North Korea in the 1990s, Kim Jong Il prioritized preventing a collapse of his regime over unification or eliminating US troops from the Peninsula. Kim Jong Un appears to have taken up North Korea's historical quest, as media continue to place rhetorical emphasis on bringing about unification. After a February 2017 missile test, for example, the Korean Central News Agency (KCNA) noted that even overseas Koreans cheered their successful demonstration, which strengthened "the fellow countrymen's conviction in the final victory of the cause of national reunification."[28] North Korea has become fond of referring to a "final victory" in its propaganda.[29] The United States holds this view of North Korea as well. As recently as October 2017, the CIA's number 2 official on Korea told an audience in Washington that Kim Jong Un's "long-term goal . . . [is to] remove US forces from the peninsula" so it has greater freedom of action against the South.[30] And in the Panmunjom Declaration, jointly issued by Kim Jong Un and South Korean President Moon Jae In, after a meeting in April 2018, both sides expressed aspirations toward peaceful unification, for Koreans and by Koreans. Unification is of interest to Kim Jong Un. The unknowns are the terms and timing.

But while nuclear weapons may make it easier for North Korea to do what it wants, its ambitions predate its nuclear program. Nuclear weapons are a means to its long desired end, but they did not *cause* North Korea to seek that end.

Regardless of its ultimate aims, there are indications that nuclear weapons may accentuate a dangerous derangement in how North Korea talks about the use of force. Consistent with the sentiment of "I die, you die," North Korean officials and public statements have stated repeatedly throughout their history that they will meet pressure with pressure, war with war. But since becoming a de facto nuclear state, it has become more common for North Korea to escalate that sentiment further. Instead of pressure for pressure, they echo the logic of gangs, drug cartels, and beleaguered national governments facing many rebellions and threats of civil war—any transgression demands manifold retaliation as a means of deterring future challenges. Deterrence, in other words, not through proportional retaliation but rather through exaggerated, disproportionate retaliation; shock-and-awe lesson-teaching. It is in this spirit that Uriminzokkiri, a state-run media site, published a statement at the height of the nuclear crisis in October 2017 that "The DPRK is ready to … cope with the enemy's dagger with a sword and his rifle with an artillery piece."[31] That is escalation, not proportionality, for the sake of deterrence. The statement linked this willingness to escalate to its nuclear capabilities, noting in the prior paragraph that "The status of force between the DPRK and U.S. at present is fundamentally different from what [it] was in the past Korean War in the 1950s."[32] Since North Korea obtained nuclear weapons, moreover, it has repeatedly stated some variation of, "The United States is not the only country that can wage a preventive war,"[33] and that the United States "dare not talk about a military option" because North Korea has achieved an "equilibrium of force" or "balance of power" with the United States.[34] All of this links the security its nuclear arsenal provides to threats of incrementally bolder, disproportionate pressure in response to pressure its enemies might bring to bear. As of this writing though, it is not at all evident that North Korean actions will eventually escalate to meet its more emboldened threat rhetoric, and if they do, it may not be because it has nuclear weapons.

In sum, we cannot definitively observe whether nuclear weapons embolden North Korea, in part because the Korean Peninsula has always exhibited the characteristics of the stability-instability paradox. We can, however, see various ways in which the existence of nuclear weapons in Korea heightens danger, and expect that nuclear weapons make North Korea more capable of pursuing what it has always sought through its foreign policy: *improved international standing and the diminution or fracture of the US alliance with South Korea so that it may unify the Peninsula on terms favorable to the North.* Those goals can be achieved any number of ways: through coercion, information operations within South Korea, a global diplomatic charm offensive, or some kind of political settlement with the South. It need not involve violence, though past attempts sometimes did. But North Korea has almost always viewed a close military alliance between the United States and South Korea as opposing its larger interests. In an alternative future that sees substantive political reconciliation between North Korea and the United States (and the Trump–Kim summit in 2018 was but a step in that direction), the former's perspective on US troops or the alliance could well change, but it would be a significant departure from the historical norm.

3 THE OBAMA YEARS: FROM ENGAGEMENT TO DETERRENCE

President Obama came to office in 2009 with the promise that "We will extend a hand if you are willing to unclench your fist."[1] This turn of phrase was a deliberate contrast with the more hawkish and confrontational image of the George W. Bush administration. The assumption underlying the Obama view was that at least part of the problem with Bush's foreign policy was dispositional: too much "us versus them," antagonism, and bad faith. Obama officials could succeed where Bush officials had failed because their engagement would be earnest. A new start. In Burma, Cuba, and Iran, this approach would bear fruit, albeit with significant caveats; with North Korea though, it would fall flat. Worse, the failure of an engagement approach in the early years of the administration undermined the ability to adopt anything but a cynical, pressure-based approach following Obama's re-election in 2012.

This chapter explains how the early Obama administration shifted from its promise of engagement to a posture of primarily deterrence and ratcheting confrontation with the North. Adherence to a maximalist goal of denuclearization, and the Six-Party Talks (6PT) as *the* model of achieving it, marked the beginning of the negative transformation. The diminishing returns from positive diplomacy in pursuit of its ambitious aims justified a commensurately harder line over time. The shift toward confrontation and deterrence was also fueled by US deference to ally South Korea amid North Korean violence in 2010. The United States faced a growing credibility problem with South Korea at the same time that it was trying to strengthen its alliances in the region;

both factors pushed the United States into adopting a harder line on North Korea even as it was trying to persist with diplomacy. In addition, South Korea's unprecedentedly aggressive posture toward North Korea after the attacks of 2010 forced a new, distortive priority on US policy-makers: preventing South Korea from triggering a war. These factors combined with the rapid collapse of the main achievement of US diplomacy with North Korea in the Obama era (the "Leap Day Deal" in 2012) to later lock US policymakers into primarily focusing on coercive pressure and military options. The policy inertia and military emphasis that defined Obama's second term in office was the logical continuation of the evolution from engagement to deterrence in the early years of his presidency.

Comprehensive, Verifiable, Irreversible Denuclearization

As much as the Obama administration may have wanted to distance itself from the attitude and style of its predecessor, on substance, the Obama era represented far more continuity than change. The United States conducted at least three comprehensive reviews of North Korea policy from 2009 to 2016,[2] always ending up in the same place: bolster the alliance with South Korea, keep the pressure of economic sanctions on North Korea, use military exercises as a signaling device, and engage North Korea diplomatically as much as circumstances allow. This was a set of reasonable enough activities, but not a strategy. Neither was it any different than the types of activities pursued as part of the Bush administration's North Korea policy. During his first term, Obama would be forced to hold to the Bush administration's 6PT as *the* model for achieving denuclearization. The even bigger problem, in hindsight at least, was Obama's seemingly uncritical embrace of the ends that Bush had sought in North Korea.

Obama's team held fast to the Bush-era formulation calling for nothing short of the complete, verifiable, irreversible dismantlement of North Korea's nuclear arsenal and programs, known as "CVID" in policy parlance. But the Bush administration, who came up with the CVID formulation, was justified in holding to it because of North Korea's active engagement with the 6PT process, which explicitly aimed at CVID. And however unlikely denuclearization might have been, under Bush, North Korea had at least superficially endorsed that end-state in the September 19, 2005 Joint Statement—a negotiated declaration in which North Korea acknowledged it had nuclear weapons and was willing to eliminate them—making it hard for the Bush administration not to demand CVID. By the time Obama took office though, North Korea had already declared 6PT "dead," its nuclear program was expanding unfettered, and there was no plausible pathway to resolving the inspection and verification issues that had bogged down the Bush administration in its final months. North Korea had no incentive to rejoin the 6PT. The goal of denuclearization was becoming implausible, and even more so as time passed. Obama had been handed a virtually unattainable goal, but instead of refining or refuting it, he doubled down on it.

The adoption of denuclearization as a US goal in 2009 and subsequently presented two major problems. First, US North Korea policy under Obama had no theory of the case; what the administration did was utterly incommensurate with what it claimed to want. A mishmash of sanctions, humanitarian assistance, military exercises, and intermittent diplomacy was no way to convince an adversary to unilaterally disarm. Insisting, moreover, on a mode of interaction (the 6PT) that your adversary repeatedly rejected was hardheaded at best, and made the entire diplomatic effort disingenuous at worst. Even the claim that denuclearization was possible became increasingly dubious as North Korea's nuclear program progressed, bilateral ties became more hostile, and both sides behaved as though time was on their side.

Second, CVID tied the hands of US policymakers in ways that short-circuited diplomacy from the outset. North Korean diplomats had, by 2009, given up the pretense that the North was willing to denuclearize, though there was some continued flirtation with the possibility of resuming 6PT, because the United States wanted it so much. If North Korea was bent on being a nuclear state, and in fact already possessed nuclear weapons, and the US purpose of negotiations was to denuclearize North Korea, then the two sides had an irreducible conflict of interest. The primary thing the United States wanted to negotiate was the one thing North Korea had no interest in discussing, unless it could somehow extract benefits from the discussion.

From Hope to Cynicism

Even as nuclear diplomacy collapsed in the waning months of the Bush administration, the incoming Obama administration publicly and repeatedly signaled its interest in renewing diplomatic engagement with North Korea, in the form of resuming the 6PT negotiating process.[3] From the outset, US officials were communicating with North Korea through the "New York channel"—a direct line with Pyongyang through the North Korean Mission at the United Nations Headquarters in New York. In the first days of the administration, Obama's point-man on North Korea policy, Ambassador Stephen Bosworth, tried to convince Pyongyang that Obama was genuinely interested in improving relations and resuming 6PT. They were simultaneously reaching out to Beijing, Seoul, Tokyo, and Moscow, in an effort to pick up 6PT where the Bush administration had left off. But it did not take long for Kim Jong Il to test the new American president, conducting a missile test under the guise of launching a "satellite" on April 5, 2009, followed by a second nuclear test a month later (May 25).

The month before the April test, which was in violation of pre-existing UN resolutions, US nonproliferation experts unaffiliated with the US Government (part of a community of "Track 2" nongovernmental interlocutors with a history of interacting with North Korea unofficially) visited Pyongyang to meet with North Korean officials. The Track 2 group explained that the Obama administration was "a new operator with a new sort of attitude and perspective and that they should expect there would be very different overtures" as compared with Bush.[4] But according to nonproliferation expert Paul Caroll, who was on the trip, "They weren't buying it."[5] Instead, the North Koreans informed Caroll's group and others (including the State Department) that they would soon be conducting the functional equivalent of a ballistic missile test. US officials warned that a missile test would set back diplomacy, but North Korea proceeded with it and the nuclear test anyway. In response, the United States pursued pressure at the United Nations, first through a UN Security Council Presidential Statement of condemnation on April 13, and then through new sanctions (UNSC Resolution 1874) on June 12. True to form, North Korea responded to pressure with pressure, following the imposition of UN sanctions with another round of missile tests, in July.

While this tit-for-tat was happening, the United States and North Korea were also negotiating the release of two American journalists whom North Korea had detained and charged with illegally entering North Korea for crossing over from the Chinese border without visas.[6] The State Department offered to send multiple high-level former US dignitaries as a gesture to earn the release of the detained journalists. But North Korea would only entertain a visit by former President Bill Clinton. So in close coordination with the State Department, Clinton prepared to visit Pyongyang, which he did on August 4, 2009.

Bill Clinton, Meet Kim Jong Il

The Clinton visit was symbolically momentous, and ultimately enlightening about subsequent problems with North Korea. Even as a private citizen, North Korea was well aware of his close ties to the Obama administration by virtue of Hillary Clinton serving as Secretary of State. And according to some Clinton-era officials like Wendy Sherman,[7] there is also an alternative history of the Korean Peninsula where, had President Clinton visited Pyongyang at the end of his presidency and affirmed a bilateral relationship with North Korea and a personal one with Kim Jong Il, North Korea would have lived up to its end of the Agreed Framework and a complementary deal to constrain its missile program.

But this is probably too sanguine a counterfactual. North Korea was already secretly developing nuclear weapons (despite its obligations under the Agreed Framework) by the time both sides were discussing a possible presidential visit in the final months of the Clinton administration. There is also no reason to think that the Bush administration would have approached Korea any differently had Clinton made the visit; and the real negative, possibly irreversible, turning point in US–North Korea relations was when Bush labeled North Korea part of the "Axis of Evil" in 2002. The downturn in relations under Bush probably would have happened regardless of anything Clinton could have done as president.

The August 4 Clinton conversation with Kim Jong Il presaged much about how US–North Korea relations would play out for the rest of the Obama administration, and so is worth addressing at some length here. Details of what they talked about were buried for years, but in a 2016 Wikileaks hack of Hillary Clinton emails, one email within the larger tranche that was put online included an eight-page memo detailing the Clinton–Kim Jong Il meeting.[8] The fact of Clinton's presence in Pyongyang is what won the release of the American journalists, so very little time was spent talking about that issue, even though it was purportedly what brought Clinton and Kim together. Instead, Kim lamented that Clinton never visited him in 2000/2001 and that if Democrats had won the 2000 election, "all agreements would have been implemented, the DPRK would have had light water reactors, and the United States would have had a new friend in Northeast Asia."[9] Kim also explained that after Bush's "Axis of Evil" labeling of North Korea, he "felt it necessary to resume nuclear development"; the 6PT negotiations were largely (but not entirely) in bad faith and at no point eliminated North Korea's existential need for nuclear weapons. Kim made two additional points that hinted at problems to come. First, he told Clinton that his early impressions of the Obama administration "were not very good. President Obama said publicly he was willing to talk even with hostile countries, but he was obstructing the DPRK's right to send satellites into orbit."[10] Second, Kim stressed the importance of bilateral US–North Korea relations over 6PT, saying in response to Clinton's plea to return to 6PT, "Pursuing Six Party Talks and neglecting bilateral talks would not resolve hostilities ... If bilateral talks went well, cooperative relations within the Six Party Talks would be possible."[11]

Clinton's remarks, in turn, similarly presaged much about the US perspective to come under Obama:

> With the right efforts, it would be possible to achieve a final peace treaty, pledges of non-aggression, and help for the DPRK from all Six Party partners, beginning with a non-aggression pledge ... *If the DPRK denuclearized* [emphasis added] ... But under the present circumstances, the president could not walk away from the Six Party Talks ... [and you] must not make President Obama pick between a bilateral relationship and the Six Party Talks.[12]

Clinton tried to convince Kim that President Obama "needed strong, cooperative relations" with North Korea's neighbors, "For reasons having nothing to do with the DPRK," which in turn necessitated the 6PT.[13]

Foreshadowing Misunderstanding and Conflicts of Interest

With hindsight, the terms of the conflict that ensued throughout Obama's time in office were readily apparent in the Clinton and Kim remarks. Kim saw 6PT as meaningless, or at least not a way to resolve the root of the problem in his view, which was mutual mistrust and hostility; he also saw nothing in Obama's early presidency to indicate he would be different from Bush. Rhetoric, Kim judged, was cheap talk. And, from Kim's perspective, with South Korea's conservative President Lee Myung-bak taking an openly hard line against North Korea, the idea of giving the South a stake in nuclear negotiations by virtue of the 6PT format would have been its own form of sabotage or disingenuous diplomacy. North Korea treated America's willingness to tolerate testing ballistic missile technology under the guise of "satellite launches" as a litmus test for America's willingness to pursue better bilateral relations. Clinton, for his part, explained why Obama was not able to jettison the 6PT model politically, but also gave no indication that he agreed the bilateral relationship with North Korea was at the root of the problem. For the United States, the problem with North Korea was as much a means of making progress in other regional relationships, especially with South Korea and China, as it was something to be resolved in its own right.

North Korea was incredibly transparent about the non-negotiability of its nuclear status at the beginning of the Obama presidency and subsequently. It declared the 6PT "dead" in 2008, "permanently" withdrew from them in April 2009 (following the UN Presidential Statement of condemnation),[14] mentioned directly to Clinton that they would not resolve the hostilities that necessitated nuclear weapons in August, and reiterated permanent withdrawal from the 6PT again in November 2009. North Korea wanted a good relationship with the United States, but not necessarily as a strict trade for denuclearization. Rather, if the fundamental character of the relationship transformed in such a way that the North no longer saw a threat in the United States, its need for nuclear weapons would diminish. This is hardly the same thing as being willing to negotiate denuclearization per se. Recognizing North Korea's position for what it was would have forced the Obama administration into either abandoning diplomacy or its goal of denuclearization. Neither option was politically tenable so early in Obama's tenure.

The Obama administration's North Korea policy started from a position of self-perceived conciliation and goodwill. After North Korea's belligerence in the early months of Obama's tenure, optimism had largely been replaced with skepticism. Still, Ambassador Bosworth, Assistant Secretary of State Kurt Campbell, and the Asia hands at the

NSC saw a possible pathway to denuclearization by using bilateral talks to resume 6PT, despite ratcheting sanctions, international condemnation, and US backing for South Korea's increasingly belligerent posture toward North Korea.[15]

The Antecedents of Strategic Patience

The events of 2010–12 would shed virtually all optimism in favor of a more openly cynical, confrontational approach to North Korea. By April 2012, the Obama administration's two-track approach of carrots and sticks had failed, but with nothing to replace it other than greater emphasis on sticks over carrots.

Opening the Nuclear Umbrella and Fearing Ally Entrapment

North Korean "provocations" would come to define 2010 and constrain much of what followed in later years. In its classical style of limited, isolated violence at a time and place of its choosing, North Korea launched two surprise attacks against South Korea that year. The first was a torpedo attack on the South Korean ship *Cheonan*, which took place on March 26 and killed 46 sailors on board. The second was an artillery barrage against South Korean Marines on Yeonpyeong Island in November. The artillery barrage killed four and wounded dozens.

Sinking of the *Cheonan*

The attack on the *Cheonan* was eventually considered an act of revenge for the North Korean Navy's poor showing at the Battle of Daecheong the prior November, though it was initially unclear why the ship sank and North Korea denied responsibility.[16] South Korea's President Lee Myung-bak wanted to retaliate for the presumed attack, but the United States urged him to first agree to a multinational investigation about the cause of the sinking.[17] That investigation, which took more than a month to conclude, confirmed that the ship was sunk by a torpedo originating from North Korea. The time delay from attack to attribution that the investigation process introduced blunted South Korea's retaliatory fervor, but animosity lingered.

Because the Obama administration had both sought to regionalize the North Korea problem as much as possible and prioritize its alliances with South Korea and Japan, the *Cheonan* attack became a catalyst for greater US solidarity with its aggrieved ally, which by definition translated into greater antagonism toward North Korea. After the *Cheonan* investigation came to a close, the United States backed all of President Lee's new hard-line measures on North Korea, and announced new sanctions of its own in July that targeted North Korean entities engaged in illicit arms trading. More consequentially, the United States also began coordinating a series of larger and more frequent military exercises with the South as a show of resolve against the North, including a controversial deployment of an aircraft carrier to the Yellow Sea, off of North Korea's western coast.[18] The amplified schedule of military exercises led to a statement from North Korea's National Defense Commission that it "will start a retaliatory sacred war of their own style based on nuclear deterrent any time necessary in order to counter the U.S. imperialists and the South Korean puppet forces."[19]

The month after the *Cheonan* sank, the Pentagon issued its Nuclear Posture Review (NPR), an infrequent document establishing America's declaratory policy and strategy regarding its own nuclear weapons. Although during Obama's first months in office he gave a high-minded speech in Prague with a vision of "Global Zero"—a world without nuclear weapons—his administration's approach to nuclear weapons was more pragmatic, even contradictory at times. The NPR reflected that pragmatism, affirming the role of extended nuclear deterrence to key allies, including South Korea. The emphasis on extended nuclear deterrence that followed might seem an odd move for a US presidency initially dedicated to the abolition of nuclear weapons, but it was propelled by the *Cheonan* incident in two connected ways. First, it needed to preempt South Korean conservative hawks, who were already murmuring about the need either for the redeployment of US tactical nuclear weapons to South Korea or for the South to develop its own nuclear weapons. Institutionalizing an extended deterrence consultation mechanism could, in theory, redirect and forestall such extreme options.

The *Cheonan* had also become a searing reminder of a historical fact that Washington had not taken seriously in decades: that North Korean provocations themselves, which were bound to occur on occasion, could be a strategic problem. Limited acts of violence such as this fell well below the threshold for justifying a retaliatory war, but disagreement over how to respond risked becoming a wedge between the United States and South Korea. In the process, otherwise small acts of violence eroded the credibility of US commitments to the South, which was what had long prevented it from going nuclear itself. Frank Sinatra famously observed that if you can make it as a lounge singer in New York, you can make it anywhere, henceforth the "Sinatra test." North Korean provocations became an inverse "Sinatra test": If the United States could not or would not handle relatively minor incidents from North Korea, how could it be counted on to protect and fight alongside the South if war broke out anew? Institutionalizing extended deterrence consultations gave South Korea a formal outlet for its angst about US credibility that promised to also incorporate South Korean suggestions for how to adapt deterrence to satisfy their political-military concerns.

Artillery Attack on Yeonpyeong-do

The second North Korean attack against South Korea was far less deniable than the *Cheonan* sinking. Not only was the second incident caught on tape (literally a smoking gun) but the attack used artillery fires, making it impossible for North Korea to deny culpability. (Who else could be firing artillery shells at South Korean forces from a northern position?) South Korean Marines in the Northwest Islands were part of an amphibious exercise called *Hoguk* ("protect the nation"). The exercise was a recurring one, not created as part of the surge in military activity following the *Cheonan* attack, though it took place against that backdrop. North Korea had threatened the South Koreans in advance that they would attack if the South went through with the exercise, but the South Korean military dismissed the threat.[20] The South Koreans were dismissive partly because they did not believe the threat, which left them caught off guard by it, but also because they had no appetite for capitulating to North Korean demands following the *Cheonan* attack.[21]

In response, South Korea immediately scrambled fighter aircraft to bomb the North Korean artillery positions that had fired on Yeonpyeong Island, and possibly the base where its artillery forces were headquartered as well. But Obama officials, after dealing with President Lee's growing obstreperousness post-*Cheonan*, already feared that South Korea might drag the United States into a war with reckless action.[22] So US officials used their close ties with South Korean counterparts, and the Combined Forces Command that integrated both countries' forces, to prevent the South from retaliation. Secretary Gates, Secretary Clinton, Chairman of the Joint Chiefs of Staff Michael Mullen, all phoned their South Korean counterparts to plead for restraint and not to bomb North Korea in retaliation, as did President Obama with President Lee.[23] Ally entreaties worked, at least in the heat of the moment; President Lee ordered the fighters to return to base without firing on North Korea.[24]

But convincing South Korea not to respond to yet another act of North Korean violence came at a price, forcing a new, competing priority on the United States—preventing ally South Korea from triggering an unwanted war. That priority locked the United States into a hardline policy toward North Korea that was at odds with its then-ongoing, but ultimately short-lived, attempts at bilateral diplomacy. President Lee, through his spokesperson, vowed "manifold retaliation" if North Korea continued with its belligerent behavior, suggesting that not only would the South retaliate against units that might attack it, but it would also attack unrelated North Korean targets like missile facilities.[25] Washington immediately announced the dispatch of the *George Washington* Carrier Strike Group to the Yellow Sea, illustrating how reassuring South Korea for the sake of restraining it outweighed even the vocal opposition of Beijing.

In the months following the artillery attack, South Korea's conservative government adopted a "never again" mindset, engaging in a belligerent rhetorical style that aped that of the North. Within a month, and against US advice, South Korea re-conducted the same amphibious exercise, daring the North to attack again, which it did not. This was just the beginning of a period of heightened hostility between North and South Korea not seen since the 1960s. On the South Korean side, the confrontational tone was set at the top and trickled down. Also the following month, President Lee said in an address to the nation, "South Korea has come to know that only a strong response to armed provocations can prevent war and keep the peace ... Being afraid of war cannot, in the end, stop war ... We must launch a merciless, massive counterattack when we are hit by a surprise attack."[26] That speech was neither the first nor the last time he would threaten disproportionate retaliation against the North. Following Lee's lead, it became common for South Korean officials and academics to make exaggerated threats and underscore newfound resolve in various ways, all of which ultimately impacted more on the United States than on North Korea. South Korea's willingness to take greater risks in the name of deterrence made US officials "concerned about the possibility that a small-scale North Korean provocation could escalate."[27]

US fears that South Korea might inadvertently ignite a war were warranted. The following spring, South Korea announced Defense Reform Plan 307 (DRP 307), which included dozens of recommendations from a "blue-ribbon panel" of eminent experts in South Korea's policy milieu. Their purpose was to refashion the South Korean military into a deterrence force rather than simply a warfighting force, though the distinction was as much about attitude as it was capabilities.[28] Among the recommendations enacted as part of DRP 307 was a redistribution of defense investments to emphasize precision-strike and other advanced weapons technologies that would allow South Korea to make good on its promises for swift and disproportionate punishment if North Korea again attacked.[29] More worryingly for US officials, DRP 307 also legitimated a decision to delegate retaliation authority to local field commanders in the event of another North Korean provocation. The ostensible reason for delegating authority for attack was to ensure a rapid response, but it also meant retaliation decisions bypassed the Blue House (South Korea's presidential residence) and the White House, making sure that alliance politics would not hold South Korea back as it had twice in 2010. This delegated authority change was part of a broader doctrinal shift that South Korea's Ministry of National Defense initially called "proactive deterrence," which promised overwhelming punishment in the event of future North Korean transgressions.[30]

Separate from the near-term concerns that South Korea might drag the United States into war was an increasingly vocal South Korean policy discourse that urged either a redeployment of US tactical nuclear weapons that were withdrawn at the end of the Cold War, or an independent South Korean nuclear capability for deterrence if North Korea was going to keep its nuclear arsenal. Some conservative lawmakers in South Korea, as well as think-tank surrogates for the conservative South Korean government, put forward the reasoning that US extended deterrence commitments were insufficient to prevent North Korean violence twice in 2010, necessitating new extreme measures in the form of nuclear weapons.[31]

South Korea's Executive Branch of government formally disavowed any claims that it sought nuclear weapons, but the Track 2 community in South Korea, which was largely an appendage of the government, persisted with this claim. So too did Assemblyman Chung Mong-joon, a hawkish conservative lawmaker and heir to the Hyundai fortune, who asserted only three months after the Yeonpyeong Island attack that as many as 67 percent of the South Korean people supported at least stationing US nuclear weapons in South Korea.[32]

South Korea's loud talk of nuclear weapons may have been deliberate. At the same time that the South Korean government was publicly distancing itself from the nuclear discourse of its policy elites, it also sought to renegotiate range and payload restrictions for its cruise missiles, which it wanted to be able to strike anywhere in North Korea.[33] A cynic would say that the South Korean government was deliberately stoking an informal nuclear discourse in order to strengthen its formal justification for longer-range missiles that would otherwise be in violation of the Missile Technology Control Regime (an international supplier's cartel agreement aimed at limiting the proliferation of missile capabilities).[34] But even if this were so, the nuclear discourse gradually took on a life of its own. Public calls by experts and lawmakers in favor of South Korean nuclear weapons *grew* substantially in the years after it successfully concluded its "New Missile Guidelines" discussions with the United States in 2012.[35]

In sum, North Korea's pair of attacks in 2010 played a major role in shaping subsequent US policy in a more rigid, confrontational direction. Ironically, this had less to do with North Korea or hawkish instincts within the Obama administration than it did with adapting to the exigencies of the moment and needing credible ways to reassure South Korea—for the sake of preventing an unwanted war, and for preserving the US alliance system in Asia.

Bilateral Diplomacy, the "Leap Day Deal," and the End of Talks

The renewed importance of reassuring and restraining South Korea after the attacks of 2010 made bilateral diplomacy with the North more difficult, but only temporarily so; the Obama administration had invested too much political capital in a diplomatic approach to abandon it. In July 2010, against the backdrop of heightened alliance military drills, the UN Security Council issued a Presidential Statement (at US urging) condemning the North Korean attack on the *Cheonan*. North Korea responded by threatening a "sacred war," denouncing alliance exercises as having "violated the spirit of the U.N. statement," and yet, paradoxically, claiming it was also willing to return to some version of multilateral negotiations.[36]

The bilateral negotiations that followed the bombast involved exceedingly modest demands. They were not even publicly described as negotiations by each side, but rather "high-level talks." The United States was asked to provide humanitarian assistance, which USAID had in abundance, and a non-aggression pledge that it had already offered many times over prior decades. North Korea was asked to reaffirm its commitment to the 2005 Joint Statement that it had previously agreed to, and to refrain from weapons testing or reprocessing activities at its nuclear facilities (specifically Yongbyon). These easily satisfiable requirements on both sides required regular communication through the New York channel and several rounds of meetings in Pyongyang, Vienna, Beijing, and New York over the course of more than two years.

Why did it take so long to clear such a low hurdle? For the same reasons the talks ultimately fell apart: because North Korea did not wish for what it termed "satellite launches" to count as missile tests, and because the only reason the United States was entertaining bilateral talks in the first place was to persuade a reluctant North Korea to return to 6PT. On a deeper level, this reflected disagreement about what the bilateral talks were for: the start of a bilateral relationship versus an on-ramp for the 6PT and CVID.

The series of formal bilateral discussions would culminate in coordinated, simultaneous, but independent (and very dissimilar) statements from the State Department and the North Korean Foreign Ministry. These parallel statements, announced on February 29, 2012, led to their being dubbed the "Leap Day Deal."[37] As part of the deal, both sides reiterated their commitment to the spirit of the 2005 Joint Statement, to returning to 6PT, and that the United States had "no hostile intent" toward the North. Beyond that, numerous technical discrepancies arose between the two statements that highlight how little agreement actually existed between the two sides, and perhaps why the "deal" took the form of separate unilateral statements.

North Korea's statement read:

> The DPRK, upon request by the U.S. and with a view to maintaining positive atmosphere for the DPRK–U.S. high-level talks, agreed to a *moratorium on* nuclear tests, long-range missile launches, and *uranium enrichment activity at Nyongbyon and allow the IAEA to monitor the moratorium on uranium enrichment* while productive dialogues continue.[38] [emphasis added]

The US statement read:

> the DPRK has agreed to implement a *moratorium on* long-range missile launches, nuclear tests and *nuclear activities at Yongbyon, including uranium enrichment activities*. The DPRK has also agreed to the return of *IAEA inspectors to* verify and monitor the moratorium on uranium enrichment activities at Yongbyon and *confirm the disablement of the 5-MW reactor and associated facilities*[39] [emphasis added]

The differences were painfully clear to pundits and reporters at the time. North Korea's statement suspends *uranium* enrichment activities, but it does not mention either plutonium or other nuclear activities, such as reprocessing spent fuel rods. In the North Korean version, moreover, IAEA inspectors were only to be allowed to monitor uranium enrichment suspension, not to confirm the disablement of the 5-megawatt nuclear reactor and "associated facilities" at the Yongbyon nuclear complex. The US statement, by contrast, specifically claims that North Korea agreed to allow IAEA inspectors a wide mandate, and that it also agreed to suspend effectively all nuclear activity. At a background press briefing, the State Department confirmed that its interpretation of what North Korea agreed to included *all* nuclear-related activity.[40]

Even more consequential was that neither statement mentioned whether "satellite launch vehicles" (SLVs) constituted "missiles" for the purposes of the testing moratorium. Given that the underlying technology was the same, the US position—that language games to work around the UN missile testing prohibition did not change the underlying reality that SLV launches *were* violations of a testing moratorium—was sensible. US officials had been abundantly clear with the North Korean Foreign Ministry that SLV launches would count as missiles and therefore violate the Leap Day Deal,[41] and they confirmed North Korea understood this. Yet North Korea never acknowledged as much publicly, and the United States could not convince North Korea to do so. That was a warning sign.

This difference of interpretation about SLVs would come to a head on April 12, when North Korea conducted a long-range missile test that it labeled an SLV launch, despite the Leap Day Deal being in place and numerous prior warnings from the United States about the consequences of conducting the test.[42] North Korea's Foreign Ministry announced its intention to move forward with the missile test on March 16, and expressed the expectation that the Leap Day Deal provisions should still hold. This put the United States in a difficult position that it should have foreseen and avoided. Either build in a discount that allows for less than perfect implementation of the agreement (especially when the "agreement" included linguistic discrepancies that gave North Korea plausible justifications for violations) or make over-the-top good faith concessions that incentivized North Korea to hold faithful to the agreement. The Obama administration had not been clear-eyed about why prior agreements with North Korea had failed, even though most of the players involved on the US side had been working Korea issues for prior administrations.

The result was the end of the Leap Day Deal, no justifiable theory of the case for a diplomatic approach to attaining CVID, and a newly deep reservoir of bad faith and cynicism among US officials.

So why did North Korea violate an agreement it had reached only a month prior? Why agree to the Leap Day Deal only to immediately break its terms in such a transparent, public way? The answer is not entirely known, but the best explanation blends dynastic succession politics and bureaucratic politics. Kim Jong Il died of a heart attack on December 19, 2011, two months after the United States and North Korea had agreed to the contours of the Leap Day Deal during the "high-level talks" that took place. Kim Jong Un's succession to his father was being publicly reported by January 15, 2009 and was therefore no surprise, but nobody knew if the younger Kim would uphold the terms of an agreement that was close but not yet finalized before he came to power. At the same time, the missile launch had been pre-scheduled for the window between April 12–16, to coincide with the 100th anniversary of Kim Il Sung's birth. So Kim Jong Un, newly in charge, was not in a position to overturn his Foreign Ministry's proposal for a profitable (and stabilizing) diplomatic deal with the United States. Neither was Kim able to cancel a pre-established missile test (an initiative outside the Foreign Ministry's purview) that was symbolically linked to his grandfather's birthday anniversary and approved while his father was still alive. Taking the path of least resistance, Kim Jong Un allowed competing bureaucratic proposals—to conclude the Leap Day Deal and conduct a missile launch in contravention of the deal—to go forward.

The Leap Day Deal was fraught because it was not really a deal to begin with. The United States was negotiating what it treated as letter-of-the-law commitments but that North Korea treated as rhetorical sentiments; Pyongyang's "commitment" language was more attitudinal than contractual. The North Korean Foreign Ministry was not in a position to make decisions on behalf of the equities of other stakeholders with competing preferences (for a missile launch, for example) in its national security system.[43] Kim Jong Un was not in a position to cancel a celebratory missile launch that his father had likely approved and that satisfied at least some stakeholders in the regime. Criticism of the United States for not getting North Korea's explicit commitment to include SLVs as satellite launches misses the point: North Korea was not in a position to negotiate a testing moratorium until after Kim Il Sung's birthday anniversary, and short of having a better bilateral relationship with the United States, neither would it sign on to denuclearization with anything more than lip service. The United States taking a legalistic approach to North Korea negotiations would not have produced a better outcome. In all likelihood, it would not have even produced a different outcome. As with the Agreed Framework and 6PT, the only two ways the United States could have secured a better, more enduring result from negotiations with North Korea was if it was willing to grant much grander concessions and symbolic gestures of good faith, or build in allowances for North Korea to fall short of perfect implementation of its commitments. The United States could do neither, so it got a brittle, quickly reversible deal that ultimately did more to exacerbate hostility than if no deal had been negotiated.

The above circumstances, and specifically the collapse of the obviously primed-for-failure Leap Day Deal, brought on the real beginning of Obama's policy of strategic patience. As long as the United States held to CVID, it had scarcely any alternative, short of military force.

Waiting Out the Threat with Strategic Patience

When the Leap Day Deal fell apart in April 2012, the conditions for a future crisis began falling into place. Kim Jong Un doubled down on his father's commitment to developing a survivable nuclear arsenal, and the Obama administration was left with either contemplating a new set of goals for North Korea, or succumbing to hawkish policy inertia. It did the latter, adopting an approach eventually dubbed "strategic patience"—part statement of policy, part bad-faith negotiating strategy. In the words of former Assistant Secretary of State Kurt Campbell, an architect of Obama's Asia policy, "the United States is playing a longer, more patient, and more strategic game than North Korea. It has demonstrated a willingness to negotiate with Pyongyang but not to budge on issues of strategic concern—such as North Korea's nuclear status."[44] In the same breath, Campbell recounted the various ways the United States has imposed continuous pressure on Pyongyang and the danger of North Korean violence. This, then, was strategic patience in a nutshell: In parallel with prioritizing the US deterrence posture toward North Korea and imposing economic pressure on Pyongyang, strategic patience entailed holding out the rhetorical willingness to engage diplomatically, but with the proviso that any negotiations be tied to impractical demands, in this case, in service of resuming the 6PT nuclear negotiating process with North Korea and denuclearization. It amounted to what Korea scholar and former White House adviser Victor Cha once described as "hawk engagement"—ultimately taking a hard line, but initially framing it in a way that makes it look like you are being reasonable and doing so reluctantly, because diplomacy had been exhausted.[45]

A Threat Looming Larger Than Ever

North Korea had a functional arsenal of rockets and missiles, as well as a modest nuclear capability, before Obama came to office. North Korean nuclear weapons, which existed only rudimentarily and as a latent threat in 2008, became very real over the course of Obama's two terms in office. The US intelligence community watched and reported as Kim Jong Un raced for reliable, diverse intercontinental ballistic missiles (ICBMs) capable of carrying miniaturized nuclear warheads, but US policy took only modest steps to impede Kim.

The most serious threat in this regard, specifically because of the difficulty of preempting and targeting it, was the development of the KN-08 and other variants that followed. The KN-08 was a road-mobile ballistic missile capable of using solid-fuel propellant. This meant it could fire a missile at US territory with little to no advance detection, change locations before the launch site was discovered, and fire again from a different launch site. If it functioned as intended, the KN-08 would effectively give North Korea a secure second-strike nuclear capability. Allowing that eventuality was unthinkable to US officials. If North Korea had the ability to reliably strike US territory with nuclear weapons, it would introduce a greater risk of strategic "decoupling"[46] with ally South Korea and diminish America's ability to credibly threaten North Korea in the name of denuclearization or nuclear nonproliferation. It would also mean that there could be no invasion of Pyongyang or attempt at regime change without North Korea resorting to nuclear war.

Road-Mobile ICBMs as the Sum of All Fears

Obama's Deputy Director of the CIA, Michael Morell, would comment after leaving government service that, in contrast with US policy on North Korea, which had been largely marked by failure, US intelligence on North Korea had been a resounding success: "over a very long period of time, the intelligence community has accurately assessed both North Korea's nuclear program and its missile program."[47] US concerns about a mobile missile like the KN-08 were rarely publicly advertised in the early years of the Obama era, but in 2011, US defense and intelligence officials (though not the White House) began going public with indications that they saw KN-08 developments as a significant and rapidly advancing threat. In June that year, former Secretary of Defense Robert Gates made one of the first open references to US concerns about the KN-08, telling *The Daily Beast*: "North Korea now constitutes a direct threat to the United States ... They are developing a road-mobile ICBM ... It's a huge problem. As we've found out in a lot of places, finding mobile missiles is very tough."[48] Gates's statement opened up a flood of more public hand-wringing by US officials, especially following an April 2012 military parade during which North Korea unveiled a static display of the KN-08. In 2013, Admiral James Winnefeld, the Vice Chairman of the Joint Chiefs of Staff, commented, "We believe the KN-08 probably does have the range to reach the United States . . . The (North) Korean threat went just a little bit faster than we might have expected."[49] In 2015, the Commander of US Strategic Command mentioned the KN-08 several times in a press briefing, explaining that "It's a threat that we cannot ignore as a country."[50] That statement was followed only a month later by remarks from the Commander of US Northern Command (NORTHCOM), responsible for military defense of the continental United States, that "Our assessment is that they have the ability to put a nuclear weapon on a KN-08 and shoot it at the homeland."[51]

These were hardly the only statements by US defense and intelligence officials about the KN-08; there were many others. But they are representative of the larger fact pattern: starting in 2011, Obama officials were increasingly warning publicly, and often without prompting, about the threat the KN-08 posed and the worrying progress North Korea was making. At a June 2013 summit between President Obama and Chinese President Xi Jinping, Obama impressed upon his guest the mounting threat the United States saw in North Korea's nuclear progress, telling Xi that "North Korea's nuclear program is now a core concern of the United States, just as Taiwan is to China."[52] The United States had never made a comparison like that before, and had not elevated the threat it saw in North Korea's nuclear program to that level since the 1994 nuclear crisis.

Of course, the KN-08 was not the only reason for America's concerns. Traditional fixed missile sites capable of launching nuclear ICBMs and shorter-range missiles were also a problem. So was the fact that North Korea had plutonium *and* uranium enrichment pathways to developing nuclear weapons, which increased the potential estimated size of its nuclear arsenal. North Korea's move to begin using solid-fuel propellant for its missiles introduced additional complications for finding and tracking North Korea's mobile missile launchers. And in May and November 2015, North Korea would claim it had successfully tested a submarine-launched ballistic missile capability that, even if an overstatement of its actual capability, indicated the direction its nuclear and missile program was going. But the KN-08 was a technical and strategic milestone; a game-changer. By 2015, US officials were publicly judging that North Korea had mastered the process of miniaturization so that a nuclear device could be mounted on an ICBM, including on the KN-08. To the extent that was true, from that point forward, North Korea had a de facto secure second-strike (assured retaliation) capability. It only needed more missile testing to improve its reliability and range, which it would do at a record pace throughout 2016 and 2017.

Beyond Mobile Missiles: Nuclear Weapons Become Status and Doctrine

North Korea's nuclear weapons capabilities became more entrenched, not less, over the course of the Obama presidency. The KN-08 may have represented a strategic milestone in the minds of US officials, but for North Korea it played only one part in its public nuclear posturing and threat-making. As Korea specialists Peter Hayes and Scott Bruce observed, North Korea underwent an evolution in how it saw its own nuclear weapons over time, from a crude and largely symbolic existential deterrent as a "substitute for a [credible] security guarantee from the United States" in 2002, to an instrument of coercion by 2010.[53] By 2016, it was also being prepared for use as an instrument of warfighting.

It was during the Obama presidency that North Korea began the practice of making offensive threats tied specifically to nuclear weapons use, which signaled a more aggressive shift in the value it saw in its nuclear arsenal. Reacting to the US Nuclear Posture Review in 2010, North Korea announced its own nuclear doctrine for the first time, ambiguous though it was: "The mission of the nuclear force of the DPRK is to deter and repel aggression and attack against the country and the nation."[54] That statement was hardly revealing of particular conditions for nuclear use, but it was a symbolic step in the process of trying to consecrate its nuclear status. Soon after the Leap Day Deal fell apart, in May 2012, North Korea went a step further, changing the preamble to its constitution to include reference to itself as a "nuclear state" (*haekboyuguk*, literally a state that possesses nuclear capability or status).[55]

From that point onward, North Korea began acting as if it were defining choices for the United States rather than the inverse. After its failed April 2012 missile launch, it conducted another in December that was successful, and whose timing had taken US officials completely off-guard. At the time of the missile launch, most Obama officials responsible for Korea policy were at a party hosted at the Japanese embassy in Washington.[56] As soon as notification of the launch came through their Blackberries, all the US officials who dealt with Korea had to leave:

"DOD, State, and the White House were just stunned by it. They were shocked."[57] Kim Jong Un would follow that missile surprise with a New Year's speech that laid out his *byungjin* line of simultaneously growing his nation's economy and consolidating its status as a nuclear power. One month later, in February 2013, Pyongyang conducted a third nuclear test, which it claimed demonstrated the ability to miniaturize a nuclear device so that it could convert its ballistic missiles into delivery systems for nuclear warheads.

The day of the third nuclear test, North Korea's Foreign Ministry issued an ultimatum to the United States:

> To respect the DPRK's right to satellite launch and open a phase of détente and stability or to keep to its wrong road leading to the explosive situation by persistently pursuing its hostile policy toward the DPRK. In case the U.S. chooses the road of conflict finally, the world will clearly see the army and the people of the DPRK defend its dignity and sovereignty to the end through a do-or-die battle ... for national reunification and win a final victory.[58]

It was the brinkmanship North Korea had often engaged in over the decades, but with the backdrop of a successful nuclear detonation and missile launch. That ultimatum was the consummation of something that should have been evident since at least 2010: nuclear weapons were officially part of North Korea's offensively oriented theory of victory.

Deepening Hostility, Growing Desperation . . . But Little Action

From spring 2013 to the end of the Obama presidency, North Korea continued to refine its nuclear and missile capabilities unrestrained, though early 2013 may have been when it transcended the most important milestone on the path to securing a reliable nuclear deterrent. US nuclear threats toward North Korea, which were once virtually cost- and risk-free, now risked putting the world's newest nuclear state on a hair trigger.

Adversely shifting circumstances should have stimulated a rethink of long-held assumptions and policies from the Obama administration. Instead, both sides were locked into a confrontational path over what now appeared an irreducible conflict of strategic interests.

Strategic Irritants

Even beyond the now-evident friction resulting from a clash of strategic interests, the various drivers and instruments of strategic patience would, on their own, have provided plenty of fuel to animosities with North Korea. America's recurring nuclear bomber overflights and alliance military exercises, for instance, elicited predictable venom from Pyongyang, even though they had more to do with reassuring South Korea. Increasingly cavalier talk of regime collapse, unification, and plans for assassinating Kim Jong Un similarly made North Korea bristle. Still other irritants appeared in US–North Korea relations from 2013 to 2016 that helped to further rigidify the antagonism of each toward the other. The December 2012 surprise missile test had been a professional embarrassment to Obama's Asia hands, providing an emotional accelerant to the decisions in the following months to escalate military signals and threats in various ways. North Korea continued to detain a number of US citizens on trumped-up charges. North Korean reconnaissance drones started appearing in South Korea. And North Korea's placement of landmines in the DMZ area, which detonated in August 2015, sparked talk of renewed conflict.

As well, the Obama administration's gradual tightening of economic sanctions amounted to a half-hearted attempt at strangling North Korea, squeezing Pyongyang hard enough that it refused to be an amenable negotiator, but not so hard that it would trigger regime collapse. But sanctions became increasingly targeted, and personal. In 2015 and 2016, sanctions moved from targeting organizations to naming select North Korean individuals as well. For the first time, in July 2016, US sanctions named ten senior officials from the Kim regime, as well as Kim Jong Un himself, blacklisting all from having bank accounts in, or doing business with, US entities.[59] Also in a departure from most past sanctions, which were reactions to North Korean nuclear or missile activity, the sanctions targeting Kim Jong Un and his lieutenants were issued for the regime's domestic political conduct, because "Under Kim Jong Un, North Korea continues to inflict intolerable cruelty and hardship on millions of its own people, including extrajudicial killings, forced labor and torture."[60]

Whether sanctioning Kim helped resolve the nuclear issue was, for the Obama administration, beside the point; the sanctions were compatible with the prevailing strategic patience approach, and an expression of righteous indignation at Pyongyang. It was the world's worst human rights abuser. True to form, North Korean media responded that the sanctions were an "open declaration of war" because the "U.S. dared challenge the dignity of the DPRK Supreme Leadership."[61] Pyongyang's threat of war for violating its "dignity" was a formulation that would become more frequent starting in 2017. The targeted sanctions also led to North Korea cutting off all diplomatic contact with the United States in the final months of the Obama administration.

Cyber Coercion from Both Sides

Eventually the US–North Korea rivalry spilled into cyberspace. Both sides resorted to cyber coercion in 2014, but for different reasons and in different ways.

That year, Sony Pictures Entertainment released *The Interview*, a raunchy comedy satirizing Kim Jong Un and his regime. The plot of the movie involved US journalists going to Pyongyang to interview Kim and then assassinating him on behalf of the CIA. Upon hearing news of the movie's pending release, North Korea charged that it would be an act of terrorism, warning the Obama administration not to allow its release.[62] In November, a hacker group that called itself the "Guardians of Peace" (which the FBI concluded were North Korean agents) accessed Sony intellectual property and thousands of e-mails of Sony executives, some embarrassing, and released them to news media outlets. Sony eventually proceeded with the movie release, but only after the hacking and facing additional threats from the Guardians of Peace group. North Korea technically refused to accept responsibility for the hack, but published a lengthy statement that seemed to take pride in having conducted it:

> The Sony Pictures Entertainment ... daring hurt the *dignity* of the Supreme Leadership of the DPRK ... was exposed to surprisingly sophisticated, destructive and threatening cyber warfare and has been thrown into a bottomless quagmire after suffering property losses worth hundreds of millions of dollars ... the DPRK is more highly praising the "Guardians of Peace" for their righteous deed which prevented in advance the

evil cycle of retaliation—terrorism sparks terrorism ... The
army and the people of the DPRK are fully ready to stand in
confrontation with the U.S. in all war spaces including cyber
warfare space.[63]

North Korea attempted to use threats to prevent *The Interview*'s
release. When that failed, it punished Sony by releasing the information
it had stolen and issuing still more threats.

At a late December press conference, President Obama reacted
to the Sony hack by saying that although not an act of war, "Imagine if
producers, and distributors, and others start engaging in self-censor-
ship because they don't want to offend the sensibilities of somebody
whose sensibilities probably need to be offended ... We will respond
proportionally. And we will respond in a place and time and manner of
our choosing."[64] The administration reviewed a list of retaliatory
options for the hack, including placing North Korea back on the
State Sponsors of Terrorism list, though it lacked legal grounds.[65]
Days later, North Korea's entire internet infrastructure was temporarily brought down by a distributed denial-of-service attack. The State
Department spokesperson, when asked if the United States conducted
the attack, simply responded that "As we implement our responses,
some will be seen, some will not be seen."[66] Two weeks later, in
January 2015, Obama signed an Executive Order imposing new
sanctions against three North Korean organizations and ten "critical
North Korean operatives," for "numerous provocations, particularly
the recent cyber-attack targeting Sony Pictures," though the operatives
it targeted were not hackers themselves, but rather senior members of
the Korean Worker's Party.[67]

As promised, the sanctions were a proportional measure in the
sense of being non-violent, yet applying them to regime elites who were
not involved in the Sony hack operation was a very modest escalation.
The administration could not simply do nothing, but its chosen
responses reveal that it had allowed itself to get locked into a futile
coercive signaling game with North Korea—one that involved no real
risk-taking. The absence of any gamble in US actions was part of the
problem; generally, risk is required for coercion to work. It is not simply
a matter of punishment, but of a willingness to escalate punishment,
even if things might get out of hand. Instead, the administration busied
itself with low-stakes decisions, making the saga a distraction for

policymakers away from the core problem: a nuclear and missile program that was rapidly growing out of control.

The entire Sony hacking incident came several months after Obama had already taken competition with Pyongyang into cyberspace. The *New York Times* eventually reported what had long been speculated but never publicly confirmed: The Obama administration, since at least early 2014, had been waging a covert campaign against North Korea's missile program that included offensive cyber operations.[68] Following North Korea's 2013 nuclear test milestone, by which time it claimed to be able to mount nuclear warheads on missiles, the United States, according to the report, started conducting "left of launch" operations designed to cause North Korean missile tests to fail either on the launch pad or shortly after takeoff. Since 2014, 88 percent of its Musudan intermediate-range ballistic missiles (IRBM) launches (capable of reaching Guam, which houses US nuclear bombers) had failed.[69] Of course, North Korea had a history of occasional failed technology demonstrations, so attributing all the post-2014 failures to a US covert cyber effort is impossible, especially since the United States has not acknowledged the program.

But four circumstantial reasons make it reasonable to infer that the *New York Times* report is basically accurate. First, suspecting sabotage, Kim Jong Un ordered an investigation into its spate of failed launches in October 2016.[70] Kim thought something was aberrant. Second, the life-cycle of a missile program typically sees the most failures in the early phases, yet the Musudan missiles had been developed over decades, and with a far higher rate of failure as they had become operationally ready than in the program's beginning.[71] Third, North Korea began experiencing greater rates of missile launch success when it shifted to surprise launches, night launches, and the use of solid-fuel propellants (which make pre-launch missile activity harder to track).[72] Finally, it would be difficult to otherwise account for such a high percentage of failures concurrent with dramatic overall technological progress by the time Trump took office. If the Musudan failures were only symptoms of organic technical problems, it is hard to see how North Korea emerged in 2017 with demonstrations of reliable long-range delivery systems.

But America's covert efforts to disrupt North Korea's missile progress were shortsighted, however necessary they may have seemed at the time. At best, covert action was a palliative that made it easier for the United States to eschew *overt* action against North Korea's missiles, whether in the form of military options or diplomatic ones. Cyberattacks may have made US officials feel like they were not just sitting idle as the threat mounted, but they were not achieving any discernible strategic effect. Even to the extent that various cyber attacks may have *caused* some missile tests to fail since 2014, it ultimately forced North Korea into being more opaque and less telegraphed about its future missile tests. And failed missile launches still generated iterative knowledge that improved the overall progress of North Korea's missile programs.

The United States would have been better off if North Korea had continued to test missiles in a transparent, public, and predictable manner, as it had in the early Obama years. North Korea started gaining experience firing missiles under duress, just as it would have to do if war broke out.

A Sign of Desperation

As one defense official recalled, "In the last year and a half of Obama's presidency, we did a global pressure campaign focused on China and alternative strategies—deterrence, sanctions. A military strike was more or less ruled out, though Defense was constantly asked for options."[73] This was a context in which the State Department was strategically marginalized, occupying itself with the burdensome task of maintaining international opinion in isolation of Pyongyang; sanctions did not implement themselves. But even as it held the line on strategic patience, the State Department, and specifically Secretary of State John Kerry, made a last-ditch attempt to get some kind of tractable dialogue going with North Korea by trying to convert one of Pyongyang's recurring offers of diplomacy into a serious negotiation.

Twice in October 2015, North Korea's Foreign Ministry delegation to the United Nations proposed holding talks with the United States that would lead to a permanent peace treaty in re-placement of the armistice that had suspended war since 1953 with-out actually ending it. This was not a new suggestion. For decades, North Korea had proposed replacing the armistice with a peace treaty. Pyongyang had always sought it as a means of fracturing the US alliance with South Korea because 1) it removed the impetus for US troops in South Korea, and 2) South Korea, who was not a signatory to the armistice, had long been opposed to peace treaty discussions. After North Korea began pursuing nuclear weapons in earnest in the 1990s, Pyongyang repeatedly sought to divert nuclear diplomacy toward a focus on the peace treaty, claiming that denuclearization could (but would not necessarily) follow the establishment of a permanent peace. North Korea's recurring calls for peace treaty discussions had always been met with US resistance. Even within the 6PT negotiations during the Bush administration—which set up multilateral working groups to address every conceivable regional issue linked to North Korea's nuclear program—there had been no discussion of a peace treaty prior to denuclearization.

Nevertheless, in response to the North's October 2015 proposal for peace treaty talks, the State Department had quietly begun probing discussions with the North to determine their seriousness, letting them know in the process that the United States would be open to resuming negotiations.[74] These contacts took place prior to North Korea's fourth nuclear test, on January 6, 2016, after which the State Department denied (falsely) it had agreed to peace treaty talks.[75] Behind-the-scenes discussions in which the United States signaled the potential for flexibility in its position presaged a public declaration of the same, which was first on display in a joint press conference with Secretary Kerry and Chinese Foreign Minister Wang Yi on February 23, 2016. Minister Wang commented that he and Kerry discussed a proposal to pursue peace treaty talks and denuclearization talks in parallel with one another. Kerry's comments implied endorsement of Wang's proposal without explicitly doing so, saying, "We are still living under the same armistice which ended the war back in the 1950s. So what our hope is is we could move down those tracks one way or the other over a period of time."[76] In March 2016, State Department spokesman John Kirby backed up that statement by commenting that "We haven't ruled out the possibility that there could be some sort of parallel process here ... but there has to be denuclearization on the peninsula and work through the Six Party process to get there."[77] Then, during an April meeting of the G-7 in Japan the following month, Kerry reiterated that "We are prepared to get back to talks ... We have made it clear [to the North Koreans] that we are prepared to negotiate a peace treaty on the Peninsula."[78]

Kerry in effect granted a tactical, rhetorical concession to North Korea—one the United States had always refrained from offering in the past. But US insistence on holding to denuclearization and the 6PT mode of negotiations caused North Korea to balk at the offer, rejecting the US olive branch symbolically (witness the January 6 nuclear test) and verbally, claiming its nuclear program was not under discussion.[79] Yet even after North Korea had repudiated the US offer, Kerry twice publicly acknowledged US willingness to pursue peace treaty talks as long as it did not require abandoning denuclearization or the Six-Party process. Both sides expressed openness to peace treaty talks, but on terms that were mutually unacceptable.

Although this last-minute diplomatic play appeared to go against the larger theme of strategic patience in the latter Obama era, there are multiple plausible incentives for having made the attempt. Had it been successful, it would have given John Kerry a legacy victory in his twilight as Secretary of State. As one State Department official commented, "he has been relentless in his effort to find a way through the impasse caused by North Korea's categorical refusal to similarly [compared to Iran] negotiate an agreement."[80] It may also have been a bureaucratic attempt to reassert Foggy Bottom in a Korea policy space that had become dominated by White House micromanagement and a clear drift in favor of empowering the Pentagon. There was also a more cynical, short-termist view circulating around Washington at the time, that North Korea conducted far fewer provocations during periods when it was engaged in diplomatic processes with the United States.[81] Diplomacy, like deterrence, might help stall North Korea's technical advancements without actually conceding on any US positions.

Whatever the underlying motivation, the State Department's diplomatic Hail Mary was making the best of an increasingly dire situation. After all, it did not entail significant costs or risks, and nothing else the United States was doing was either freezing or rolling back North Korea's rapidly advancing capabilities. Cyber disruption was a stalling action. Sanctions were more about signaling disapproval and providing an object around which international consensus could rally. And the various nuclear bomber overflights, military exercises, and extended deterrence consultations were really about mollifying South Korea. If pressure was eventually to yield "credible negotiations," then talks with the North had to resume at some point. The Obama administration was running out of time.

4 HISTORY'S HINGE POINT: THE CLINTON COUNTERFACTUAL

Nearly everyone in the Washington foreign policy community expected Clinton to win the presidency in 2016, and many appointees from the Obama administration played prominent roles as advisers to and surrogates for Clinton's presidential campaign, among them Michele Flournoy, Kurt Campbell, Laura Rosenberger, and Jake Sullivan.[1] Prior to November 8, 2016, the Obama White House also assumed it would be handing its foreign policy problems, with North Korea foremost among them, to a Clinton team staffed with likeminded, familiar faces.

The widespread expectation of a Clinton victory is one of the reasons it makes sense to construct what a Clinton North Korea policy would have looked like. From the Obama perspective, there was no reason to accept the risks of action today for a problem whose resolution you believe can be delayed until tomorrow. And the ideological overlap between Obama's and Clinton's foreign policy mandarins implied a steady, if somewhat hawkish, hand would continue to steer the ship of state, whatever differences between the two might have existed. Obama was prepared to pass the buck on North Korea to his successor, just as every US president had done since the end of the Cold War.

The other impetus for counterfactually examining a Clinton North Korea policy is to rigorously imagine what would have been possible in an alternative history and consider how closely it resembles what actually happened under Trump. Was the 2017 nuclear crisis inevitable, or an artefact of the Trump team's idiosyncrasies? How much blame does Trump deserve for America's renewed anxieties about nuclear war and North Korea's relentless threats of as much? Answering those questions requires baselining US–North Korea policy under Trump against the only alternative.

The advisers surrounding Clinton saw the flaws of Obama's policy but struggled to formulate meaningful alternatives. They were also split initially into opposing camps: those who favored a renewed attempt at engagement versus those who sought a version 2.0 of strategic patience. Added to that was the witches' brew of North Korea's behavior, the growing and unprecedented threat its capabilities posed, and the Obama administration's rhetorical coarsening in its final days, and what you have is a situation that was primed for crisis in 2017 *even if* Trump lost and Clinton won.

Constructing a Hillary Clinton Doctrine

By almost every available indicator, Clinton would have adopted a muscular, confrontational policy toward North Korea that looked similar to, but more active than, strategic patience under Obama. Part of the reason to expect this is dispositional. Clinton was a pragmatic foreign policy hawk. In 2007, during a debate with then presidential candidate Obama, both candidates were asked if they would meet with Kim Jong Il "without preconditions."[2] Obama agreed he would and Clinton declined, describing Obama's response as "irresponsible and frankly naïve."[3] As Secretary of State, Clinton was an early proponent of the strategic patience policy that would come to define the Obama era on North Korea. Along with Secretary of Defense Robert Gates, who repeatedly portrays Clinton as an interventionist and hawk in his memoir, she only reluctantly got behind the Obama administration's early attempts at extending an olive branch to North Korea.[4] And even her support for diplomatic engagement seemed filtered through a prism of pressure. At her Senate confirmation hearing in January 2009, she said, "it is our strong belief that the six-party talks ... is a vehicle for us to exert pressure on North Korea in a way that is more likely to alter their behavior."[5]

The experts advising Clinton also ended up favoring a more aggressive pressure campaign on North Korea. Her Asia policy team during the 2016 presidential campaign was initially divided into two camps. Some supported a renewed attempt at diplomacy akin to what the Obama administration pursued in 2009; others supported a more hawkish posture that would try to convince other Six-Party players, especially China, to ratchet up their own coercive pressure on Pyongyang. Everyone on the Asia team agreed that Obama's strategic patience policy was the wrong branding, but struggled to pivot away from its substance—policy change would be "a bit more rhetorical than it is actual. There is not a whole lot that can be done with [North Korea] given the limits of the regime and our relationship with [South Korea]."[6] One adviser summarized the views of the group: "There were a testable set of propositions behind 'strategic patience' that we tested ... The Obama administration, for whatever reasons, has not moved on from that effort."[7]

But with the group somewhat divided, it was unclear how to move on from strategic patience. Denuclearization was not a priority, but neither was it abandoned. Attacking North Korea was more or less ruled out ("nobody talked about conducting a nuclear or a first strike ... and if it came up later they would never have talked publicly about it"[8]) but the military instrument played a central role all the same. The internal dispute was whether to emphasize a containment posture or an engagement posture. That debate was settled when momentum shifted decisively in favor of the more hawkish camp following North Korea's fifth nuclear test in September 2016. That test "foreclosed on any possibility of early engagement with North Korea. Dovish voices had no response ... it narrowed the options facing Clinton's would-be North Korea policy to basically Trump's maximum pressure policy but without the war rhetoric."[9] The policy advocated within the campaign lacked a compelling slogan, but in substance amounted to Strategic Patience v.2.0. They were going to elevate the public profile of North Korean human rights abuses (and unification planning), draw a hard redline against North Korean proliferation of nuclear and missile materials (which could involve preventive attacks, but it was not discussed), prioritize extended deterrence for allies, impose maximum sanctions pressure on regime elites, and expend whatever political capital was necessary to persuade China to prod North Korea back to the negotiating table.[10]

A Publicly Hardening Line

After the September 2016 nuclear test, the Clinton campaign surrogates and advisers started publicly touting an aggressive tilt on North Korea that emphasized several of these positions. Michele

Flournoy, who served as Obama's Undersecretary of Defense during his first term, was widely considered the frontrunner to be Clinton's Secretary of Defense. Following the North's fifth nuclear test, Flournoy called talks with Pyongyang "a waste of time,"[11] and foreshadowed a hard line: "The only way you're going to get them to consider [genuine denuclearization] is through additional sanctions ... that involve pressure from China."[12] Mira Rapp-Hooper, who was Asia policy coordinator for the Clinton campaign, went even further: A President Clinton would invoke a "secondary boycott to put sanctions on Chinese companies that are illegally trading with North Korea in order to force China to cooperate, as well as strengthening trilateral security cooperation with South Korea and Japan, deploying THAAD, and improving our missile defense system."[13] And Wendy Sherman, who had espoused collapsism while serving as an Undersecretary of State in the Obama administration, carried those beliefs over to the Clinton presidential campaign in 2016. Sherman was one of the most influential foreign policy veterans surrounding Clinton, and openly urged the United States, South Korea, China, and Japan to collaborate on a plan for fomenting regime change in the North.[14]

The rhetoric coming out of the Obama administration in its final months seemed to urge the would-be Clinton administration to adopt a much tougher, more skeptical approach toward North Korea than it had pursued, and once Trump was declared presidential victor, the Obama administration continued to lay the groundwork for its successor to adopt a hard-line policy. On October 25, 2016, only weeks before the presidential election, James Clapper, the Director of National Intelligence, commented publicly, "I think the notion of getting the North Koreans to denuclearize is probably a lost cause," the first such admission from a senior-level US official.[15] Clapper went on to say that negotiating limits on North Korea's nuclear program in a way that allowed it some weapons was the best that could be hoped for. Despite this assessment, the State Department's spokesman repudiated Clapper's comments and reiterated the administration's longstanding commitment to nothing short of "the verifiable denuclearization of the Korean Peninsula."[16] Also the month before the presidential election, John Hamre, president of the Center for Strategic and International Studies in Washington and a Deputy Secretary of Defense to President Bill Clinton, commented, "I've been at meetings with senior US officials who say we need to change policy to formally embrace regime change."[17] The Obama administration showed no sign of such an extreme policy shift, yet it had become a normal part of public but off-the-record think-tank discussions around Washington by 2016, and it was in the context of a growing sense of urgency about North Korea's ability to strike US territory with nuclear-armed missiles.[18]

Preemptive strikes on North Korean nuclear facilities or missile sites were also discussed,[19] but Obama himself had already ruled out a military option against North Korea in 2015 because of the risks involved. Even John Kerry, who had previously taken the most concil-iatory tone toward North Korea of anyone in the administration, said on January 10, 2017:

> China provides 100 percent of the fuel that goes to North Korea ... and because China also is the facilitator, through Beijing, for the banking system ... So we really think China needs to increase its focus ... My counsel to the next adminis-tration will be to work with China very, very closely and try to get the Chinese to, in fact, have a greater impact on the North in order to affect their behavior.[20]

This emphasis on pressuring North Korea indirectly through China closely resembles what the Clinton Asia policy team and campaign surrogates had indicated they would do. It was also the same recom-mendation put forward by the Council on Foreign Relations' bipartisan North Korea Task Force only months prior. But Kerry did not stop at advocating pressure. He went on to accommodate the possibility that the Trump administration might need to launch preemptive or preven-tive strikes on North Korea, saying, "Now, there comes a point here where this gets dangerous, and it's getting close to it right now. Because if he [Kim Jong Un] persists, as he said he would the other day, in moving forward on the intercontinental ballistic missile front, it more immediately drags the United States into an immediate threat situation."[21]

Why a Clinton Crisis Was Plausible

The more emphasis the United States placed on denucleariza-tion, the more it was backing itself into an unsavory choice: either reveal US rhetoric to be unrealistic and hollow, or take riskier and more extreme measures in pursuit of denuclearization, even though US intelligence publicly acknowledged the Quixotic nature of the goal. While Obama would take no great risks on North Korea policy, he was also unwilling to set more realistic definitions of policy success. The would-be Clinton doctrine promised to be, initially at least, an amplified version of Obama's legacy on North Korea.

Kerry's public remarks on North Korea only ten days before Trump became president illustrate a basic continuity in the conflict between the United States and North Korea, regardless of who was president: a nuclear-armed intercontinental ballistic missile (ICBM), which Kim Jong Un declared essential at all costs and Obama officials declared unacceptable at all costs, even in Obama's final days in office. A Clinton administration would have held to the goal of denuclearization, at least initially, and would also have been boxed into the nearer-term goal of preventing North Korea from obtaining a functional, nuclear-armed ICBM, which Kim Jong Un was bent on obtaining. These conflicts of interest were necessary and sufficient for a nuclear crisis with Clinton; all that was missing was a triggering moment.

The consequence of the Obama administration's posture of strategic patience and a deepening mutual antipathy between the United States and North Korea was an unprecedented (and more or less unrestrained) expansion and improvement of Kim Jong Un's nuclear and ballistic missile capabilities. By the time Clinton would have assumed office, North Korea would have been beyond rollback of its nuclear and missile program. Under Clinton, fears of South Korean aggression would wane as the South underwent its own domestic political transition, but North Korea's growing capabilities and the diplomatic impasse would remain.

Of course, all crises are not equal, and meaningful differences between Clinton and Trump also surface. A Clinton presidency would have avoided needlessly inflammatory rhetoric, making it possible to retaliate in response to North Korean aggression—or to conduct limited preemptive strikes if necessary—with a comparatively lower risk of igniting nuclear war. Clinton was famous for her careful, measured use of language, and even derided for it during her campaign. Clinton would have also been apt to seize diplomatic opportunities to unwind the crisis rather than repeatedly foreclose on them as Trump would end up doing.

Most importantly, a Clinton administration would have been much more likely to reconcile itself to the reality of a deterrence-and-containment approach, as opposed to comprehensive denuclearization, soon after North Korea demonstrated the ability to reach US territory with its missiles. Prior to the September 2016 nuclear test, some of Clinton's advisers were already advocating a deterrence and containment approach. Being presented with that fait accompli in 2017 would have forced the hard choice of launching a strike against North Korean missile targets or adapting to the reality of a nuclear-armed adversary with a posture focused on deterrence, containment, and crisis stability. Her team would have included many advocates of the latter, and doing so would have significantly reduced later risks of inadvertent nuclear conflict.

5 PRESIDENT TRUMP AND THE MAXIMUM PRESSURE STRATEGY

President Obama sat down with President-elect Donald Trump for the first and only time on November 10, two days after the 2016 election results came in. The meeting had been unimaginable only a week prior. Obama and his team were in total shock that Trump had just won. Trump's election was a stunning repudiation of everything Obama stood for, and Obama had gone out of his way on the campaign trail to advocate for Clinton as an extension of his own legacy. Although it would only become public later, Obama's national security officials had also briefed him at the time on the likelihood that Trump's campaign conspired with Russia to tilt the election in Trump's favor.[1] And by some accounts, it was Trump's embarrassment from Obama's comic roasting of him during a 2011 White House Correspondents' Dinner that may have prodded Trump into running for president in the first place.[2] There was no love lost between Obama and Trump. It was a meeting of opposites. And their discussion fore-shadowed the priority that the United States would place on dealing with the threat it saw in North Korea during the Trump era.

This chapter charts how the Trump administration ended up with the strategy that brought it to the brink of nuclear war with Pyongyang. The weeks after Trump's presidential victory were colored with uncertainty in every sense and across every issue, including North Korea policy. But even with North Korea policy formally undecided, forces outside and within the Trump administration were urging some form of what would ultimately be labeled "maximum pressure." Kim Jong Un was still bent on securing a reliable nuclear-capable intercontinental ballistic missile that could reach the continental United States, but how quickly, and how belligerently, depended on what the United States decided.

Priming Trump for a Hard Line

Obama's meeting with Trump on November 10 proved surprisingly cordial. In their 90-minute discussion, the most urgent foreign policy issue Obama impressed upon Trump was North Korea. Obama told his aides after that he thought Trump "seemed to 'sit up and take notice.'"[3] Trump reportedly came out of that meeting remarking, "I will be judged by how I handle this [North Korea]."[4] Jon Wolfsthal, a nonproliferation expert at the NSC at the end of the Obama administration, told VOA News that Obama "presented two options to Trump for dealing with the nuclear threat: Seek a freeze on North Korea's nuclear and missile programs through direct engagement, and increase pressure on North Korea through China."[5] These options were variants of what Obama had attempted. By 2016, the latter, in particular, had crystallized into conventional wisdom in Washington: "Making it clear to China that ... we would increasingly have to take steps to protect our interests in a way that might undermine China's own security."[6] Trump had repeatedly judged Obama a weak, failed president on the campaign trail, casting him as someone who was unwilling to do what was necessary to bolster American security and standing in the world. For Obama to then be appealing directly to Trump to bring down greater pressure on Pyongyang must have made an impression.

Ambiguity—Strategic and Otherwise

During the interregnum between election day on November 8 and inauguration day some two and a half months later, it was unclear what posture Trump would ultimately take. North Korea did not feature heavily in the presidential campaign, and his most revealing comment on the subject was one that contradicted Washington orthodoxy: that he would be willing to sit down with Kim Jong Un and have a hamburger with him. Plus, Trump's campaign obsession with pillorying US allies South Korea and Japan as free-riders seemed to signal a willingness to either extort allies or outright abandon them. These very limited data points raised the possibility that, paradoxically,

Trump's bombastic disposition might not lead to a hawkish policy on North Korea.

But opacity about the direction of Trump policy stretched on for several indecisive months, primarily because the Trump campaign had been unprepared to win the presidency. They scrambled to pull together a transition team on short notice.

Compounding difficulties for the transition team was the significantly limited pool of available and qualified candidates for senior positions in the administration. Most Republican foreign policy talent had been blacklisted from the Trump administration for signing #NeverTrump letters that damningly rejected his candidacy, and few of the transition team's members had any political or foreign policy experience at all. The transition team's late start, its inner turmoil, and its lack of experience with politics and policy all combined to make identifying shortlist candidates for positions an urgent priority, but one that took much longer than was normally the case. Neither North Korea nor foreign policy in general were immediate concerns of the Trump transition team.

North Korea was, however, a major national security concern of the bureaucracy and of Obama political appointees, the latter of whom would be transitioning out of government en masse on January 20. But because the Trump team was both inexperienced and dealing with its own internal challenges, the hand-off of foreign policy from Obama to Trump was not smooth.

The final year of the Obama administration was spent piling sanctions on North Korea, and heightening the presence in Korea of nuclear-capable bombers and submarines through escalating deployments. The buildup of pressure was partly a response to the growing nuclear threat from Pyongyang, but it was also a deliberate effort to give maximum optionality to the next administration, regardless of who won the election. The logic of US officials at the time was "setting up the next team [president] for success ... By ramping up pressure at the end, we were either going to give the next guys a head start on sanctions pressure or something to alleviate should they want to pursue diplomacy."[7] But the nuance of pressure for the sake of greater optionality was lost in the transition because there was no hand-off of policy portfolios. Before the inauguration, there was no contact below cabinet level. At the State Department, Kerry had been in touch with Tillerson on only one occasion prior to inauguration, by phone.[8] At the Pentagon,

Mattis and his chief of staff had been in contact with his predecessor, but Trump's transition team had made no contact at all with anyone in the Office of the Secretary of Defense (who runs defense policy on behalf of the Secretary) below the Undersecretary.[9] The lack of preparation and lack of prior contact with Obama's foreign policy team meant that Trump, who started off his presidency with minimal insights about foreign policy issues, did not take advantage of the institutional memory of his predecessor, other than to "sit up and take notice" that North Korea would likely end up being both a near-term threat and a legacy issue for his presidency.

Washington's Hawkish Consensus

But even while Trump had not yet seriously contemplated what to do about North Korea, the policy landscape in Washington was changing in anticipation of his arrival to office. Specifically, there was an impossible-to-miss shift in US discourse about North Korea that increasingly focused on launching first strikes against Pyongyang. Korea watchers of every political stripe—even progressive foreign policy doves—agreed that the Obama-era line of strategic patience inadvertently abetted North Korea's surging missile and nuclear capabilities and was therefore a dead letter. The question was what should succeed strategic patience, and the deck was stacked in favor of maximum pressure.

Talk of Preventive Strikes Begins

In Washington at least, that near-consensus against strategic patience tended to favor the hawkish approach Hillary Clinton would have taken, leveraging China to pressure North Korea, isolating Pyongyang in every way imaginable, and prioritizing deterrence in the name of protecting US allies. The irony was that this *was* strategic patience, only more so. Before Trump even took office, the Washington consensus on North Korea had become sufficiently aggressive that it started accommodating and normalizing a discourse about preventive attack. General Walter Sharp, who had served as commander of USFK during the Obama administration, said on December 1, 2016 that he believed the United States ought to launch a preemptive attack if North Korea put an ICBM on a launch pad and was uncertain whether or not it had a nuclear warhead.[10] Admiral Mike Mullen, who had been Chairman of the Joint Chiefs of Staff under Obama, had signaled the same.[11] Crucially, both were widely viewed in Washington as respectable, mainstream officials, far from wild-eyed about security policy. Even Secretary of State John Kerry, in a speech to the US Naval Academy the following month, implied that military action of some kind might be necessary if Kim continued pursuing nuclear ICBMs.[12]

During this same period, national media outlets and commentators started regularly churning out stories with headlines such as "What Would Happen in the Minutes and Hours after North Korea Nuked the United States?," "Pre-empting a North Korean ICBM Test," "What the US Would Use to Strike North Korea," and "Should Washington Strike North Korea's Dangerous ICBMs Before It's Too Late?"[13] Commentaries strongly opposed to attacking North Korea were forced to focus primarily on the question of military strikes rather than some non-violent alternative, with headlines such as "Washington's Dangerous Drums of War on North Korea" and "Attacking North Korea Would be a Disaster."[14] Not only had the North Korea policy landscape developed a hawkish tilt; the terms of debate about North Korea policy had shifted dramatically into the military realm. This was the prevailing state of mind among Washington policy elites as Trump entered the White House.

South Korea Sidelined

As Washington's discourse about Pyongyang coarsened, South Korea was becoming marginalized. It would have been a significant enough thing for South Korea to have to adapt to the shock of the Trump presidency given his vocal skepticism toward alliances during the presidential campaign, but the month after the US election South Korea became engrossed in its own political crisis. Late in 2016, South Korea's President Park Geun-hye was implicated in a corruption scandal that revealed she had been receiving, and even acting upon, the policy advice of a "Rasputin-like" friend, Choe Soon-sil, who promoted a fringe religiosity. Park stood accused of a range of charges, from giving Choe classified information to embezzlement.[15] The South Korean Parliament voted on December 9, 2016 to impeach President Park.

For months while Park's fate was uncertain, Seoul, the South's capital, was filled with competing mass protests and candlelight vigils.

Some protestors sided with Park, but the overwhelming majority demanded Park's ouster and to have her brought up on charges of corruption. South Korea's uncertain political transition left it with little choice but to avoid making big foreign policy decisions and instead try to hold to the status quo as much as possible; there was no political mandate to do anything else until elections were held the following May. The entire Park saga served as a distraction that froze South Korean strategy, but its internal crisis may have been opportunely timed. With the novelty of the still inchoate Trump administration, South Korea's smartest foreign policy move was probably to wait and observe continuity or change in Trump policy and then react to that. And while South Korea was not directly fueling Washington's hardening discourse about the North, that tough talk was entirely consistent with the direction that South Korean officials and think tank analysts had been urging consistently since 2010.

Kim Jong Un's Two-Front Game

The month prior to the US presidential election, US scholars and former officials met with North Korean Foreign Ministry officials to urge the North Korea to freeze

> nuclear testing, missile launches, and fissile material production ... as a gesture to the new administration ... It was presented as a confidence-building measure from Pyongyang. They in turn would expect a confidence-building measure from the U.S., primarily dealing with their security concerns, thus joint military exercises were mentioned ... as was the beginning of a dialogue on a Peace Treaty.[16]

Kim Jong Un therefore knew what the United States would look for to determine his seriousness about pursuing negotiations or détente of some kind.

A Feeling-Out Period

After the US election, North Korea remained relatively quiet for months. No nuclear detonations, minimal missile activity (none, in fact, until after Trump's inauguration) and significantly toned down apocalyptic rhetoric compared to its historical norm. Through December and January, North Korea's Foreign Ministry was meeting behind closed doors with the Trump team and its surrogates, but part of this was also likely not to distract from South Korea's political crisis, which was to Kim Jong Un's advantage in a propaganda sense. There was, moreover, an element of holding back until Kim knew where the Trump administration stood on Korea policy. Once it was clear that Trump would be at least as "hostile" toward the North as Obama had been, Kim accelerated his plans to achieve a secure nuclear arsenal that could range the continental United States.

Two weeks after Trump's electoral win, North Korea's Foreign Ministry issued a nine-page statement (one of its first since the election) that excoriated the Obama administration and was widely interpreted as a message to Trump. Its tone was not threatening, and quite explicitly aimed at shaping the next administration's policy toward the North: "The U.S.," it said, "should face up to ... scrap its anachronistic hostile policy and nuclear threat against the DPRK."[17] It then tried to define the narrative frame through which the Trump administration might make future North Korea policy, charging the Obama administration with committing a long series of transgressions that led to the present moment. It claimed that the United States "aimed at political suffocation and system collapse," and catalogued 19 specific instances, starting from the end of the Leap Day Deal in 2012 through October 2016, nearly all of which focused on US attempts to elevate the profile of North Korean human rights abuses. North Korea interpreted these attempts as "defam[ing] the supreme dignity of the DPRK ... the gravest of all sins." It catalogued 18 examples of US "military provocations" that risked war, again emphasizing the period from mid-2012 through October 2016.[18] Most of the examples it cited involved the deployment of nuclear-capable bombers to South Korea. And it identified 13 instances in which the Obama administration imposed new sanctions on it, claiming strategic patience "is none other than an aggressive and heinous 'strategic suffocation.'"[19] The Foreign Ministry statement thus betrayed North Korea's keen interest in nudging the Trump administration not to follow Obama's policy of strategic patience and instead rewind the clock to US policy prior to the Leap Day Deal.

Following the Foreign Ministry statement, North Korea continued to keep a low international profile until Kim Jong Un made his 2017 New Year's speech, the tone of which was rather muted and primarily focused on the North Korean economy. The speech nevertheless lauded the regime's "first H-bomb test, test-firing of various means of strike and nuclear warhead[s] ... and enter[ing] the final stage of preparation for the test launch of an intercontinental ballistic missile" capable of striking the United States.[20] This, Kim claimed, "remarkably raise[ed] the strategic position" of North Korea.[21] International media, especially in the United States, fretted about the prospect of North Korea actually demonstrating that it could reach US territory with a nuclear-armed missile, even though experts and US officials had warned for years that North Korea likely already possessed such a capability.

By the time of Kim's New Year's speech, Trump had already taken a number of intelligence briefings on North Korea. He must have been told that demonstrating a reliable ICBM capability would amount to an undeniable breach of the invisible, and arguably artificial, threshold between Pyongyang as a local threat and a global one, because on January 2, 2017, Trump tweeted two missives on North Korea. The first was widely interpreted as drawing a red line against Pyongyang demonstrating a capability that US military commanders and intelligence officials had already assessed it possessed: "North Korea just stated that it is in the final stages of developing a nuclear weapon capable of reaching parts of the U.S. It won't happen!"[22] Given Kim's declaration of a forthcoming ICBM test only one day before, the subtext of "It won't happen!" seemed to imply that the United States would act with military force or covert action if necessary. Later in the day, Trump followed that message with another, tweeting, "China has been taking out massive amounts of money & wealth from the U.S. in totally one-sided trade, but won't help with North Korea. Nice!" These were the first real signs of what Trump's North Korea policy would become, as well as the first time the Trump administration (which would not formally take office for two more weeks) crossed rhetorical swords with the Kim regime.

Trump's tweets were followed by other ominous signals in subsequent days. On January 4, 2017, South Korea's Ministry of National Defense held a press conference announcing it was creating a "special brigade with the goal of removing or (at least) paralyzing North Korea's wartime command structure."[23] On January 5, 2017, Obama's outgoing Deputy Secretary of State, Tony Blinken, held a Vice Ministerial Trilateral Summit with the Vice Foreign Ministers of Japan and South Korea. They reiterated the call for total denuclearization (CVID) and claimed that the United States, Japan, and the South would continue to "put extraordinary pressure on the North Korean regime—sustained, comprehensive pressure ... pressure that we hope will lead it to make the smart decision to come back to credible negotiations to end its nuclear weapons program."[24] These early, sparse signals boded ill for any promise of change on North Korea policy.

The day before Trump's inauguration, on January 19, 2017, reports emerged that North Korea had placed ICBMs on two mobile missile launchers in preparation for a missile test that would be timed with any belligerent declaration from the Trump team about its North Korea policy.[25] This presented the very scenario that a number of senior officials, including former USFK commander, General Walter Sharp, had warned should be met with what they characterized as a "preemptive" strike against the launch site: long-range missiles, placed on mobile launchers, with a lack of certainty about whether they were armed with a nuclear warhead. But the Trump administration was not yet in office, had not yet settled on a strategy for dealing with the North, and the context was one in which North Korea's only incentives to launch first strikes from its mobile missile launchers would have been if it misperceived the United States as imminently launching some kind of attack itself. Reasonable powers of deduction could still conclude that these missiles were intended for testing and signaling, not attacking.

The newly minted Trump administration displayed virtually no public angst or consternation about North Korea's preparations for a missile launch, despite Trump's January 2 tweets indicating, "It won't happen!" But on January 29, Trump had his first phone call with Hwang Kyo-ahn, South Korea's interim president, while Seoul sorted through its domestic political crisis. In the alliance phone call, both sides avoided raising any points of controversy, and Trump affirmed the traditional US position on Korea—that the alliance is "ironclad," agreeing with Hwang's suggestion that any North Korean provocation be met with a firm response jointly, as allies.[26] This was fairly anodyne as far as alliance statements of solidarity go, but it was the strongest sign yet that the Trump administration would, at a minimum, continue riding the policy inertia of the Obama administration's final days. The week after the Trump–Hwang call, on February 3, an even stronger indication of continuity in US policy toward North Korea appeared in Secretary of Defense James Mattis's first overseas trip of the administration, to Japan and South Korea. The symbolism spoke for itself, and all of Mattis's talking points were standard fare for alliance management, assuring Tokyo and Seoul of the reliability of the US commitment to extended deterrence and their defense. Notably though, Mattis affirmed that "any use of nuclear weapons would be met with a response that would be effective and overwhelming."[27]

These early signals from the Trump administration were hardly definitive of the direction it would take, but they were enough to compel North Korean media to reply to Mattis's remarks venomously, decrying that Washington and Seoul "worked out a plan for a preemptive attack on the North ... pushing the situation on the peninsula to the brink of a nuclear war."[28] Given how predisposed North Korea was to rendering the most malign conclusions about US intentions (recall its dismissal of Obama's many benign signals in 2009) Pyongyang clearly concluded after Mattis's visit to Seoul that Trump policy would not be a radical departure from the Obama administration. So on February 12, 2017, North Korea went ahead with the first missile test since the US presidential election—and the first on Trump's watch. The missile, successfully launched, was the KN-15/Polaris-2, a road-mobile medium-range ballistic missile (MRBM) whose engine used solid-fuel propellant. The KN-15 was a slightly shorter-range version of the KN-08 missile that had been the Obama administration's nightmare. The missile, moreover, was fired from a "transporter-erector-launcher," a mobile launch pad. In past decades, North Korea's missile tests were tests in the name of research and development. By 2017, as nuclear expert Jeffrey Lewis warned, North Korea was no longer simply testing missiles for program analysis, but rather "preparing for a nuclear first-strike."[29] Its tests now transcended experimentation and the collection of technical data to actually be part of operational readiness.

Assassination with a "Weapon of Mass Destruction"

The day after the successful KN-15 missile test, North Korea conducted a brazen assassination on foreign soil. It was the first North Korean action since the 1980s that could plausibly be labeled "terrorism." On February 13, 2017, North Korean agents assassinated

Kim Jong Un's older brother, Kim Jong Nam, with a chemical weapon at an airport in Malaysia. By that time, Kim Jong Un had already purged hundreds of North Korean officials in a bid to assert greater control over the regime, including Jang Song-thaek, who was Kim's uncle, former regent, and the de facto number two in charge of the regime.

Jong Nam was a marked man from the beginning of Kim Jong Un's rule. Hereditary succession in Korea customarily favored the eldest son and Jong Un was the youngest. There were rumors that Jong Nam was working with the CIA, and possibly with the South Korean or Chinese governments to play the future role of a figurehead for a North Korean government in exile. Jong Nam also reportedly sent an email to a Japanese reporter when his youngest brother first came to power, suggesting that Jong Un's regime would not last. A former South Korean intelligence official, Nam Sung-wook, estimated that Jong Un ordered the hit to be carried out the way it was—in public view, on camera, and with a chemical weapon—in order to strengthen general deterrence: "Pyongyang wanted to horrify the rest of the world by releasing a chemical weapon at an airport ... Jong Un wants to reign a long time and negotiate as a superpower. The only way to do that is to keep the world in fear of his weapons. He has a grand design and this is part of it."[30]

For all these reasons and perhaps more, Jong Un had ordered Jong Nam's death years prior to the 2017 assassination, and Jong Nam had previously dodged at least two known attempts on his life.[31] By all accounts, Kim Jong Un's string of assassinations and purges, of which Jong Nam was a high-profile part, had the effect of consolidating his control over the regime; a bloody form of coup-proofing. But the regime-control explanation does not account for the way in which Jong Nam was assassinated. Kim attempted to use the assassination of his brother as a tool to generate fear that would in turn strengthen deterrence against external threats, and it may have half-worked.

Following the Kim Jong Nam assassination, a Trump transition team official commented, "You can't help but think, Jesus, maybe [Kim] *is* crazy."[32] Such a statement confirms that Kim's aggressive posture did stimulate fear on some level, but without the effect that Kim had hoped for. The Trump administration would repeatedly use the notion that Kim is crazy as a justification for taking a zero-tolerance line against North Korean nuclear weapons. A preventive war with North Korea made sense to some Trump national security officials because they believed that Kim could not be trusted to behave rationally with nuclear weapons.

Maximum Pressure: Strategic Patience with a Loaded Gun

From the time of Trump's inauguration through the end of March 2017, the Trump team undertook a comprehensive review of US policy toward North Korea. While that review was ongoing, the administration continued to carry out Obama's script on Korea policy: "In the early months ... the bureaucracy in general was a caretaker that didn't feel empowered to start new things or redirect Asia policy in any way, especially on Korea. So we used the same talking points from the end of the Obama administration unless we got redirected."[33]

Going through the (Saber-Rattling) Motions

Much of that continuity involved pro forma phone calls and meetings with allies, but on March 1, 2017, the United States and South Korea also began pre-scheduled military exercises, called Key Resolve and Foal Eagle, which ran through April 30. Key Resolve and Foal Eagle, or some version of them, had occurred annually in the spring since 1976, and the alliance historically treated the exercises as an essential way to ensure both militaries were ready and able to respond to a war brought on by North Korean aggression. The exercises were also ritualistic in the sense that they symbolically affirmed (and both allies routinely vocalized that affirmation) the US commitment to South Korea's defense.

After the Leap Day Deal fell apart in 2012, the spring military exercises also began incorporating more US strategic assets every year, including nuclear-capable bombers and aircraft carriers, which made North Korea chafe because these same types of capabilities would be involved in any US war against the North. The 2017 exercises were no exception to the trend since 2012, and, specifically, made good on the promise of the Extended Deterrence Strategy and Consultation Group meeting in December 2016 to more regularly contribute strategic assets to South Korean deterrence and defense, by sending the USS *Carl Vinson* Carrier Strike Group and B-1 bombers from Guam.[34] But as predictably as the United States and South Korea conducted the exercises each year, North Korea predictably responded to each one with invective, accusations of US war plotting, and, often, with counter-military maneuvers or mobilizations of its own. The regularity of the alliance's spring exercise regimen made it something that Pyongyang could reliably plan around and politicize for its own purposes.

It was therefore unsurprising that Pyongyang met the start of the alliance's annual exercise regimen with in-kind saber-rattling. Beyond its resumption of apocalyptic threat-making, on March 6, it launched a new series of operationally oriented missile tests—four extended-range Scud missiles—followed by four additional (but failed) missile tests through the end of April. As part of Kim's dash to secure an operationally ready, reliable retaliatory nuclear capability that could reach US territory, his regime had conducted an unprecedented number of missile tests in 2016, and after a multi-month pause, would resume that pace during the Trump administration. The classic Washington playbook on North Korea (coercive diplomacy tied to the maximalist goal of denuclearization) was eliciting a classic North Korean response of greater intransigence as it continued to meet pressure with pressure.

By the time of North Korea's March missile launches, the Trump administration had not technically completed its North Korea policy review, but its outcome was by then preordained. Secretary of State Rex Tillerson followed Mattis's February trip to Seoul and Tokyo with a trip of his own a month later (adding a stop in Beijing on the backend) to give its allies a status update on the nearly finished North Korea policy review. During the trip, State Department officials twice noted in background briefings to the press that "all options are on the table" for achieving comprehensive denuclearization (specifically the CVID formulation) of North Korea.[35] On March 17, in Seoul, Tillerson repeated that phrasing publicly, twice, in the same remarks. While the use of military force is often "on the table" for consideration among other alternatives for any given policy decision, there is never an explicit need to say so unless deliberately implying the possibility of using it. In context, the phrasing "all options are on the table" explicitly refers to a military force option, which itself is a thinly veiled threat. That is also precisely how international media (including in

North Korea) interpreted it. That the phrase was mentioned on back-ground *and* through official remarks suggests it was a scripted rhetorical formulation, not merely a gaffe. When Tillerson repeated the phrase a second time, he was sure to note the military nature of the implication, stating with regard to the "military option. All of the options are on the table ... if North Korea takes action that threatens the South Korean forces or our own forces, then that would be met with an appropriate response. *If they elevate the threat of their weapons program to a level that we believe requires action, that option is on the table.*"[36]

A further indication of the Trump administration's policy to come, which reinforced the public perception that the United States was actively contemplating the use of preventive force against Pyongyang, was Tillerson's declaration during his stop in Seoul that "The policy of strategic patience has ended."[37] By this time, nobody any longer suspected that the Trump administration would adopt a conciliatory policy toward North Korea, yet Obama's strategic patience policy seemed to bring as much pressure on the North as was possible without resorting to military force. If not strategic patience, and if not a diplomatic strategy, it appeared that the only "options on the table" were military in nature.

Prior to returning to Washington, Tillerson's stop in Beijing signaled still another aspect of the Trump strategy on North Korea: convincing Beijing to squeeze Pyongyang to a degree that it had never before done. It had become Washington wisdom on the political left and right that any solution to the North Korean nuclear issue required Chinese quiescence, if not its full-throated activism, on behalf of US interests. Yet it was never clear that China could actually change North Korea's behavior in any meaningful way, despite exercising a near-monopoly over Pyongyang's trade ties. Tillerson came out of his meetings in Beijing with a statement that was a virtual copy-and-paste of the bipartisan consensus on North Korea called for in a Council on Foreign Relations task force report from 2016: cooperate with China to pressure North Korea when you can, and pressure China, in turn, to pressure the North when you must.[38] Tillerson was still in a phase of soliciting Chinese cooperation while he could. Trump, though, had already signaled his own willingness to cajole Beijing to induce changes in North Korean behavior, and while Tillerson was meeting with Chinese officials, Trump tweeted on March 18 that "North Korea is behaving very badly. They have been 'playing' the United States for years. China has done little to help!"

By this time, the Trump team had finally gotten the bulk of its national security team in place, and congressional Republicans had reached their own conclusions about what North Korea policy ought to be. Everything converged on a hard-line policy consistent with the evolving Washington consensus, and similar to what Hillary Clinton would have pursued. On the personnel side, the political appointees that Trump brought in to national security positions overwhelmingly skewed toward active-duty and retired military officers, some of whom had no policy experience and whose primary qualifications were nothing more than having previously served with either McMaster or Mattis in the past. These officers shared in common an understanding of national security policy through the very narrow lens of military operations and tactics. As one White House official observed, "The NSC has a bunch of colonels with no policy experience talking about 'strategy' to describe what are really battlefield tactics and military campaigns."[39] The military's dominance of the national security staff was accentuated by the concomitant gutting of US diplomacy taking place under Tillerson. The State Department's senior ranks hollowed out, as senior positions that were forcibly vacated after Obama left office went unfilled under Tillerson. A common refrain in Washington is that personnel *is* policy. To the extent that was true, the Trump administration's policies were blinkered to positive-sum, institutional, and other non-combative thinking about the problems facing the United States abroad because of its military bias, and North Korea policy was a case in point.

Congressional Republicans, meanwhile, had a long history of urging a hawkish approach to North Korea. Since the 1990s and their staunch opposition to Clinton's Agreed Framework deal, congressional Republicans had consistently taken a confrontational, pressure-based approach to North Korea.[40] That historical continuity was on full display during a March 21 hearing of the Republican-led House Committee on Foreign Affairs, Subcommittee on Asia and the Pacific, which took place the week before the conclusion of the administration's North Korea policy review. Republicans at the hearing, which carried the suggestive title, "Pressuring North Korea: Evaluating Options," uniformly recommended that the Trump administration press harder on sanctions, specifically by embracing the "secondary sanctions" on Chinese banks and firms that the Obama administration had been reluctant to impose, and to introduce what would gradually become a more general embargo on North Korea rather than just targeted sanctions.[41]

The prevailing logic was to cause the regime enough pain that it would come to see its nuclear program as a dangerous liability rather than the guarantor of its security. As we have seen, there were plenty of reasons to doubt the soundness of that logic. But by the end of March, the McMaster-led policy review had concluded that the United States must continue to pursue nothing short of comprehensive denuclearization, and that the best approach to achieving it was a strategy that relied on escalating the pain the Kim regime felt until it changed its views about its own nuclear weapons.[42] The McMaster strategy, dubbed "maximum pressure," expressly rejected Obama's strategic patience label, yet appeared to be an intensified version of it in practice. The centerpiece of the strategy was convincing China to impose a greater squeeze on North Korea by any means necessary, including secondary sanctions against Chinese businesses in contact with North Korea. That China-centric effort would be buttressed by ratcheting sanctions on North Korea directly, isolating Pyongyang diplomatically, elevating the profile of North Korea's human rights abuses, and relying heavily on coercive signaling via military deployments and exercises. If none of that worked, the administration intimated that it was willing to resort to the preventive use of military force rather than just give up on denuclearization. The goal was fixed. The question was what it would take to achieve it.

Circumstances thus overwhelmingly favored the Trump administration strategy of maximum pressure on the North: congressional Republicans wanted it, Korea hands in Washington repudiated Obama's risk aversion, North Korea had begun conducting ever-more alarming missile tests, the administration's national security team was stacked with military bias, and the default setting of US policy execution during the policy review continued to prioritize coercive diplomacy. Maximum pressure was the policy path of least resistance. In this political and institutional context, it is difficult to imagine arriving at a meaningfully different strategy for dealing with what Washington saw as a rapidly growing threat.

Maximum Pressure's Debut at Mar-a-Lago

McMaster expedited the Trump administration's North Korea policy review so that the relevant details, and first steps toward implementation, would be ready when China's President Xi Jinping would meet with Trump on April 6–7, 2017. Rather than meeting at the White House for a formal State Dinner or Summit though, Trump invited Xi to his Mar-a-Lago estate in Palm Beach, Florida. It would serve as the debut for the maximum pressure strategy, which only became public through background briefings and the odd remark from administration officials when talking about North Korea.

A few days before the Mar-a-Lago meeting, Trump gave an interview to the *Financial Times* as a preview of his thoughts about Xi Jinping's imminent visit. He was overwhelmingly concerned about North Korea and confirmed that China was the centerpiece of its strategy. Trump also indicated a willingness to unilaterally resort to either military or covert action to prevent North Korea's nuclear and missile programs from advancing further. "China has great influence over North Korea. And China will either decide to help us with North Korea or they won't ... If they do, that will be very good for China, and if they don't, it won't be good for anyone ... if China is not going to solve North Korea, we will. That is all I am telling you."[43]

The day after Trump's *Financial Times* interview, White House officials indicated that they were going to impress upon Xi two major issues: the seriousness they saw in the North Korea threat, and the need for China to offer greater "reciprocity" (referring to the bilateral trade balance and import tariffs) in the economic relationship. Trump had made clear that he was willing to link these two issues, and that progress on North Korea took priority. As an anonymous official told the press, the North Korea issue "is now urgent because we feel that the clock is very, very quickly running out ... the clock has now run out, and all options are on the table for us."[44]

The run up to Xi's April 6–7 visit to Mar-a-Lago promised that Trump was going to issue some dire warnings to Beijing. The publicly telegraphed expectation was not only that Trump would force Beijing to get tough on North Korea by conjuring an image of a region awash in US missile defenses that encircled China in the name of defending against Pyongyang's missiles, but also that China itself would become the target of sanctions if it failed to curb

North Korean behavior and more faithfully implement UN Security Council sanctions. Trump had also signaled his intention to confront China about its economic practices, currency manipulation, and the need to rectify America's trade deficit with China. Trump told reporters before that event that "We have been treated unfairly, and have made terrible trade deals with China for many, many years. That's one of the things we are going to be talking about."[45] He also tweeted on March 31 that "The meeting with China next week will be a very difficult one."

The actual outcome of the Trump–Xi meeting thus came as a surprise. Trump, on the advice of his son-in-law Jared Kushner, treated the visit as an opportunity to build a bond with China. Kushner had been working quietly for weeks with Cui Tiankai, China's ambassador to the United States, to make sure the Trump–Xi meeting did not take the sharp, confrontational tone that Trump's national security team (and Trump himself) had presaged in media interactions prior to the event.[46] Kushner's efforts largely worked, as Xi Jinping won Trump's affections by flattering him and offering token conciliatory gestures toward more favorable economic cooperation.[47] Crucially, as Xi and Trump privately walked the Mar-a-Lago grounds on April 7, Xi explained to Trump the difficulties that China faced in trying to pressure North Korea, and, in the moment at least, convinced Trump that China did not quite possess the leverage over North Korea that US policymakers had long claimed it had. There is no record of what specifically Xi might have told Trump, but Beijing's longstanding priority of both preventing the North Korean regime from collapsing and preserving North Korea as a geographic buffer state against democratic encroachment on its border gave Xi strong incentives to avoid squeezing North Korea as hard as Trump seemed to wish for. Trump gave an interview the following week, noting that during his walk with Xi, "After listening for 10 minutes, I realized it's not so easy ... I felt pretty strongly that they had a tremendous power over North Korea. But it's not what you would think."[48] While Trump's aides claimed he did bring up issues of disagreement generally, there was no public indication that Trump raised regional missile defenses or the threat of secondary sanctions for failing to curb North Korea's nuclear and missile programs. The public messaging coming out of both sides following their meeting was that the two established a rapport grounded in trust. This surface-level harmony masked a major victory for China, which temporarily won Trump's favor and avoided making any costly or specific commitments on either North Korea or economic policy.

The meeting did not go entirely Beijing's way, however. On North Korea, H. R. McMaster later claimed publicly that Xi agreed that a nuclear-armed North Korea was a threat to China, that a proposal of "freeze for freeze [suspending US military exercises in return for suspending nuclear and missile testing] doesn't work anymore ... it's intolerable," and that China acknowledged its "coercive economic influence" over North Korea.[49] All three claims, to the extent they were accurate, represented Beijing backpedaling on some of its long-held positions toward North Korea.

But more significant than discussions about North Korea was a coming attack on Syria. Hours before Xi's plane arrived in Florida, Trump convened a meeting of his NSC at Mar-a-Lago to determine how to respond to Syria's repeated use of sarin nerve gas against civilians as part of the Bashar Al-Assad regime's unending civil war. In 2013, President Obama had stated publicly that the United States did not have sufficient interests in Syria to get embroiled in its civil war, but that a "red line" for him would be the use of battlefield chemical weapons. After the United Nations found that the Syrian government was indeed using chemical weapons, Obama refused to follow through on his "red line" threat, instead working through Russia diplomatically to dispose of some of Syria's chemical weapons stockpile. Before Trump ran for president he had tweeted, "Syria is NOT our problem," but Republicans, and most of the foreign policy establishment, lambasted Obama for not only appearing weak on national security, but for playing fast and loose with America's reputation for following through on the threats it makes.

Trump, sitting at Mar-a-Lago with his national security team, now faced a virtually identical situation. He was reportedly presented with images of a child who had been the victim of nerve gas dropped from aircraft owned by Assad's Air Force and it impacted him emotionally.[50] He decided almost immediately that the United States must respond. So at 3:45pm, Trump ordered US Navy destroyers armed with Tomahawk land-attack cruise missiles (TLAMs) to fire at Shayrat airfield, the base responsible for conducting the most recent gas attack.[51] Ninety minutes later, Xi and his delegation arrived at Mar-a-Lago. The Navy launched 59 TLAMs at 7:40, while Xi was sitting down for dinner with Trump. Mid-meal, Trump leaned over to Xi and quietly informed him that he had ordered a strike on Syria that was being executed at that moment.[52]

For Xi, this had not been part of what was otherwise a carefully choreographed plan. The harmonious relationship coming out of the meeting was a secondary headline, significantly diluted by the larger news story—that Trump had ordered an attack on Syria.[53] It diminished the importance of Xi's visit, and made it harder for him to frame the Mar-a-Lago visit back home as the United States treating China as its top priority. The strike, and its surprise timing, also lent credence to the then-dominant image of an unpredictable president at the helm of a superpower with global reach.

The loud-talking president who seemed like all swagger and no substance had just intervened in a new conflict that Obama had tried desperately to keep America out of. Nobody knew if this strike was an aberration or a new era of military interventionism abroad.

6 MIMICKING PYONGYANG

Coming out of the Trump–Xi summit at Mar-a-Lago, the Trump administration seemed emboldened, almost cocky in its foreign policy rhetoric and military signals, especially those aimed at North Korea. Xi convinced Trump that China had less leverage over Pyongyang than conventionally thought, but that it would nevertheless do more to faithfully implement existing UN Security Council sanctions against it. Crucially, Xi made no specific public commitments to do anything. Trump saw this as a win anyway. More importantly, Trump garnered widespread approval from the US foreign policy establishment—even many Democrats—for his impromptu missile attack on the Assad regime in retribution for it using chemical weapons on its own people. The administration felt confident, it identified North Korea as its foremost foreign policy challenge, and it had settled on the direction of US policy.

But as the Trump administration's maximum pressure strategy clashed with Pyongyang's pressure-for-pressure instincts, the United States and North Korea ended up locking themselves into a tit-for-tat dynamic. Washington and Pyongyang traded intensifying rhetorical barbs and military gestures, ironically aimed mostly at deterring each from attacking the other. The total absence of what anyone could recognize as a predictable or stable hand steering events started compounding public concerns about the risk of nuclear war.

Swaggering into an Unplanned War Scare

Basking in the glow of Mar-a-Lago, the Trump administration wanted to conduct "shows of force" aimed at Pyongyang. It was time to implement the maximum pressure strategy, and the NSC had been asking the Pentagon for a range of "military options." While still deterring North Korea from attacking, Secretary of Defense Mattis was simultaneously called on to offer preemptive strike options to hit North Korean missiles (before they launched) if they appeared to be aimed at the United States, deter North Korea from conducting another nuclear or ICBM test, and deliver options that would add to the gradually escalating pressure on Pyongyang until it agreed to negotiate away its nuclear program. In other words, the administration sought options to achieve four different objectives to influence the same actor (North Korea) in different ways, each with varying levels of feasibility, but using the same instrument of statecraft (the military). Mattis was being asked for the impossible.

By mid-April, the United States began showing signs of mimicking North Korea's assertive theory of victory. It generated deliberate friction with Pyongyang through military saber-rattling and tough rhetoric. North Korea's capabilities were on the verge of crossing a threshold that official Washington had established as the point of greatest threat: demonstrating a mobile ICBM capability in tandem with proving it could adequately miniaturize a nuclear device to fit on the ICBM. Nearly every day through the end of April produced a new threat or hostile act from either the United States or North Korea.

Picking Up Steam, Losing an Aircraft Carrier

The day after the Mar-a-Lago summit, April 8, the Commander of US Pacific Command, Admiral Harry Harris, was away from headquarters in Honolulu when navy staff under his command proposed changing the schedule for the USS *Carl Vinson* carrier strike group. They suggested cancelling a planned port visit and exercise with Australia in favor of sending the entire carrier strike group to sail in waters off the Korean Peninsula. Harris had been pressing his staff for more "military options" to give Secretary Mattis and Chairman Dunford, both of whom were, in turn, responding to an ongoing request from General McMaster and his staff at the NSC to implement maximum pressure.[1]

The thinking at Pacific Command and by Admiral Harris was that redeployment of an aircraft carrier to the Korean Peninsula would be a highly visible deterrence signal, showing America's readiness to act on its enhanced resolve.[2] Harris had recently given a number of speeches in which he expressed the belief that "Deterrence = Capability × Resolve × Signaling."[3] This was incorrect, and a distortion of how security scholars think about how deterrence works; it was also a mirror image of the highly combustible way North Korea thought about deterrence. Most scholars believed deterrence could not be expressed as a mathematical formula at all—it was overly simplistic—but the crucial elements of deterrence were always the fluid combination of capability, interests, and reputation for resolve.[4] Signaling for the purpose of deterrence was typically heavily discounted "cheap talk" because adversaries always had incentives to posture aggressively. A signal could be many things—an indicator of imminent conflict, a statement of hostility, or an escalation of tensions—but it was not a reliable indicator of simply a willingness to fight. Harris's emphasis on "signaling" translated into policy recommendations that involved chest-thumping and generating friction with adversaries in the mistaken belief that such actions enhanced deterrence. But in fact, the status quo situation with North Korea deterred it from attacking, and military signaling ironically risked causing deterrence to fail by triggering North Korea to do the same. This thinking, which justified increasing the frequency of strategic bomber deployments and nuclear submarines to Korea, also justified rerouting the *Carl Vinson* aircraft carrier.

So Harris agreed to the proposed plan because it nested well within his beliefs about deterrence *and* the NSC's call to increase pressure on Pyongyang. He told the 3rd Fleet to issue a press release announcing that the *Carl Vinson* "will be operating in the Western Pacific rather than the previously planned port visits to Australia," which it did on April 9.[5] But there is no public evidence that Harris's decision was coordinated with or approved by Mattis's rank-and-file policy staff in the Office of the Secretary of Defense (OSD), who would normally provide oversight on such matters. At that point in the Trump presidency, Mattis had created an alternative structure, called "The Machine," to support his decision-making that relied on a small cadre of personally selected front-office staff, in lieu of the professional Pentagon bureaucracy.[6]

But apart from inadequate OSD oversight of Pacific Command decisions, there was no indication that Harris formally directed his headquarters staff to issue orders to the 3rd Fleet to cancel the Australia visit and redirect to Korea. At the time, the 3rd Fleet was in the habit of only acting on Harris's routine orders if they came through a formal written instruction; an oral or email command was not necessarily sufficient to undertake a big schedule change.[7] For the next week, the *Carl Vinson* gradually made its way from Singapore southward to Australia—not northward to Korea—but every senior official in the Trump administration believed it was steaming for Korea, as the 3rd Fleet announced on April 9, and said as much publicly. White House Press Secretary Sean Spicer, Mattis, Tillerson, and McMaster were all asked about the reason for suddenly sending an aircraft carrier to Korea, and each gave different answers, but all confirmed they believed it was heading to Korea and not Australia.[8]

Consequently, when the White House was asked about the *Carl Vinson* sailing to Korea on April 11, it rationalized the change of plans as "The forward deployment [of the *Carl Vinson*] is deterrence, presence ... when you see a carrier group steaming into an area like that, the forward presence of that is clearly, through almost every instance, a huge deterrence."[9] The White House was echoing Harris's offensive belief about how deterrence works: through antagonism and deliberate friction. That same day, Trump tweeted another in a series of increasingly routine barbs aimed at Pyongyang: "North Korea is looking for trouble. If China decides to help, that would be great. If not, we will solve the problem without them! U.S.A." It was unclear what prompted the tweet. The next morning, on April 12, Trump appeared on Fox News and was asked about his thinking on North Korea. Trump at first replied coyly, "You never know, do you? You never know ... I don't want to talk about it." He then blurted out, "We're sending an armada. Very powerful. We have submarines, very powerful, far more powerful than the aircraft carrier, that I can tell you. And we have the best military people on Earth. And I will say this. He [Kim Jong Un] is doing the wrong thing. He is doing the wrong thing."[10]

The statement was significant not only for the hyperbole of "an armada," which aped the North Korean style of over-the-top threat-making, but also in the sense of risking war in a way that was probably not fully appreciated. It was not a trivial thing to place an aircraft carrier in the vicinity of an adversary armed with nuclear weapons and anti-ship ballistic missiles. The North Korean military had studied the American way of war in operations since the Gulf War in 1990–91, and understood that the United States only launched military campaigns after first massing forces in a staging area accessible to the battlefield. The North Koreans also understood that the local presence of an aircraft carrier would be a necessary component of any US-initiated conflict. Promises that "an armada" was on its way to the Korean Peninsula, and especially that an aircraft carrier strike group would soon be parked off the Korean coast, were confirming some of the early indicators that North Korea used to determine if a US attack was imminent.

This was a problem because, since the 1990s, North Korean officials had repeatedly warned that if they believed the United States was going to attack, they would launch a preemptive assault to blunt, forestall, and hopefully deter the United States.[11] As the militarily inferior state, it would be the only strategic move North Korea would have under such circumstances. Thus, Trump's April 12 armada statement—particularly in the context of an unexpected attack on Syria, surprise rerouting of an aircraft carrier, and Trump's foreboding threats-by-tweet—carried a heightened risk that Kim Jong Un would misinterpret what Trump meant or what the United States was doing in a manner that would encourage Kim to preemptively launch his own limited attack on South Korea or US forces.

Yet, being in a swaggering foreign policy mood, there was no indication that Trump or anyone around him appreciated the elevated danger it was engendering by pursuing an Obama-like approach to North Korea in substance, while becoming much tougher and even offensive in rhetorical style. As much as maximum pressure represented a more vigorous version of strategic patience under Obama, the rhetorical backdrop of Obama's policy was not one where US officials intimated a willingness to go to war; Obama even publicly rejected a military option in 2015.[12] By contrast, the Trump administration was going through a lot of the same military movements as Obama had, but in a context now defined by a deliberate sense of urgency and a declared willingness to launch strikes against the North under certain conditions. Rhetoric was the main difference, and the difference elevated the risk of war.

Threats of a "Preemptive" Strike

April 15 was the anniversary of the birth of Kim Jong Un's grandfather, an occasion that had historically been cause for celebrations that sometimes included weapons demonstrations. Speculation abounded that North Korea would conduct its sixth nuclear test on the anniversary—something the Trump administration had repeatedly implied it would act to prevent. That pending date for some kind of standoff hung over events in the first half of April, amplifying tension that came to a head the day after Trump's armada remark, when unnamed senior US intelligence officials leaked something that had been rumored around Washington since before the North Korea policy review was completed. The officials told *NBC News* that the United States was preparing to launch a strike on North Korea, not to preempt an imminent attack on America or its allies, but to preempt a North Korean missile test: a demonstration of missile technology as it had done countless times before.[13] It was an unprecedentedly low threshold for violence, and might have been illegal under both domestic and international law. At that point, it was still unclear on what legal basis the Syria strikes were conducted the week prior, and while preempting an imminent North Korean attack would have been legally defensible, preempting a non-violent North Korean action with strikes would have simply been wanton aggression; a *preventive*, rather than preemptive, attack.

The story also noted that two US Navy destroyers were positioned off of North Korea's eastern coast and armed with Tomahawk cruise missiles, the kind that had just been launched against Syria, without warning.[14] One of the intelligence officials commented "It's high stakes . . . we're trying to communicate our level of concern and the existence of many military options to dissuade the North first . . . there is a new sense of resolve [in the White House]."[15] In the context of an aircraft carrier supposedly heading to Korea, the strike on Syria, a lack of transparency about what precisely "maximum pressure" entailed, and the administration's universal emphasis that "all options are on the table," the warning alarmed the public. That public concern, in turn, put the White House in a position where it had no choice but to disavow the NBC News story. From the outset, the administration had been clear that if it launched a strike, it would want it to be a surprise and therefore not publicly telegraph the move.[16] Admitting that it was considering a first strike in response to a missile test before actually launching one would put the action in legal jeopardy, because it would reveal the attack to be unprovoked and premeditated; it would be an admission that there was no imminent threat to justify attacking the North.

But White House denials about its contemplating low-threshold *preventive* strikes did not stop it from continuing to make veiled threats that encouraged the world to fearfully anticipate a pending attack. On April 14, Vice President Pence stoked concerns further after launching a 10-day trip around Asia. In Seoul, Pence said he hoped North Korea could denuclearize peacefully, "But all options are on the table." Then, linking the recent missile strikes on Syria to the North Korean nuclear issue, he commented, "The world witnessed the strength and resolve of our new president in Syria and Afghanistan ... North Korea would do well not to test his resolve or the strength of the armed forces of the United States."[17] During the Tokyo leg of that trip, Pence stood beside Japanese Prime Minister Shinzo Abe and repeated that "all options are on the table," and "the United States will continue to work directly with Japan, our allies across the region, and China to bring economic and diplomatic pressure to bear on the regime in North Korea until they once and for all abandon their nuclear and ballistic missile programs."[18] It was the rationale of confrontation—maximum pressure—but stopping short of admitting to or advocating the use of preventive force, even if it was a logical conclusion. In every capital Pence visited on his Asia trip, he sought to shore up an international consensus that the Kim regime ought to be subject to increasing pressure and that total denuclearization was the only acceptable goal. In that narrow task he was largely successful.

While Pence was traversing Asia though, North Korea continued with its own confrontational approach to the United States, undaunted by American tough talk or its actions in Syria. Just before Pence arrived in Seoul, North Korean media warned, "If the U.S. dares opt for a military action ... the DPRK is ready to react to any mode of war desired by the U.S."[19] As Pence visited South Korea, and urged North Korea to heed Trump's order to strike Syria as a warning, North Korea's Vice Foreign Minister told the Associated Press, "We certainly will not keep our arms crossed in the face of a U.S. pre-emptive strike ... We are comparing Trump's policy toward the DPRK with the former administrations and we have concluded that it's becoming more vicious and more aggressive." North Korea, its Vice Foreign Minister warned, "will go to war if they [the Trump administration] choose."[20] And amid public beliefs that "an armada" was heading to Korea, on April 15, the much-awaited anniversary of Kim Il Sung's birth, Pyongyang held a large military parade, followed by a test of a "carrier killer" anti-ship ballistic missile.[21]

The next day, April 16, H. R. McMaster went on the Sunday news shows to condemn the launch, label it as destabilizing, and generate a sense of urgency, declaring, "This is a situation that just can't continue. And the president has made clear that he will not accept the United States and its allies and partners in the region being under threat from this hostile regime with nuclear weapons." Asked what Trump would have done if North Korea had conducted a nuclear test in the prior week, McMaster noted that "all options are on the table," and referred to Trump's cruise missile strike on Syria, noting, "I think what you saw last week with the president's decisive response to the Assad regime ... our president is clearly comfortable making tough decisions and respond[ing]." McMaster then invoked a characterization of Kim Jong Un that he would repeat and clarify over subsequent months:

> this regime ... is unpredictable. This is someone who has demonstrated his brutality by murdering his own brother ... I mean, what Kim Jong-Un is doing is a threat to all people in the region and globally as well. I mean, this is someone who has said not only does he want to develop a nuclear weapon, but he wants to use it to coerce others. He's said that he was willing to proliferate nuclear weapons once he develops them. And so this is a grave threat to all people ... in the coming weeks, months, I think there's a great opportunity for all of us—all of us who are really the threat now of this unpredictable regime—to take action short of armed conflict, so we can avoid the worst.[22]

Mixed Messages Amid Escalating Pressure

The administration was consistent in claiming that it did not seek regime change and it did seek nothing short of comprehensive denuclearization through a campaign of escalating pressure. But that distinction appeared lost on a regime in Pyongyang that equated one with the other. The administration also failed to consistently size up the North Korean regime and Kim Jong Un, it undermined its own pressure campaign through recurring errant remarks that took a soft line on Pyongyang, and it unnecessarily triggered public fears by being unable to control leaks from within the administration about what the United States was planning.

Everything Is Signal, Everything Is Noise

At times, the internal contradictions of the administration's North Korea policy were between its actions and its rhetoric. The most egregious example was the snap decision in April to announce rerouting an aircraft carrier to Korea, even though it was not true at the time. Admiral Harris had not technically ordered the 3rd Fleet to change the aircraft carrier's schedule, even though he did order a press release about it. Yet it was not until April 17, more than a week after the press release, that *Defense News* discovered that the carrier was thousands of miles away from Korea and still heading to Australia, even while Trump bragged about his armada steaming in the opposite direction.[23] Everybody looked bad.

The Trump administration was also undisciplined in how it talked about North Korea, and especially about Kim Jong Un. Trump was by far the most erratic, speaking and tweeting bellicosely about dealing with North Korea on the nuclear issue while at times speaking respectfully, even fawningly, about Kim Jong Un per se. Injecting confusion into a high-pressure environment encourages everyone to assume the worst.

Trump Evokes War, Provokes Confusion

The same day that the aircraft carrier mishap was revealed, Trump was asked in passing about how he would handle North Korea's nuclear and missile programs. He quipped condescendingly, "He's [Kim Jong Un's] gotta behave."[24] It marked the beginning of Trump's personalization of the nuclear standoff as if it were something between him and Kim Jong Un. In an extension of his longstanding practice of public feuds with celebrities, at times he was insulting toward Kim, and at other times he was unusually conciliatory. Through a series of subsequent interviews with different news outlets, Trump began simultaneously speaking ominously about military conflict with North Korea while lavishing praise on Kim Jong Un as a leader.

In one interview, he regarded Kim's control over the regime as impressive: "He's 27 years old. His father dies, took over a regime. So say what you want but that is not easy, especially at that age. I'm not giving him credit or not giving him credit, I'm just saying that's a very hard thing to do. As to whether or not he's rational, I have no opinion on it. I hope he's rational."[25] In another interview, he added, "Obviously he's [Kim] a pretty smart cookie." And on April 30, he told Bloomberg Politics that "If it were appropriate for me to meet with [Kim Jong Un], I would absolutely, I would be honored to do it ... Most people would never say that. But I'm telling you under the right circumstances, I would meet with him. We have breaking news."[26] Trump's motives were unclear, and nobody yet knew if Kim Jong Un grasped the signal through all the noise. But even as the Korean Peninsula lurched toward crisis, in part due to Trump's rhetoric, Trump was simultaneously signaling an openness to something unprecedented. A once unthinkable presidential summit between the United States and North Korea was being foreshadowed.

Saying he would be "honored" was an unprecedented statement for a sitting US president to make about a North Korean leader, and it was one that Trump had arguably foreshadowed during his presidential campaign when he then stated he would be willing to meet with Kim. But the clearly positive, even friendly valence of the statement contradicted the larger tone the administration was trying to strike with its maximum pressure campaign. It also contradicted Pence's remarks during his Asia trip, where he ruled out negotiating with Pyongyang until it agreed to halt its missile testing and to denuclearize. The White House thus rushed to qualify Trump's statement by saying that "clearly conditions are not there right now ... we've got to see their provocative behavior ratcheted down."[27] White House Chief of Staff Reince Preibus went even further to knock down the idea of talks with North Korea, stating a Trump meeting with Kim could never happen unless North Korea would agree to "disarm and give up what he's put in mountainsides across his country and give up his drive for nuclear capability and ICBMs."[28]

Even as Trump spoke respectfully of Kim, he intimated a willingness to attack the North and described the trajectory of North Korean behavior as unacceptable. The same series of interviews that produced his adulation of Kim Jong Un were also used to convey that "There is a chance that we could end up having a major, major conflict with North Korea. Absolutely ... We'd love to solve things diplomatically but it's very difficult."[29] On April 18, Trump was asked, "Have you ruled out a military strike?" He replied:

> I don't want to telegraph what I'm doing, or what I'm thinking ... We'll see what happens ... but you know they've been talking with this gentleman [Kim Jong Un] for a long time. You read Clinton's book, he said, "Oh we made such a great peace deal" and it was a joke. You look at ... President Obama, everybody ... they've all been outplayed by this gentleman.

When asked, "What happens if North Korea launches another missile?" Trump answered, "We'll find out."[30] Whether by instinct or strategy, Trump's interviews were always laced with the innuendo of violence. Far from dispelling rumors of a willingness to use preventive force against Pyongyang, Trump's comments encouraged that perception.

At the end of April, North Korea launched an intermediate-range ballistic missile that failed about one minute after launch, exploding on North Korean territory.[31] Asked about the missile test, Trump downplayed North Korea's testing of shorter-range missiles generally, even when they served as building blocks for ICBM advancements, yet he also appeared to draw a line against North Korean nuclear testing. He remarked, "I didn't say don't test a missile. He's [Kim] going to do what he's going to do ... this was a small missile. This was not a big missile. This was not a nuclear test, which he was expected to do three days ago ... I will not be happy, if there's a nuclear test, I will not be happy."[32] Asked whether by "not happy" he meant military action against the North, Trump said, "I don't know, maybe. I mean, we'll see."[33]

Nobody's Controlling the Message

Even putting Trump's inscrutable intentions aside, administration officials were invested in trying to draw nuanced distinctions without difference about what was, at its core, a blunt policy of pursuing comprehensive denuclearization at any cost. The message was further muddled by leaks from officials in the administration who were raising alarm bells about the violent direction of internal deliberations. Ultimately, there was enough variation and contradiction in what administration officials said about North Korea policy that it was difficult for anyone to know what to believe. Everything had a subtext of eventual military intervention, but the rationale for it was muddled at best. As a result of a rampant lack of confidence in the stability of the situation, everything that both the United States and North Korea did took on greater meaning and amplification in public discourse. This had the effect of needlessly heightening tensions, though some cynical commentators surmised that creating public anxiety was part of the White House's maximum pressure strategy to begin with.[34] Even if the administration's war threats were deliberate attempts to stoke a crisis mood, that did not preclude the administration from acting on its threats in the future. What starts out as a bluff can end with follow-through.

As Trump proceeded with media interviews in which he made repeated veiled threats toward Pyongyang, *The Guardian* spoke with two administration officials claiming that the Trump administration was considering using ballistic missile defenses positioned on US ships to intercept future North Korean missile tests.[35] According to the report, the idea had been considered during the Obama administration, but was fraught with risks incommensurate with any plausible benefit. Did the United States expect Kim to no longer launch missiles after the United States intercepted one? What if he retaliated or escalated? At minimum, it seemed likely that, for political reasons if nothing else, Kim would be forced to repeatedly launch missiles in defiance. If that happened, would the United States be willing to continually trade expensive US missile interceptors for taking out far less costly North Korean missiles? And what if the United States attempted to intercept a missile and missed? It would puncture the mythically high expectations surrounding what missile defense can do. That would have strategic consequences, not just against North Korea, but in US competition with China and Russia too. When asked about the missile intercept option—which had come out of the North Korea policy review and was discussed ahead of the Mar-a-Lago meeting with Xi Jinping—the Pentagon spokesperson did not deny it, but reiterated that "We are exploring a new range of diplomatic, security, and economic measures and all options are on the table."[36]

That leak was followed shortly after by something that had never happened before when it came to foreign policy. On April 26, Trump invited the entire Senate to the White House (literally bringing them in on buses) for a closed-door briefing on North Korea. The briefing was led by Tillerson, Mattis, Director of National Intelligence Dan Coats, and Chairman of the Joint Chiefs of Staff Dunford. The secretive and unprecedented nature of the gathering betrayed an ominous symbolism that again fueled public fears and speculation, regardless of whether that was the meeting's intention. Despite the appearance of something grave being discussed behind closed doors, senators came out of the meeting saying that the briefing was anodyne and that nothing new was offered. The one meaningful deviation came in remarks about the meeting from Senator Ted Cruz, who commented, "The military is obviously planning for a number of options, as they should—minimal military action to more significant action ... If there's a clear and imminent threat to the U.S., our military needs to be prepared to act."[37]

The next day, Tillerson went on Fox News and National Public Radio to give the first real public, but not detailed, explanations of the administration's maximum pressure strategy. "We're just in the early stages of executing [our strategy]. And it is one that involves bringing significant pressure to bear on the regime in Pyongyang. It also involves calling on China to play a role in how we deal with this threat. So again, you're right, tensions are running a bit high right now."[38] When his interviewer suggested that maximum pressure looked like Obama's strategic patience, Tillerson tried to differentiate it by saying:

> I think it's different in terms of both the intensity, and the expectations we have for global participation ... I first spoke to the Chinese ... to make clear to them that we were unwilling to negotiate our way to the negotiating table ... I think in the past the assumption has been the Chinese would only take limited action. We're going to test that assumption.[39]

Asked if he thought Kim Jong Un was unstable, Tillerson contradicted McMaster's previous portrayal of Kim, replying, "All indications are he is not crazy. He may be ruthless ... by our standards is irrational, but he is not insane ... In the past, when certain events have happened, he has made rational choices."[40] Despite both McMaster and Tillerson being publicly portrayed as part of an "axis of adults"—essentially moderates who believed in sustaining a traditional US foreign policy—they frequently clashed at both a bureaucratic and personal level. Consequently, the NSC engaged in significant informal policy and planning discussions that excluded the State Department's Asia bureau, just as the State Department's diplomatic activity and public messaging was often conducted without pre-coordination with the NSC.[41] Occasionally, as in characterizations of Kim Jong Un, their disagreements and lack of coordination spilled over into the public view.

Tillerson also took pains to distinguish the goal of comprehensive denuclearization from other goals that it thought might be perceived as more threatening: "We do not seek regime change. We do not seek a collapse of the regime. We do not seek an accelerated reunification of the peninsula."[42] The problem was that this nuance was tone-deaf to the situation. North Korea viewed nuclear weapons as necessary for survival, and it had reached that view by experience and observation over time. It was willing to endure decades of costs, isolation, and threats from the United States in order to secure what it saw as its only assurance of survival. To Pyongyang, demanding comprehensive denuclearization was not meaningfully different than demanding regime change. Even if Kim Jong Un took Trump administration attempts at nuance more seriously than mere cheap talk, he had a view about the relationship between his country's nuclear weapons and its survival that was the opposite of what the White House wanted it to be.

China Gets "Tough," North Korea Bides Its Time

China was the Trump administration's primary line of effort as part of its maximum pressure strategy. Experts in Washington had long since converged on the belief that any progress on the North Korean nuclear issue ran through China, especially if pressure was to be the primary instrument of change. Yet solid consensus that China was the solution belied how China could be made to be the solution. Was Chinese cooperation best secured by pressure on China or solicitous ingratiation of China? The question about the merits of carrots versus sticks on North Korea extended to China too. The Trump–Xi personal bond translated in the near term to increased reliance on working with China to solve North Korea, not unlike the final years of the Obama administration.

As part of the cooperative China effort on North Korea, the Trump team had agreed to a package of four assurances that China relayed to its contacts in Pyongyang. If North Korea would agree to enter talks aimed at abandoning its nuclear weapons, the Trump administration was prepared to promise "it will not push for regime change; it will not seek the end of Kim's government; it will not launch an invasion above the 38th parallel ... and it will not try to hurry along reunification of the Korean Peninsula."[43] But of course this was not substantively different than the Obama administration's posture toward North Korea. If it made a difference in US actions at all, it would have been on the relative prioritization of touting North Korean human rights abuses and some of the State Department's information penetration operations into North Korea. To be sure, human rights criticisms and information operations were major irritants in the relationship between Washington and Pyongyang, but they were trivial in a strategic sense as they were askew of the central problem of nuclear-armed missiles.

Nevertheless, the United States had begun extensive coordination with Beijing after Xi Jinping's Mar-a-Lago visit. Armed with the White House's "four assurances" and the threat of greater pressure to come, China's envoy for nuclear negotiations visited Pyongyang in April to warn them against conducting a sixth nuclear test, and to relay America's verbal carrot and stick to North Korean Foreign Ministry officials. China and the United States also consulted on an additional round of UN sanctions, as well as increased Chinese inspections of vehicles going to and from North Korea across its long, shared border.

But none of this had any observable effect. Kim Jong Un's posture toward China had been openly hostile since taking power in 2011, and China's supposed effort to pressure Pyongyang was more symbolic than it was actual in the first half of 2017. China's border inspections, which were designed to prevent trafficking of illicit goods prohibited by UN sanctions, allowed companies crossing the border to self-verify (as opposed to physically conducting inspections) that they were not in violation of sanctions by filling out a standard form.[44] Chinese trade with North Korea also expanded through the spring and summer of 2017, and exports of grain actually increased by more than 400 percent from January to April 2017 compared with the year prior.[45] So while China put on a cooperative face with Trump administration officials and was frustrated by Pyongyang's intransigence, it did little to try to meaningfully change the situation with North Korea.

Rather than influencing Pyongyang, China seemed more focused on nudging the United States into a calmer posture. As it had always done, China repeatedly called for restraint on the part of both the United States and North Korea, striking a tone of moral equivalence with statements that portrayed the countries as "two accelerating trains coming toward each other."[46] It also renewed calls for a proposed "suspension for suspension" process, whereby the United States suspended military exercises with South Korea, and North Korea suspended missile and nuclear testing.[47] The United States and South Korea summarily rejected that proposal on the grounds that they would not trade legal actions (military exercises) for illegal ones (nuclear and missile testing).

As this cooperative approach to pressuring Pyongyang through Beijing played out, Trump offered public yet backhanded encouragement for China to take greater action to pressure North Korea, with tweets like, "I explained to the president of China that a trade deal with the U.S. will be far better for them if they solve the North Korea problem," and "North Korea is looking for trouble. If China decides to help, that would be great. If not, we will solve the problem without them! U.S.A." Trump was betting that China had the key to convincing North Korea to denuclearize (and he was, on balance, still on chummy terms with Xi Jinping), but was doing so in a way that tried to minimize China converting that reliance into leverage against the United States. In effect, Trump tried to project that it was in China's interests to successfully influence North Korea, but the United States had recourse (through options Beijing would find problematic) should it fail.

North Korea Doubles Down

While spring 2017 was among the quietest periods in the Trump administration's standoff with the Kim regime, it was also a time when North Korea took active diplomatic steps to shape the future in its favor; it was not a static adversary. Pyongyang persisted with missile tests and bombastic external propaganda threatening "thermonuclear war," but as it did so, it also tried to create international political space that would permit it to continue advancing its nuclear and missile capabilities while staving off an acute crisis showdown with Washington.

By April, the Trump administration had already issued many pressure-oriented statements, hinted at war in media interviews, promised Chinese pressure on the North would be forthcoming, increased the frequency of strategic bombers and nuclear submarines appearing in Korea, announced additional sanctions, and carried out a larger-scale version of its two-month-long annual military exercises with the South. Cumulatively, this did nothing to sway Kim Jong Un from the course of consolidating his nuclear and missile programs, and neither did any of it encourage North Korea to tone down its own threatening rhetoric. It is possible that Kim took seriously America's warnings not to test a nuclear weapon or ICBM in March and April, since it did not do so. But even in that generous interpretation—that is, that American deterrence threats against nuclear testing were successful in forestalling them for a time—the United States was using threats to delay the inevitable. Deterrence is not an end in itself, but rather a way of buying time.

In the final week of April, after Tillerson tried to explain maximum pressure to the public and distinguish the denuclearization goal from regime change, North Korea tested yet another ballistic missile, and North Korean media released a video that went viral in the United States. The video, released from the North Korean site, Arirang Maeri, which rarely received attention outside Korea, was a montage set to Soviet-style music involving North Korean missiles aiming through crosshairs at images of US aircraft carriers and the White House. The video ended with an explosion of the US Capitol and the message, "The final collapse will begin." With images of the aircraft carrier as a target in particular, North Korea was calibrating its threatening propaganda to meet whatever instruments of pressure the United States trotted out. North Korea did not appear dismissive of the Trump administration's various threats, but neither did it betray any sign of acquiescence in its already hardened posture, especially on the nuclear issue.

In early May, as the White House began toughening its sanctions measures against Pyongyang, North Korea sought to counteract them through diplomatic outreach that routed around the White House. North Korea's newly reconstituted Foreign Affairs Committee—a body that functioned like a Potemkin foreign ministry but had not operated since the 1990s—distributed a letter to missions at the United Nations, urging their governments not to implement UN Security Council sanctions resolutions. That outreach prompted US Ambassador to the United Nations, Nikki Haley, to make a divisive declaration: "You either support North Korea or you support us. The United States is not past looking at third-country entities who are helping North Korea and putting sanctions against them. If you're supporting North Korea, you're against the rest of the international community."[48] The Foreign Affairs Committee also sent a letter of protest to the US House of Representatives, warning them that "As the U.S. House of Representatives enacts more and more of these reckless hostile laws, the DPRK's efforts to strengthen nuclear deterrents will gather greater pace, beyond anyone's imagination."[49] Pressure for pressure.

And when South Korea elected political progressive Moon Jae-in president on May 9, North Korea took the occasion to try to drive a wedge between Washington and Seoul. Under successive conservative governments in Seoul, the prior decade in North–South relations was among the worst and most hostile in their history. Upon news of Moon's victory (a political progressive whose candidacy included a platform favoring a more conciliatory approach to North Korea and the nuclear issue) North Korea sought to use the change to its advantage. North Korea's most popular newspaper, *Rodong Shinmun*, published a message carried in Seoul, calling on Moon to cancel military exercises with the United States and urging that "The two Koreas should respect each other and open a new chapter to move toward an improvement of their ties and inter-Korean unification."[50] Prior to Moon's assumption of the presidency, South Korea had been a bystander in the burgeoning nuclear crisis. But now North Korea was laying the foundation to take a separate approach to South Korea than to the United States.

Less than a week after the South Korean election, on May 14, North Korean media announced the successful test of an intermediate-range ballistic missile capable of carrying nuclear warheads, launched from a mobile platform. The missile (the Hwasong-12) was among the longest-range missile demonstrations North Korea had ever conducted. As was often the case, the media announcement included a colorfully ominous retaliatory warning: The US "mainland and Pacific operation region are in the D.P.R.K.'s sighting range for strike ... If the U.S. dares opt for a military provocation against the D.P.R.K., we are ready to counter it."[51] In a loss of face for China, the test occurred in conjunction with its hosting of the One Belt One Road (OBOR) conference in Beijing, to which it had invited a North Korean delegation. The OBOR meeting was the most symbolically important event instantiating

Chinese ambitions for extending its political and economic influence in the region. It was thus ironic that North Korea, China's only formal ally in the world, could not only steal the spotlight from China, but act so intransigently in clear contravention of Chinese preferences. If nothing else, North Korea's defiant launch of a missile after extensive consultations and warnings from China called into question the Washington wisdom that China could or would rein in Kim Jong Un.

Without overstating the relative quietude of the transition from spring to summer (even these months were marked by continuing rhetorical bombast and missile tests) a series of North Korean diplomatic engagements with the United States gave reason for a degree of restraint by Washington and Pyongyang.

In May, while North Korea conducted several ballistic missile tests, it was also engaging with the United States about the possibility of releasing detained US citizens charged with various crimes and sentenced to hard labor in North Korea. By this time, Pyongyang had made a common practice of arresting US citizens visiting North Korea on trumped-up charges and then holding them as de facto hostages until US representatives negotiated their release. It was this pattern of interaction that saw Bill Clinton visit Pyongyang in 2009. Although strictly a humanitarian issue distinct from nuclear negotiations, both sides often treated these detainee negotiations as a litmus test of the overall relationship. North Korea started out the month of May by arresting the fourth such American, Kim Hak Song, and charging him with "hostile acts" against the regime.

For more than a year the State Department had been intermittently engaging with the North Korean Foreign Ministry—sometimes through the Swedish diplomatic mission in Pyongyang and sometimes through the New York Channel at the United Nations—to seek the release of all US citizens, though North Korea had effectively cut off direct contact with the United States in the final months of the Obama administration, in reaction to targeted sanctions naming Kim Jong Un. Later in May, Joseph Yun, US Special Envoy for North Korea Policy, met informally with Choi Son-hui, then Pyongyang's Director-General for American Affairs and a ubiquitous presence in past nuclear negotiations, in Oslo, Norway. The scope of the meeting was limited to seeking the release of the Americans detained in Pyongyang. Several months prior, in February, before the North Korea policy review was complete,

Trump instructed Tillerson to make a priority of recovering Americans being held there. Yun was originally scheduled to hold this meeting back in February, but the State Department canceled North Korea's visas when news of the Kim Jong Nam assassination broke. Yun's Oslo meetings succeeded in gaining North Korean agreement to allow Swedish diplomats to check on and report back about the status of US detainees, but not in releasing them. Ultimately though, Pyongyang would only allow Swedish access to one of the four detainees.

As the humanitarian discussions were playing out in early June, North Korea fired off a series of short-range anti-ship ballistic missiles. Very routine, but they were a kind that was capable of striking at the US Navy destroyers and frigates that were best positioned to launch a first strike against North Korea should the White House make the call to do so. But the missiles had temporarily become background noise relative to the humanitarian negotiating track. On June 6, North Korea's ambassador to the United Nations suddenly informed Joe Yun that the teenager Otto Warmbier (one of the four American detainees, and the only one who was not ethnically Korean) was in critical condition. Warmbier was an American college student who was visiting Pyongyang as part of a multi-country tour of Asia—a slightly more daring and exotic version of any normal trip abroad to soak and poke in a foreign culture. North Korea claimed Warmbier was caught trying to steal a poster from the hotel where he was staying, and imprisoned him on that basis. They also asserted that, while in North Korean custody, Warmbier contracted botulism, but doctors who looked after him upon his release on June 13 ruled that out and pointed instead to severe "neurological damage."[52] The Swedes had previously been barred from checking on Warmbier.

In parallel with the rapidly changing situation leading to the release of Warmbier, a group of former US officials and experts met with representatives of North Korea's foreign ministry in Stockholm, Sweden. Their purpose was to probe for any opening in North Korea's position on the nuclear issue that might allow for the possibility of resumed government-to-government negotiations. The tone of the discussions in Sweden was cordial but serious and fairly rigid, which was typical of US–North Korea diplomacy. According to two of the participants on the US side, there was no give whatsoever in the North Korean position. They recalled the North Koreans declaring, "The most perfect weapons system will never become the exclusive property of the United States ... accept us as a nuclear state, then we are prepared to talk about a peace treaty or fight. We are ready for either."[53] Suzanne DiMaggio, who helped arrange the talks, told the North Koreans that if they "immediately released the remaining three prisoners, it could set up an atmosphere for potentially serious talks."[54] The North Koreans declined the proposal without an explanation. At the time, it was unclear whether the release of Warmbier should have been interpreted as a gesture of good will or a way of North Korea preemptively making sure that it would not be blamed for killing Warmbier in their custody. The severity of Warmbier's condition may have necessitated his release whereas the others remained detained because their health was not in jeopardy.

The Otto Aftermath

The surprising and unsettling death of Warmbier so quickly after being returned to US care struck a nerve, with Trump personally, and with the administration. It also coincided with Trump's growing frustration at China's lack of results in pressuring North Korea as Xi Jinping had previously intimated it would. By late June, a contradictory pattern in America's approach to China started to emerge—and would continue for several more months—whereby Trump took an openly antagonistic tone toward China while his cabinet officials proceeded with a steady and more nuanced approach to China, especially on the North Korea issue. Trump expressed a degree of outrage at Warmbier's treatment. On June 19, the day of Warmbier's passing, Trump was at a roundtable of the American Technology Council when he told the press, "I just wanted to pass on word—Otto Warmbier has just passed away ... A lot of bad things happened [to him] ... he was in very tough condition ... It's a brutal regime, and we'll be able to handle it."[55] The next day Trump tweeted, "While I greatly appreciate the efforts of President Xi & China to help with North Korea, it has not worked out. At least I know China tried!" Trump had pressuring North Korea on his mind, and China was not delivering as he hoped.

The day after Trump's tweet trolling China, Mattis and Tillerson met their Chinese counterparts in Washington for a Diplomatic and Security Dialogue, which had been agreed to at the Mar-a-Lago summit. While there were whiffs of disagreement between

Washington and Beijing in the follow-up press remarks—Mattis called them good "philosophical-level discussions," which in a military context was a euphemistic pejorative for uselessness—Tillerson spoke of solidarity with China on North Korea:

> The most acute threat in the region today is posed by the DPRK. We both call for complete, verifiable, and irreversible denuclearization of the Korean Peninsula ... We reaffirmed our commitment to implement in full all relevant UN Security Council resolutions ... we both agreed that our companies should not do business with any UN-designated North Korean entities in accordance with these resolutions. China understands that the United States regards North Korea as our top security threat ... they have a diplomatic responsibility to exert much greater economic and diplomatic pressure on the regime if they want to prevent further escalation in the region.[56]

At a bureaucratic level, then, the United States persisted with a conventional, nuanced approach toward China that was a blend of cooperation, competition, and rhetorical restraint, even after Trump put down more antagonistic markers in the public discourse about China when it came to dealing with the North. But the China issue had become entwined with indignation about Warmbier's treatment by North Korea, which placed an emotional overlay on the White House's already hardened posture. Mattis was asked about Warmbier during the press availability for the Diplomatic and Security Dialogue, and he revealed a disgust and outrage that is difficult to overstate, and that was a publicly shared sentiment in news headlines across the United States at the time:

> We see a young man go over there healthy, and with a minor act of mischief, come home dead, basically ... There is no way that we can look at a situation like this with any kind of understanding. This is—goes beyond any kind of understanding of law and order, of humanity, of responsibility towards any human being.[57]

During Trump's first six months in office, Kim Jong Un approved firing off multiple long-range missiles, continued with bombastic rhetoric, released propaganda videos depicting attacks on the United States, assassinated his own brother on foreign soil with a chemical weapon, and promised to test a nuclear weapon and an ICBM at some point in the near future. Now the Kim regime had tortured and killed an American—the only non-ethnically Korean American in its custody—offloading him to the United States just in time for his family to see him die. Rage fueled resolve, and the Warmbier incident poisoned the atmosphere for any near-term diplomatic engagement between Washington and Pyongyang.

7 ON THE BRINK OF NUCLEAR WAR

By July 2017, the conditions were set for the first US nuclear crisis since the Cold War. That month, North Korea twice demonstrated a missile capability that the White House implied it was never going to allow. The spark for the crisis would follow shortly after those tests, in early August, when Trump threatened North Korea in a manner that no US president had ever done. Its content and tone were unprecedented. Other than Trump's rhetoric—which was at times hyperbolic and highly personalized, and grew more so throughout the crisis—US actions toward North Korea were almost entirely consistent with what policy had been under Obama. But combining new threats with the old policy looked a lot like North Korea's offensive theory of victory, which was a recipe for disaster.

As the crisis ensued, both sides threatened and indicated a readiness for war. Each made clear that nuclear catastrophe depended entirely on the decisions of the other. Kim showed no sign of abandoning the trajectory that so alarmed Washington, yet the Trump administration deliberately created a sense of global urgency around forcing Kim to do precisely that. By September, the prevailing view in the Trump administration, which persisted throughout the crisis, was that denuclearization was worth drawing first blood over: "Everyone wants a 'preemptive war' now except [Secretary of Defense] Mattis," said one official.[1] The United States had not faced a risk of nuclear war this palpable since the 1962 Cuban Missile Crisis.

Crossing the Line

On June 27, 2017, James Clapper, Director of National Intelligence under President Obama, gave a keynote speech for an event hosted at the Center for Strategic and International Studies in Washington. Clapper, who had a long reputation as a foreign policy hawk, but had also become a vocal critic of President Trump, reflected on a November 2014 visit to Pyongyang he had made to seek the release of Kenneth Bae, an American who was being held captive like so many before and after him. His remarks came only a week after Warmbier's death and Washington's newly elevated hostility toward Pyongyang.

While in North Korea, Clapper met with two of the regime's senior-most officials responsible for national security decision-making, after Kim himself: the Director of the Reconnaissance General Bureau and the Minister of State Security. The former was in charge of the organization that, historically, planned and executed North Korean acts of asymmetric violence (including terrorism) and cyber attacks, which would include the 2014 Sony hack and the 2010 torpedo attack on the South Korean ship *Cheonan*. Clapper said he was:

> amazed at the magnitude and depth of paranoia, and the over-whelming sense of siege that seems to prevail among the elite leadership in the north. Everywhere they look, as I heard repeatedly, they see enemies who threaten their very existence. They find [South Korea's] military capability quite formidable, and superior to theirs, and when they then consider the US military force, it compounds the paranoia, and [this] amplifies their siege mentality.[2]

The status quo mentality among North Korean policy elites was one of paranoia about being attacked or invaded. The early months of the Trump presidency heightened that fear considerably. But because of North Korea's deeply engrained strategic beliefs about what it takes to survive in the world, Clapper judged, "if we were to mount a pre-emptive attack, the North, I am convinced, would react reflexively ... to make Seoul a 'sea of fire.'"[3] North Korean fear would translate into hardened resolve, not capitulation. The more North Korea feared being attacked, the greater the pressure to lash out or pull its hair trigger.

In all likelihood, heightened fear among Pyongyang elites was what engendered both its intense hostile rhetoric and its urgent need to demonstrate the capability that it possessed in some form since at least 2015 the ability to deliver an ICBM armed with a nuclear warhead against US territory, and ideally against Washington itself. Only by holding the US homeland at risk of attack could Kim Jong Un be certain that the United States would not invade.

From Kim's Missiles to Trump's Fire and Fury

Consequently, on July 4, North Korea tested an ICBM that could reach the continental United States. It flew 580 km for 40 minutes, and was capable of striking Alaska and Hawaii.[4] In the wake of Otto Warmbier's death, dialogue between Washington and Pyongyang (even the administratively focused New York Channel) ground to a standstill. Tillerson, who, throughout the Trump presidency tried to carve out a more moderate, careful stance on North Korea policy, called the test "a new escalation of the threat to the United States, our allies and partners, the region, and the world."[5] While continuing with the nuanced distinction between eliminating North Korean nuclear weapons and regime change, Tillerson reiterated that "we will never accept a nuclear-armed North Korea."[6]

North Korean media issued an unusually hostile statement that the missile was a "gift" for the "American bastards," and that Kim Jong Un, "with a broad smile on his face, told officials, scientists and technicians that the U.S. would be displeased to witness the DPRK's strategic option as it was given a 'package of gifts' on its 'Independence Day.'"[7] North Korea's belligerent statements and threats were usually cast with a defensive rationalization, but this was willfully antagonistic. Even the Fourth of July timing was intended to raise the ire of Washington. Kim deliberately adopted a "screw you" posture in his foreign policy toward the Trump administration, consistent with the belief that friction added to deterrence.

Later the same day, US and South Korean forces launched retaliatory demonstration missiles of their own, which they explicitly justified as "countering North Korea's destabilizing and unlawful actions on July 4."[8] Underscoring the precariousness of the situation that North Korea's ICBM launch set off, the Commander of US Forces Korea, General Vincent Brooks, observed that "Self-restraint, which is a choice, is all that separates armistice and war ... It would be a grave mistake for anyone to believe anything to the contrary."[9]

Separating Kim from His Missiles

Two weeks later, several senior Trump national security officials appeared at the Aspen Security Forum, a who's who event in defense and intelligence policy. General Joseph Dunford, Chairman of the Joint Chiefs of Staff, commented that "it is not unimaginable to have military options to respond to North Korean nuclear capability. What's unimaginable to me is allowing a capability that will allow a nuclear weapon to land in Denver, Colorado ... so my job will be to develop military options to make sure that doesn't happen."[10] Dunford was aware of the cost of a war with North Korea, and betrayed no sign that he wanted a war. But his much-publicized comments implied that the administration preferred to resort to military strikes than to allow North Korea to retain nuclear-armed ICBMs. H. R. McMaster and other anonymously quoted White House officials had been saying as much since April.

That interpretation of Dunford's remarks was amplified because of CIA Director Mike Pompeo's comments at the same event two days earlier. Pompeo noted that he, along with Director of National Intelligence Dan Coats, personally delivered the President's Daily Brief to Trump most days, and that Trump "rarely lets me escape the Oval Office without asking a question about North Korea, it is at the front of his mind."[11] Pompeo went on to say that Trump had asked the CIA for options for neutralizing the North Korean nuclear threat in the same sense that he asked the military for options; the CIA, he implied, was looking for ways to either overthrow the regime or assassinate Kim:

> the thing that is most dangerous about it is the character who holds the control over them today. So from the administration's perspective, the most important thing we can do is separate those two, right, separate capacity, and someone who might well have intent, and break those two apart. And I am confident the intelligence community will present a set—a wide range of options for the President about how we might go about that.[12]

Pompeo was among Trump's most hawkish cabinet officials, so it was unsurprising that he would make tough comments. But nobody in the US government had ever spoken publicly about "separating" Kim Jong Un from his capacity to launch nuclear weapons, not least an intelligence official who might be charged with that mission. For Pompeo, eliminating Kim was not necessarily about any expectation that Kim was as reckless as McMaster had taken to describing him; it was about delivering options for Trump and taking a zero-risk approach to national security. Kim, Pompeo said, was utterly rational: "we've watched Kim Jong-un respond, right, he measures his responses, he's trying now to figure out how to work with the South Koreans to get us to back off, to get America to stop pressing just as hard as he is . . . So in that sense he certainly has the capability of responding to what are in his best interest [and] in his regime's best interest."[13]

Only days later, on July 28, Kim again seemed to do what was in his regime's best interest, launching yet another ICBM, this one flying further than the previous one. Through state media, Kim declared, "We have demonstrated our ability to fire our intercontinental ballistic rocket at any time and place and that the entire U.S. territory is within our shooting range."[14] Kim needed to both generate friction with his adversary and further prove his ability to do the unthinkable—launch a nuclear weapon against the United States—without actually doing so. A clearly frustrated Trump responded orthogonally to the test by fuming via tweet, "I am very disappointed in China. Our foolish past leaders have allowed them to make hundreds of billions of dollars a year in trade, yet they do NOTHING for us with North Korea, just talk . . . We will no longer allow this to continue. China could easily solve this problem!" Trump's cooperative approach to securing Beijing's influence was giving way to something more confrontational.

Through July, Trump's ambassador to the United Nations, Nikki Haley, had been working to secure additional sanctions on North Korea, expanding their scope to include not only named individuals and firms as targets of sanctions, but also the regime's access to foreign currency generally. But China and Russia, both of whom exercised vetoes over UN resolutions as permanent members of the Security Council, were stalling further sanctions announcements. That changed with the July 28 ICBM launch, which forced their hand, leading to a new sanctions resolution against North Korea on August 5. The new sanctions imposed a ban on North Korean coal exports, which were one of the Kim regime's primary sources of revenue.

Tough action was accompanied by even tougher talk, not only within the Trump administration, but among some Republicans too. Appearing on *The Today Show* on August 2, Senator Lindsey

Graham (who was a #NeverTrump Republican during the presidential election, but eventually became a Trump confidant on foreign policy) spoke of recent discussions he had held with Trump about North Korea. His comments appear extensively here because of the tone they struck, the way they framed the question of war, and because they give some insight into Trump's mindset on North Korea. Graham noted:

> President Trump has said "I will not allow them to get an ICBM with a nuclear weapon on top to hit America." They're headed that way. The only way they're going to change [is] if they believe there's a credible threat of military force on the table ... [Trump's] got to choose between homeland security and regional stability ... There is a military option—to destroy North Korea's program and North Korea itself ... If there's going to be a war to stop [Kim] it will be over there. If thousands die, they're going to die over there. They're not going to die here. And he's told me that to my face ... Kim Jong Un is threatening America with a nuclear-tipped missile.[15]

Matt Lauer tried to clarify if Graham was saying it was acceptable to invoke a military option that would kill thousands of people in East Asia and Graham responded affirmatively and fatalistically:

> It's inevitable unless North Korea changes because you're making our president pick between regional stability and homeland security ... They've kicked the can down the road for twenty years. There's no place else to kick it. There will be a war with North Korea over their missile program if they continue to try to hit America with an ICBM. He has told me that, I believe him.[16]

Graham's comments foreshadowed Trump's public position to come on North Korea. They also restated themes from prior comments by the administration, but in a more explicit way. Whereas McMaster and others would refer obliquely to "military options" or it being "unthinkable" that North Korea would be allowed to retain a nuclear ICBM capability, Graham made his (and by extension Trump's) beliefs plain: homeland security and regional security were different things, war in the region prevented war against the homeland, and war would be inevitable if Kim did not denuclearize. With Graham's comments, a senior US statesman was now on the record explicitly supporting a preventive war against a nuclear-armed adversary if that adversary did not unilaterally disarm, and he claimed Trump shared that view.

Fire and Fury

The nuclear standoff exploded onto the world stage on August 8. By this time, the atmosphere was already heavy with talk of war, and sanctions were buttressing an ever-enlarging slate of military activity. The United States had increased the frequency of its now routine nuclear bomber deployments to Korea (which started occurring regularly in 2013 under Obama) from a few times a year to at least once per month, in addition to nuclear submarines regularly calling on South Korean ports and US Navy destroyers patrolling in waters off North Korea's eastern coast. Those destroyers had been given orders to program North Korean targets and prepare to fire on command. North Korea was militarily encircled even as its diplomatic and economic isolation grew. That morning, the *Washington Post* reported a Defense Intelligence Agency assessment about North Korea that concluded Pyongyang had successfully miniaturized nuclear warheads to fit on ICBMs, as it claimed to have done already in 2013.[17]

Later that day, a press gaggle covering Trump attending an unrelated event asked him about the report. Trump stopped, sat back in his chair, crossed his arms, and sternly declared: "North Korea best not make any more threats to the United States—They will be met with fire and fury like the world has never seen. [Kim Jong-un] has been very threatening, beyond a normal statement. And as I said, they will be met with fire, fury, and frankly, power the likes of which this world has never seen."[18] The statement was emotional and hyperbolic, and it left open the interpretation that Trump was implying US use of nuclear weapons. The fire and fury threat, moreover, was not about a strategic goal or denuclearization or any established objective; it was aimed at the vague and low-threshold purpose of getting North Korea to stop threatening the United States.

The threat went viral and became a priority concern in capitals around the world, especially in Washington. It was entirely Trump's doing. As an administration official told Reuters, "There had not been any discussions about escalating the rhetoric in response to North Korean leader Kim (Jong Un)'s statements or about the possible effects of doing that."[19] Notwithstanding the improvisational nature of the fire and fury remark, it locked in an elevated level of confrontational rhetoric in the administration's subsequent talking points on Korea. Mattis, whose words were typically measured, seemed to endorse Trump's remarks by urging, "The DPRK must choose to stop isolating itself and stand down its pursuit of nuclear weapons ... The DPRK should cease any consideration of actions that would lead to the end of its regime and the destruction of its people."[20] The implication was that the destruction of North Korea could follow for reasons other than North Korea launching an attack, such as nuclear or missile testing, or simply continuing to possess nuclear weapons. Yet Tillerson downplayed Trump's utterance, remarking: "nothing that I have seen and nothing that I know of would indicate that the situation has dramatically changed in the last 24 hours."[21] It was neither the first nor the last time that Tillerson would publicly contradict the valence of his boss.

In the spirit of pressure for pressure, only hours after Trump's fire and fury remark, the North Korean military issued an unusually specific threat that was no less alarming than what Trump bellowed. The statement read that US bomber aircraft:

> threaten and blackmail through their frequent visits to the sky above South Korea ... The KPA strategic force is now carefully examining the operational plan for making an enveloping fire at the areas around Guam with medium- to long-range strategic ballistic rocket Hwasong-12 in order to contain the US major military bases on Guam, including the Andersen Air Force base ... It is a daydream for the US to think that its mainland is an invulnerable heavenly kingdom.[22]

That statement's precision suggested careful planning rather than a throwaway line: "They [the missiles] will fly for 3,356.7 km for 1,065 seconds and hit the waters 30 to 40 km away from Guam," it said.

Threatening to use missiles to bracket-fire a US territory that hosts a nuclear bomber base was novel, and a statement aimed at intimidation. If North Korea could deliberately fire missiles on either side of Guam, it would incontrovertibly demonstrate the ability to hit Guam with a degree of control and precision that it had not yet shown for its long-range missile arsenal. The demonstration itself would generate a considerable risk of triggering US military action, either preemptively because of uncertainty about where North

Korea's missiles would land, or in retaliation. Despite being defensively motivated, North Korea's threat to "envelope" Guam with missile fire could have brought about the very war North Korea was attempting to prevent through deterrent threats. As North Korean General Kim Rak Gyom said in response to Trump's threat, "Sound dialogue is not possible with such a guy bereft of reason and only absolute force can work on him."[23]

What started as errant, emotionally driven bluster from Trump not only quickly elicited a startling and unprecedented warning from Pyongyang, it also crystallized into an administration-wide attitude toward North Korea that would only harden in the coming months. Increasingly, that hardening stance put it at odds with Seoul. South Korea, which had heretofore been a bystander in the emerging crisis, could do little other than reiterate that "South Korea can never accept a war erupting again on the Korean Peninsula."[24]

But Trump and his staff were on a different page than South Korea's president Moon Jae-in. Two days after Trump's fire and fury remark, Trump addressed reporters in Bedminster, New Jersey while on vacation. A reporter asked what he thought about North Korea's response that his threat was "nonsense."[25] Trump replied, "Maybe it wasn't tough enough. They've been doing this to our country for a long time . . . That statement may not be tough enough . . . What they've been doing, and what they've been getting away with is a tragedy, and it can't be allowed."

After more questions, Trump was then asked what assurances he might offer an American public growing worried about North Korean missiles striking the United States, to which he replied:

> If North Korea does anything in terms of even thinking about attack—of anybody that we love, or we represent or our allies or us—they can be very, very nervous . . . Things will happen to them like they never thought possible . . . North Korea better get their act together, or they're going to be in trouble like few nations ever have been in trouble in this world.

Asked about North Korea's threat against Guam, Trump responded, "Let's see what [Kim] does with Guam. He does something in Guam, it will be an event, the likes of which nobody's seen before, what will happen in North Korea."[26] Trump then tweeted on August 12, while still on vacation, "Military solutions are now fully in place, locked and loaded, should North Korea act unwisely. Hopefully Kim Jong Un will find another path!" His threats against North Korea were getting more explicit and bellicose.

Kim Briefly Signals Restraint

On August 14, Kim Jong Un visited his military's Strategic Force Command to "inspect" the plans proposed for launching an enveloping fire of Guam, as the military had warned it was considering on August 8. After reviewing the plan and agreeing that it was ready for execution, Kim seemed to walk it back, or at least pause it. Kim showed a degree of restraint that may have prevented the crisis from escalating further at that moment, saying, "if the Yankees persist in their extremely dangerous reckless actions on the Korean Peninsula and in its vicinity, testing the self-restraint of the DPRK, the latter will make an important decision as it already declared ... it will be the most delightful historic moment when the Hwasong artillerymen will wring the windpipes of the Yankees and point daggers at their necks."[27] It was restraint packaged in highly threatening terms, but restraint all the same.

While Kim lavished praise on the Command, it was possible the military's threat against Guam was not approved by Kim directly, and a visit to the Strategic Force Command intended to impress upon his generals the degree to which operational actions could have strategic consequences and therefore must not proceed without his expressed direction. The media statement hinted as much when it said Kim stressed the importance of "the Strategic Force to firmly establish the monolithic leadership system, command and management system of the Supreme Commander over the nuclear force."[28] Kim was stressing centralized command and control of North Korea's strategic assets.

Tillerson went out of his way to publicly acknowledge Kim's show of modest restraint, and expressed hope that it would lead to an opening for dialogue. Yet Tillerson was the only one in the administration to publicly express that hope, and Kim's gesture of restraint ultimately went unreciprocated at any rate. Trump actually interpreted it during a public speech in Phoenix, Arizona as evidence that "[Kim] is starting to respect us."[29] After the fact, Trump taunted Kim and drew a post hoc red line, saying on Twitter, "Kim Jong Un of

North Korea made a very wise and well reasoned decision. The alternative would have been both catastrophic and unacceptable!" As Trump persisted with goading Kim, the administration also continued working to make economic sanctions on North Korea as comprehensive as possible, even at the expense of spillover costs for other countries. Making good on Trump's threat-by-tweet toward China the previous month, the Treasury Department announced on August 22 "secondary sanctions" against Chinese and Russian individuals and firms who do business with North Korea, as well as cutting off funds sent to the regime from North Korean laborers working overseas.[30] It was a move that the Obama administration was reluctant to pursue because it undermined incentives for Beijing to work together with Washington to solve the North Korea issue.

But Trump's exasperation at what he saw as China's fecklessness, combined with Kim Jong Un's continued defiance of US warnings against his pursuit of a retaliatory nuclear strike capability, were gradually turning the US sanctions regime into a general embargo aimed at preventing North Korea from having any access to the global economy. It was a process of gradual strangulation, and it required sanctioning not only North Korean entities, but also third-country entities that did business with North Korea, and those entities were primarily Chinese. Haley's divisive statement in June that "You either support North Korea, or you support us"[31] was now manifesting as policy.

Adding Insult to (Threats of) Injury

The events of August started a process of escalating rhetorical exchanges and military posturing that would carry through the end of 2017. America's cumulative threats and pressure were engendering the same from Pyongyang. Rather than convincing Kim Jong Un to return to the negotiating table, maximum pressure appeared to fuel Kim with a maximum sense of urgency to convince the Trump administration that his missiles could attack the United States, which required demonstration tests. Meanwhile, widespread uncertainty plagued North Korean officials about whether a US attack really was impending. War could have come at any point, and it was equally plausible that it would follow from deliberate escalation or miscalculation.

A Competition in Desperation

Kim was increasingly in dire straits. The Trump administration acknowledged Kim's restraint against Guam, and then met it with even more comprehensive sanctions. Nothing in the US position had changed (indeed, nothing in Trump's public trolling of Kim had changed) and that, in a perverse way, freed North Korea to fire the Hwasong-12 IRBM on August 28, which flew over Hokkaido in northern Japan to the east rather than southward toward Guam. As an ally of the United States for more than half a century, a threat against or attack on Japan would be just as calamitous as one against South Korea. North Korea had proven its ability to strike US territory yet again, but did so in the least provocative way; it could have fired toward Guam or Hawaii, but did not. Had US rhetoric been at a higher level of bellicosity in weeks prior, North Korea may well have fired missiles at Guam.

After the test, the White House issued a condemnatory statement: "This regime has signaled its contempt for its neighbors, for all members of the United Nations, and for minimum standards of acceptable international behavior ... all options are on the table."[32] Then, on August 31, following a spate of expert commentaries urging restraint and engagement of North Korea, Trump preemptively foreclosed on a diplomatic resolution of the crisis by tweeting, "The U.S. has been talking to North Korea, and paying them extortion money, for 25 years. Talking is not the answer!" He closed the door to dialogue for the time being, again removing any incentive for North Korea to show restraint in its rhetoric or missile testing.

By this time, it was clear that the Trump administration was following a classic playbook on coercion—a competition in risk-taking—making threats that implied things could get out of control, and seeming to tie its own hands in the process. But was the administration serious, or was it bluffing? Was its threat rhetoric even strategically motivated, or just the byproduct of Trump's emotional impulses combined with what was by now a hawkish bureaucracy? And was the administration unaware of North Korea's strategic belief in offense-as-defense, which meant that maximum pressure unknowingly risked war even if Trump was bluffing, or was the administration trying to goad North Korea into an action that would justify US retaliation? For maybe the first time in a generation, uncertainty about *US intentions* created a public mood of heightened sensitivity and fear.

Against that backdrop, on September 3, North Korea conducted its largest ever nuclear test, which its state media claimed was a hydrogen bomb; it was plausible given the magnitude of the blast. Once again, fear among North Korean elites translated into resolve and defiance, not quiescence. At around 100 kilotons, it was several times the size of the bomb dropped on Hiroshima in 1945. The test was conducted underground, just as all its past tests had been. Trump immediately issued a series of tweets in response, stating, "North Korea has conducted a major Nuclear Test. Their words and actions continue to be very hostile and dangerous to the United States ... North Korea is a rogue nation which has become a great threat and embarrassment to China, which is trying to help but with little success."

Later in the morning after the nuclear test, Trump took to Twitter again for a dig at South Korea's progressive government: "South Korea is finding, as I have told them, that their talk of appeasement with North Korea will not work, they only understand one thing!" The tweet was needlessly antagonistic. Facing a common threat, the United States had every incentive to maintain alliance solidarity and therefore avoid remonstrating with an ally publicly. What is more, South Korea's posture at that point was not one of appeasement; its military immediately responded to North Korea's nuclear test with exercises that simulated attacks against North Korean nuclear facilities—hardly an act of conciliation. Trump's tweet aimed at South Korea was thus not about South Korea's response to North Korea, but rather intra-alliance policy debates that were heretofore taking place behind closed doors. Trump was making no secret that he disagreed with President Moon's preference for a more conciliatory approach to North Korea.

With the September 3 nuclear test, once again North Korea crossed a line that the Trump administration earlier held out as something it implied it would not allow. Trump's April 29, 2017 interview with CBS News suggested a nuclear test on his watch might force him to undertake a military response. Trump clearly believed that North Korea would only respect the logic of force. Nikki Haley said Kim was "begging for war," and Mattis warned of a "massive military response" if the United States believed North Korea was actually going to attack anything.[33] The world wondered what would happen next.

The answer came days later, on September 12, when the United States convinced the UN Security Council to pass yet another round of sanctions on North Korea, this time restricting oil imports and textile exports, and banning new international visas for North Korean overseas workers. North Korea's economy had never faced this degree of economic deprivation as a result of an isolation strategy by the international community. North Korea's ambassador to the United Nations decried the sanctions as "illegal," promising retaliation: "The forthcoming measures by DPRK will make the US suffer the greatest pain it has ever experienced in its history ... the Washington regime finally opted for political, economic and military confrontation, obsessed with the wild dream of reversing the DPRK's development of nuclear force—which has already reached the completion phase."[34]

It was a decades-long recurring theme: sanctions spawned still more defiance. Only two days after the sanctions announcement, on September 14, North Korea conducted another Hwasong-12 intermediate-range ballistic missile test, which was again successful and again flew over Hokkaido, Japan rather than in the direction of Guam. It was unclear if North Korea was willing to launch a first strike against US bases in the region, but it had become abundantly clear that it could. North Korean state media quoted Kim Jong Un as saying: "Our final goal is to establish the equilibrium of real force with the U.S. and make the U.S. rulers dare not talk about [a] military option."[35] Since 2016, North Korean media had made more frequent reference to nuclear weapons as a means of achieving a "balance of power" or "equilibrium of force" with the United States. These were crude references to a secure retaliatory nuclear strike capability: the guaranteed ability to turn any conflict into a nuclear one. Kim was now making plain his strategic need to prove to the United States that it had such a capability and was willing to use it. Trump responded by publicly trolling Kim on Twitter, remarking, "I spoke with President Moon of South Korea last night. Asked him how Rocket Man is doing. Long gas lines forming in North Korea. Too bad!" The White House Spokesperson added, "now is not the time to talk to North Korea."[36]

Dropping a Bomb at the United Nations

Even though the Trump administration had postured itself against diplomacy, the week after the missile test nevertheless offered an opportunity to engage North Korea. On September 19, Trump gave a much-anticipated address to the UN General Assembly. Notwithstanding Trump's trolling of Kim in response to the most recent missile test, public commentators expressed hope that—given the multilateral, peace-oriented nature of the body he was addressing—Trump would use the speech to cool some of the hot rhetoric coming from the United States, which in turn might encourage North Korea to do the same. Some even speculated the US delegation might meet with the Pyongyang delegation on the sidelines. There was hope, in short, that Trump's address would be an off-ramp from what had become a bona fide nuclear crisis. Trump's actual delivery of the speech dashed those hopes.

In it, he took occasion to again threaten North Korea in hyperbolic terms, and in the process insulted Kim personally. Referring to North Korea and Iran, Trump said, "The scourge of our planet today is a small group of rogue regimes that violate every principle on which the United Nations is based."[37] He then extensively singled out North Korea: "No one has shown more contempt for other nations and for the wellbeing of their own people than the depraved regime in North Korea." He went on to mention North Korea's torture of American college student Otto Warmbier, and Kim's assassination of his brother. The line that went viral and was widely construed as a direct insult to Kim Jong Un was that if the United States "is forced to defend itself or its allies, *we will have no choice but to totally destroy North Korea. Rocket Man is on a suicide mission for himself and for his regime*" [emphasis added]. At an organization dedicated to world peace, Trump threatened the "total destruction" of one of its members. In the weeks to come, Trump would take the insult "Rocket Man" and render it more explicitly diminutive.

Kim Jong Un issued a rare public and darkly fatalistic statement in response to Trump's speech. The two leaders were now publicly trading harsh words of the highest stakes, in a context where each side's military was postured to launch attacks against the other with literally no advance warning. Kim called Trump a "dotard" (*nulk-dari michi-gwangi*), an antiquated English word for a senile, bumbling old man, and decried Trump's assault on his dignity, exclaiming, "Trump has denied the existence of and insulted me and my country in front of the eyes of the world."[38] This, Kim claimed, confirmed that "the path I chose is correct and that it is the one I have to follow to the last." The path Kim was referring to was the decision to double down on North Korea's nuclear arsenal, but it may have also been a reference to a recent decision to close what was already a very small window of opportunity for diplomacy with the United States. After Trump's UN speech, even Track 2 (non-governmental) dialogues with North Korea went silent for a time. Kim also issued his own personal threat, and not the normal defensive kind that would be contingent on some hypothetical act of US aggression, but rather a direct promise of harm against Trump himself and the United States: "I will make the man holding the prerogative of the supreme command in the U.S. pay dearly for his speech calling for totally destroying the DPRK ... I will surely and definitely tame the mentally deranged U.S. dotard with fire." Kim expressed the will to vengeance in an obviously personal way.

Reinforcing his leader's rare and ominous response to Trump's speech, North Korea's Foreign Minister Ri Yong-ho gave an address of his own to the United Nations the next day. Shortly before Ri's speech, reports emerged that the underground tunnel North Korea had been using to conduct nuclear tests had collapsed, raising concerns that Kim's next nuclear test would have to take place above ground, which would be more provocative and potentially more dangerous. Ri's speech did not address the tunnel collapse or Pyongyang's nuclear tests, instead taking occasion to match Trump's threats and insults with a litany of his own. Ri said Trump was "a mentally deranged person full of megalomania," and that he "has turned the White House into a noisy marketing place full of crackling sounds of abacus beads, and now he has tried to turn the U.N. arena into a gangsters' nest where money is respected and bloodshed is the order of the day."[39] Ri labeled US military exercises and nuclear bomber deployments as acts of hostility that threaten North Korea's "sovereignty, dignity, and national security," and noted that in the current environment, the slightest miscalculation could bring a war. He also argued that Trump's threats and ignorance have made a strike against the

United States almost inevitable: "Due to his lacking of basic common knowledge and proper sentiment, he tried to insult the supreme dignity of my country by referring it to a rocket ... he committed an irreversible mistake of making our rocket's visit to the entire U.S. mainland inevitable all the more." Trump immediately tweeted another threat aimed at Kim Jong Un: "Just heard Foreign Minister of North Korea speak at U.N. If he echoes thoughts of Little Rocket Man, they won't be around much longer!"[40]

8 WHEN WILL THE WAR BREAK OUT?

Trump's belittling, blustery UN speech in September blunted an opportunity for diplomacy, but the trend of growing antagonism was having other effects as well. The air was thick with war rhetoric, mutual taunting, and military deployments that were swelling in frequency and scale. The public mood, especially in the United States, became more panicked.

An Accidental Indicator of War

In late September, Elizabeth Cordray, a deputy assistant secretary in the Pentagon, made an unusual trip to the US logistics component command in South Korea in order to check on the procedures and preparations for evacuating US civilians. Although Cordray tried to be low-key and the trip was billed as a "routine inspection," it was highly uncommon for someone at that level to get dispatched to Korea for that specific purpose.[1]

On the heels of her visit to South Korea, US forces and civilians living in the South started receiving text messages and Facebook alerts instructing civilians to evacuate South Korea immediately. These messages proved to be fake, and the US Army in South Korea had to issue instructions clarifying as much. But North Korea had seen them as serious enough that when the United States conducted a civilian evacuation drill the following month, the North accused the United States of "creating tension on the eve of war."[2] In conjunction with news of Cordray's visit, even Americans living in South Korea who normally brushed off North Korean war threats were scared. Some American expats felt the need to pack "go-bags" that included first aid, water, granola bars, and the like. They had good reason for concern.

One of the key indicators of an imminent alliance attack against the North was a noncombatant evacuation operation (NEO) to minimize the loss of American civilian lives once conflict began. Pyongyang would have made this association between a NEO and expectations of imminent war because North Korean hackers stole alliance war plans in 2016.[3] So public talk of a NEO, and especially spreading news of a NEO hoax, literally risked triggering a North Korean preemptive attack.

An ongoing dialogue with North Korea, in theory, could have mitigated some of the risk of miscalculation, but by this point, US interaction with North Korea had effectively stopped. Post-Trump UN speech, North Korea cut off every avenue of communication with the United States. At the end of September, Tillerson said the State Department was still "probing" for dialogue with North Korea, and that it had "lines of communication" with the North, though none were active at the moment. Tillerson and his Special Envoy Joe Yun were still seeking a diplomatic way out of the crisis their boss had helped fuel.

Kneecapping Tillerson, Spurning Pyongyang, Burning Capitol Hill

The day after Tillerson's "probing" comment, Trump reprimanded him in a tweet with the rejoinder, "I told Rex Tillerson, our wonderful Secretary of State, that he is wasting his time trying to negotiate with Little Rocket Man … Save your energy, Rex! We'll do what has to be done!" Trump publicly undermined whatever credibility Tillerson and the State Department may have had as interlocutors with North Korea. It was the second time in as many weeks that Trump's rhetoric shut down a potential diplomatic off-ramp from the nuclear crisis. As if to ensure his hostility toward diplomacy was not lost in translation, Trump tweeted a few days later, "Presidents and their administrations have been talking to North Korea for 25 years … hasn't worked, agreements violated before the ink was dry, making fools of U.S. negotiators. Sorry, but only one thing will work!" He was again making veiled threats of preventive force amid strangulating sanctions, diplomatic silence, and an increased tempo of nuclear-capable bombers to Korea, the deployments of which were now taking place twice per month.

Seeing the needless risk-taking involved in simultaneously avoiding communication with North Korea while making threats and insults—and all in service of the seemingly impossible goal of comprehensive denuclearization—nuclear experts began publicly warning of concerns not only of miscalculation, but also the excessive ease with which Trump might launch a nuclear attack given the virtually unchecked prerogative of the president to order nuclear strikes under the existing US system of nuclear command and control. Expert worries eventually helped trigger congressional oversight of the issue, however fleeting. On October 6, the day before Trump took to Twitter to again foreclose on diplomacy, Senator Bob Corker, Chairman of the Senate Foreign Relations Committee, channeled the prevailing view among many in Washington at the time when he remarked, "I think Secretary Tillerson, Secretary Mattis, and Chief of Staff Kelly are those people that help separate our country from chaos."[4]

In context, the statement had several meanings. Corker had grown concerned about Trump's stability as commander in chief, the prospect of a US-launched war with North Korea, and Trump's executive control of US nuclear weapons. Recognizing the effect that Trump's threats were having on the situation, Corker accused Trump of "kneecapping" Tillerson's efforts to keep open a dialogue with Pyongyang.[5] At the same time, some of the nativist political appointees within Trump's administration opposed the tradition of American internationalism that had been the basis of US foreign policy since World War II, leading to pitched internal battles over the direction of policy. For multiple converging reasons, then, there was a prevailing perception that the Trump administration might not be able to make stable, rational foreign policy decisions. All the while, Trump administration officials continued making elliptical references to launching a war of choice. H. R. McMaster appeared at a conference in mid-October and repeated his oft-made claim that the United States was "in a race to solve this short of military action," alluding to the preventive use of force if North Korea did not denuclearize soon.[6] Combined with a total absence of diplomacy, these threats caused Capitol Hill to worry about the situation; Corker's voice was the most high-profile of a much larger group of elected officials concerned about the prospect of war.

Shortly after Corker's remark implying that Trump was the "chaos" that faced America, Corker ended up in a brief public feud with Trump that led him to call the White House "an adult day care center," saying that Trump's loose rhetoric and tweeting habit would put America "on the path to World War III."[7] This from a respected senior senator of Trump's own political party. Thereafter Corker scheduled a Senate Hearing to review the command and control policy on US nuclear weapons, which he eventually held, in mid-November. Command and control arrangements lingered from the days of the Cold War as a system designed for speed of execution rather than caution or a system of checks and balances. Strategic deterrence during the Cold War depended on rapid retaliation, which empowered the presidency with significant discretion. For the first time since the Cold War, that system of nuclear authority was being called into question.

Congressional concerns not only about the stability of the Korean Peninsula, but also of the US presidency reflected the concerns of a jumpy public that was by now conditioned to fear the worst. An NBC News/Survey Monkey poll conducted in October showed, for the first time, that a majority of Americans (54 percent, Republican and Democrat in comparable proportions) saw North Korea as the country's most immediate threat.[8] An even larger percentage though (64 percent) believed the situation needed a diplomatic resolution. With the public increasingly nervous, misinformation abounded, and with high stakes. On October 22, the website Defense One reported that Barksdale Air Force Base, which hosts nuclear-capable B-52 bombers, was preparing to be placed on 24-hour alert status.[9] The United States had not maintained that "ready-to-fly" posture with its strategic nuclear assets since the Cold War. If true, it was a sign of America positioning itself for war, and the news spread rapidly across social media and the community of experts as if it were.

The story sparked another short-lived cycle of public worry before the Air Force and the Pentagon denied its very premise. The following day, several newspapers ran stories aimed at correcting the record, explaining that the B-52s would not be placed on alert but simply could be. During the intervening period though, there was a risk that North Korea believed the original report, which, if accurate, would considerably shorten the window for North Korea to launch preemptive attacks before facing squadrons of B-52 bombers. There was also a risk that North Korea would believe the original story despite later corrections, because it was something that fit with their own worst-case expectations about what the United States intended to do. And because there was no diplomatic communication with North Korea, there was no opportunity to directly shape North Korea's perception of news reports it received from the outside world. Only two days before the Defense One story appeared, Choi Sun-hui, North Korea's Foreign Ministry counterpart to the State Department's Joe Yun, appeared at a conference in Russia where she stated that the North had no intention of re-engaging the United States as long as it made daily threats against them, and its nuclear weapons were a "matter of life and death," not something to be abandoned through talks.[10]

Three weeks after the B-52 misreporting incident, US Strategic Command, responsible for US nuclear weapons, tweeted a link to an article claiming that US B-1B bombers were capable of dropping nuclear payloads, housed in "secret silos" in the United States.[11] Neither claim was true. Many of the US bomber deployments to Korea had been the B-1B, which was reconfigured years prior to no longer be capable of carrying nuclear weapons. But North Korea's military could not necessarily distinguish a B-1 from a nuclear-capable bomber in real time, and it was inclined to dismiss US military claims that the B-1 was not a nuclear bomber as American deception or disinformation. Although Strategic Command later had to correct the record, the original (inaccurate) information confirmed North Korea's bias in favor of interpreting B-1 bombers as nuclear bombers, which—as past North Korean media statements confirmed—they viewed as much more threatening.

Trump Does Asia

Come November 2017, the United States and North Korea seemed at the apogee of the nuclear crisis. Admiral Dennis Blair, former commander of US Pacific Command and a respected analyst, urged that if North Korea conducted an atmospheric nuclear test over the Pacific, the United States and South Korea should launch an "air and missile strike against all known DPRK nuclear test facilities and missile launching and support facilities."[12] The idea of war had become acceptable. If nobody backed down, there appeared little place else to go. Blair's comment reflected a discourse in Washington that seemed unmoored from the constraints the situation imposed on anyone who sought to avoid a nuclear war.

Despite Washington's war talk, Pyongyang had not tested a missile since September 15. The reasons for the lack of missile demonstrations were seasonal and programmatic rather than strategic: North Korea always slowed its testing during the fall. But the relative quiet provided another window to potentially bring stability to the situation, by America either somehow reciprocating Pyongyang's restraint or rekindling dialogue.

A new possibility for precisely that was Trump's long-scheduled visit to Asia, his first as president, in early November. It was scheduled to be a five-stop tour over 12 days: Japan, South Korea, China, Vietnam, and the Philippines. North Korean media warned Trump as he headed to Seoul, "Nobody can predict when Trump does a reckless act ... The only and one way for checking his rash act is to tame him with absolute physical power."[13] A Trump insult, they implied, would be cause for an unspecified act of force. Even without that warning, North Korea was the topic on everyone's mind. But as much as Trump, too, was concerned with North Korea, he also gave a high priority to securing more favorable trade balances in bilateral economic relationships. Squeezing Asian governments for "better" trade deals risked coming at the expense of the international consensus to impose maximum pressure on Pyongyang. Achieving both goals would require staying on-script.

Trump did show message discipline for most of his trip. North Korea was raised in every meeting in every capital, but Trump's public remarks about the North veered away from personal insults, direct threats, and hyperbole. That changed slightly on November 7, when Trump delivered a speech that was highly critical of North Korea before South Korea's National Assembly, remarking:

> North Korea is a country ruled as a cult ... there have been hundreds of North Korean attacks on Americans and South Koreans ... The regime has interpreted America's past restraint as weakness. This would be a fatal miscalculation. This is a very different administration than the United States has had in the past ... Do not underestimate us, and do not try us ... History is filled with discarded regimes that have foolishly tested America's resolve.[14]

It was a tough speech. If delivered during any other presidency, it might have been seen as provocative and threatening. But in the context of events since August, it was hostile but restrained, even mild. It contained no gratuitous insults. Shortly after the speech though, it was revealed that Trump wanted to use much tougher, more bellicose language that would have put North Korea on notice in an unprecedented manner. The delivered version of the speech was entirely due to interventions by Trump's national security team, who launched "a group effort" to ensure the speech would be "toned down."[15] But on Twitter, Trump was less restrained, commenting two days later that "NoKo has interpreted America's past restraint as weakness. This would be a fatal miscalculation. Do not underestimate us. AND DO NOT TRY US."

By the end of Trump's Asia tour, his discipline slipped more fully. On November 12, from Vietnam, Trump issued the most personal insult of Kim to date: "Why would Kim Jong-un insult me by calling me 'old,' when I would NEVER call him 'short and fat?' Oh well, I try so hard to be his friend—and maybe someday that will happen!" While nobody expected the United States to launch a war while Trump was in the region, and especially not while in South Korea or Japan, provoking Kim rhetorically risked Kim provoking America militarily. Ratcheting up the stakes even further was an unprecedented amount of military force appearing in the region coincident with Trump's trip. For the first time since 2007, three aircraft carrier strike groups converged on the Pacific, and it was while Trump traversed the region. A submarine carrying 66 Navy SEALs and Tomahawk cruise missiles—the kind launched against Syria without warning in April that year—also made port in Busan, South Korea. If the United States were to attempt an assassination of Kim Jong Un, US special operations forces such as the SEALs were the most likely candidates to pull the trigger. All told, it was a staggering amount of firepower when combined with America's continuous troop presence, and could easily be mistaken for a prelude to preventive war or assassination, especially if any of the newly brought in military assets lingered after Trump departed the region.

North Korean Fear and Loathing

The diplomatic silence from North Korea, which started even before Trump's Asia trip, was deafening. After Trump returned to

Washington, Joe Yun attended a meeting on the South Korean resort island of Jeju, where reporters asked him about how he interpreted North Korea's lack of missile tests in the preceding months. It was Yun who previously told the press that if North Korea avoided testing for a period of 60 days it would be a sign to the administration that Pyongyang was serious about diplomacy, and it was now 60 days and counting.

Nevertheless, when asked in mid-November about Pyongyang's lack of missile activity, Yun replied, "I hope that they will stop [testing] forever. But we had no communication from them so I don't know whether to interpret it positively or not. *We have no signal from them*" [emphasis added].[16] The breakdown of communication with North Korea as a result of the insult exchanges between Trump and Kim made it impossible to take advantage of a moment of North Korean military restraint.

North Korean elites did probe every foreigner they could access in hopes of piecing together Trump's intentions. Since the summer, North Korea's Foreign Ministry had ceased meaningful contact with the US government, but it was still busy trying to discern whether Washington was planning a preventive war. When *The New Yorker*'s Evan Osnos traveled to Pyongyang in August—a week after Trump's "fire and fury" bluster—his Foreign Ministry interlocutors relentlessly queried him as they had so many other journalists: "Is the American public ready for war ... Does the Congress want a war? Does the American military want a war? Because if they want a war, then we must prepare for that ... If [Trump's] not driving toward a point, then what is he doing?"[17]

For months, North Korea had been courting Republican policy analysts no longer in government, including inviting some to visit Pyongyang, in hopes of figuring out Trump's thinking, but to little avail.[18] North Korea even futilely reached out through a business intermediary to Trump's son-in-law, Jared Kushner, trying to arrange a backchannel dialogue with Trump's inner circle, as the Chinese had done.[19] As Suzanne DiMaggio, a think-tank analyst who had played a central role in Track 2 dialogues with North Korea during Trump's first year in office and before, told *POLITICO Magazine* in November, the North Koreans "want to know if he's crazy or this is just an act."[20] North Korea's very existence was at stake, so naturally its policy elites placed a premium on understanding whether signs of war from

Washington were cheap talk or honest intentions. To the extent that Pyongyang assumed the worst, it would not be cowed. As Osnos's host remarked, "The United States is not the only country that can wage a preventive war."[21] Kim Jong Un might have been willing to go to war, but he was not suicidal and would not have wanted to go to war over a misreading of Trump's theatrics.

The Ultimate Act of Missile Defiance

But after Trump's personal mockery of Kim Jong Un's height and girth on November 12, it was hard to imagine Kim then authorizing his diplomats to pursue dialogue with the United States. Following Trump's Asia trip, moreover, South Korean intelligence was also reporting indications that North Korea was likely preparing to conduct another missile test, giving further cause to refrain from inferring too much from Pyongyang's lack of missile testing in the preceding months. Within days, those reports about missile preparations proved correct.

On November 28, North Korea launched an ICBM (the Hwasong-15) from an indigenously constructed mobile platform (an 18-wheel truck). The missile demonstrated an unprecedented capability, landing in Japan's exclusive economic zone, roughly 1,000 kilometers away, and reaching an altitude of more than 4,400 kilometers, several times higher than many US satellites. It reached such a remarkable height because the ICBM was fired at an angle that ensured it would avoid the appearance of attacking US targets. In so doing, it proved beyond any doubt that it could fire a missile capable of carrying nuclear warheads at any part of the United States—not just US territories in the Pacific, but the eastern seaboard of the United States as well.[22]

North Korean media treated the missile test as a consummation of its status as a bona fide nuclear weapons state, reporting, "Kim Jong Un declared with pride that now we have finally realized the great historic cause of completing the state nuclear force, the cause of building a rocket power."[23] They released a photo of the memo ordering the missile launch with Kim Jong Un's signature on top—proof that this test was by and from him—and later a video of Kim witnessing the launch. And they referred to themselves as a "responsible nuclear power" that had succeeded in outmaneuvering "the U.S. imperialists' nuclear blackmail policy and nuclear threat."[24] A North Korean official separately told CNN, "Before we can engage in diplomacy with the Trump administration, we want to send a clear message that the DPRK has a reliable defensive and offensive capability to counter any aggression from the United States."[25] The test was necessary to make that pivot.

The United States had no immediate answer other than to reiterate the tropes of maximum pressure. Mattis seemed discomfited, admitting, "It went higher, frankly, than any previous shot they've taken, a research and development effort on their part to continue building ballistic missiles that can threaten everywhere in the world, basically."[26] Trump stated, "I will only tell you that we will take care of it. We have General Mattis in the room with us, and we've had a long discussion on it. It is a situation that we will handle."[27] The obvious implication was that the United States was being backed into a corner: there was nothing it could do to stop North Korea's missile program, short of military force, so Trump intimated that military force would be in the offing. Later that day, during a speech on tax reform, Trump referred to Kim as a "sick puppy," which he followed with another tweet reiterating his commitment to maximum pressure: "Just spoke to President XI JINPING of China concerning the provocative actions of North Korea. Additional major sanctions will be imposed on North Korea today. This situation will be handled!"

The cumulative weight of pressure, threats, insults, increased and expanded military deployments, and intermittent scaremongering must have put North Korean regime officials in a state of high anxiety. Whatever trepidation the American public might have felt was surely orders of magnitude worse in Pyongyang. North Korean elites looked out past their borders and saw the United States preparing to launch a preventive war. If they became certain of that eventuality, whether they were correct or not, they would launch a preemptive attack. That fear drove Kim Jong Un to race to prove it had the ability to launch a preemptive attack, not just against US military bases, but against the US homeland.

The late November missile test did just that. Having achieved and demonstrated the baseline nuclear capability he sought, Kim was now prepared to turn to a charm offensive, pursuing more ambitious, but also more stabilizing goals than just nuclear deterrence, including sanctions relief and laying the groundwork for potentially decoupling the United States from South Korea. But the United States seemed more resolved than ever to use military force; administration officials repeatedly promised to prevent a North Korean nuclear ICBM at any cost, and now North Korea seemed to be flaunting that capability. Following North Korea's latest missile test, Senator Lindsey Graham, who had discussed North Korea with Trump on multiple occasions, took the hardest public line: "If we have to go to war to stop this, we will. If there's a war with North Korea it will be because North Korea brought it on itself, and we're headed to a war if things don't change."[28] It was time to prepare the American public for the next phase.

Putting Odds on War

At the end of 2017, the Trump administration found itself embroiled in a nuclear crisis with no exit in sight. It was the closest the United States had come to nuclear war since the Cuban Missile Crisis. Many experts saw what was playing out between Trump and Kim as something much more dangerous and much less controlled than what had occurred between Kennedy and Khrushchev.

The United States ended up in this position for multiple converging reasons: the trajectory of US policy under Obama and the corresponding US demand for nothing short of North Korean unilateral disarmament; Kim Jong Un's steadfast commitment to securing a nuclear capability that ensured it could attack the United States with a nuclear weapon; the Trump administration's pursuit of "maximum pressure" on Pyongyang with the aim of denuclearization; and Trump's predilection for taunting, insults, and obstinacy toward diplomacy. If even one of these factors were absent or different, the danger of the situation would have been both less immediate and less intense.

Around Washington, talk of war had been growing louder from the day Trump took office, but by December 2017, it was reaching a gratuitous crescendo. Some serious politicians and foreign policy specialists were now publicly making the case for preventive war against Pyongyang. The administration itself peddled all the rhetorical building blocks that led to the logical conclusion of accepting a preventive war without explicitly advocating preventive war per se. And some on Trump's national security team began anonymously floating the idea of giving Kim Jong Un "a bloody nose" as an alternative to war—that is, conducting a limited preventive attack rather than a full-blown war, even though the former was the most likely way of bringing about the latter.

In the weeks after North Korea's record-breaking ICBM test on November 28, the US position on Pyongyang hardened considerably, even though the damage was already done: North Korea had more or less proven its ability to strike the United States with a nuclear-armed missile. Whether it could strike with precision was in doubt, and the size of its operational arsenal was still modest, but Kim Jong Un had achieved the most crucial of his strategic goals: he could now make any conflict one with seemingly unacceptable costs for the United States by turning it nuclear, and potentially even bringing the fight to the US homeland in the process.

In parallel with North Korea's strategic strides, America's policy discourse about North Korea had shifted for the worse. Commentators and experts of every kind were being asked by the media to weigh in with their odds that the United States would end up in an inadvertent war with the North. Retired Admiral James Stavridis, who was briefly considered as Hillary Clinton's running mate in 2016, put the likelihood at 50/50.[29] John Brenan, Obama's CIA director, thought the odds were between 20 and 25 percent.[30] Richard Haass, who headed the Council on Foreign Relations, which published the 2016 North Korea policy task force report that became a blueprint for the maximum pressure strategy, argued there was a 50 percent chance of war in Korea.[31] These experts were taking the temperature of the situation, not delivering probability estimates based on hard analysis. Still, the fact that the consensus of the pundit class saw war as plausible, and certainly more likely than at any point in recent decades, reflected the unique severity of the current crisis compared to anything in recent memory.

But the odds-making commentary was primarily about *inadvertent* war—the idea that a deliberate decision by either side would have unforeseen escalatory consequences. Two weeks after North Korea demonstrated its ICBM capability, Senator Lindsey Graham, who had more foreign policy contact with Trump than any person outside his administration, promoted the idea of a deliberate preventive war. In a December interview with *The Atlantic*, Graham again channeled Trump and made the bleakest prediction yet as part of his case for war: "I would say there's a three in 10 chance we use the military option" unprovoked, and if North Korea conducted another nuclear test, "I would say 70 percent."[32] He reminded his interviewer that the topic of North Korea came up all the time when he played golf with Trump, and that Trump:

> has 100 percent made up his mind that he's not gonna let Kim Jong Un break out [possess an ICBM with a nuclear warhead] ... if you ever use the military option, it's not to just neutralize their nuclear facilities—you gotta be willing to take the regime completely down ... *if they test another [nuclear] weapon, then all bets are off ... I am literally willing to put hundreds of thousands of people at risk, knowing that millions and millions of people will be at risk if we don't* ... [because] North Korea is the ultimate outlier in world order ... the person who's inherited the mantle is, on a good day, unstable ... I don't know how to put North Korea in a historical context. [emphasis added]

During the interview, Graham acknowledged a role for diplomacy, but conceived of it as something to rule out prior to going to war rather than something that was likely to ameliorate the crisis: "I'm not taking anything off the table to avoid a war ... When they write the history of the times, I don't want them to say, 'Hey, Lindsey Graham wouldn't even talk to the guy.'"[33]

Fatalism and False Hope

Maximum pressure was reaching its logical limit short of applying military force: sanctions continued to take their toll on the North Korean economy; the United States reinstated North Korea on the State Department's largely symbolic list of state sponsors of terrorism; and the United States continued military exercises, including Vigilant Ace in December, a large-scale air force exercise that brought hundreds of military aircraft to the Korean Peninsula, including the F-22 and F-35 (stealth fighters) and B-1B bombers (which were not nuclear-capable, but which North Korea assumed were nuclear bombers).[34]

North Korean media predictably responded that the drill would "push the already acute situation on the Korean peninsula to the brink of nuclear war."[35] Days later, they added that war with the United

States had become "an established fact ... The remaining question now is: when will the war break out?"[36] A sense of fatalism about war had always played a role in North Korea's strategic culture, allowing the Kim dynasty to take risks and respond to pressure with pressure, even when circumstances appeared entirely unfavorable to it doing so. Its nuclear arsenal did not seem to change that. Meanwhile, McMaster quietly met with his Japanese and South Korean counterparts in San Francisco, and publicly urged the international community to fully abandon and isolate North Korea because it "might be our last best chance to avoid military conflict."[37] If sanctions could not bring about denuclearization, then war would.

But Tillerson, taking a tone at odds with the moment, offered a brief glimmer of optimism that the United States might depart from the war path it now appeared to be on. At a think-tank event on December 12, he commented that the United States had "no pre-conditions" on diplomacy with North Korea, and that "We're ready to talk any time North Korea would like to talk ... we can talk about the weather if you want ... But can we at least sit down and see each other face to face?"[38]

It sounded like a dramatic reversal of policy—contrary to the logic of maximum pressure—and given that it followed Kim's declaration that his "state nuclear force" was complete after the November 28 missile test, it was an opportune off-ramp from crisis. It was the kind of statement that might have signaled to Pyongyang that the United States was more open to talks than it had been previously. The problem was that Tillerson lacked the credibility to speak on behalf of the administration, having been repudiated publicly by Trump himself on multiple occasions.

Less than 24 hours later, Tillerson's comments had proven dangerously counterproductive. The White House countermanded Tillerson's remarks, saying, "The administration is united in insisting that any negotiations with North Korea must wait until the regime fundamentally improves its behavior ... clearly right now is not the time."[39] Tillerson's spokesperson even had to walk back his statement, tweeting the clarification, "Our policy on #DPRK has not changed. Diplomacy is our top priority through our maximum pressure campaign."[40] Prior to Tillerson's attempt to jump-start diplomacy, it was at least ambiguous whether the United States might be amenable to re-engaging North Korea. Such ambiguity permitted the State

Department to reach out and probe North Korea independently, and then report back to the White House if it gained diplomatic traction. But the White House's explicit rejection of everything Tillerson said sent a harsh signal that nothing in the US posture, substantively or emotionally, had changed. That inhibited Tillerson and his special envoy on North Korea, Joe Yun, from any meaningful steps to break North Korea's worrying diplomatic silence.

Bloody-Nose Theory

A few days later, on December 20, *The Telegraph* reported on administration sources who claimed that the White House was leaning toward giving Kim Jong Un a "bloody nose."[41] The report, which the *Wall Street Journal* also reported later with separate sourcing,[42] gave a more detailed rendition of what McMaster and others had been saying in a more oblique way for months. Although the White House denied that anyone in the administration had used the term "bloody nose," they never denied being enamored by its underlying logic, which they had publicly touted since the end of their March 2017 policy review.

From the beginning of the Trump administration, a belief prevailed among some senior officials that the United States could strike North Korea out of the blue and not trigger a larger war if done in a limited way.[43] The strike, which would target nuclear facilities, missile facilities, or a missile launcher used in a long-range missile test, would be coercive. The primary purpose was not to materially set back North Korea's nuclear or missile program by destroying a specific target. Instead, the belief among bloody-nose advocates was that going on the offensive in an unprecedented way, by actually drawing first blood, would demonstrate America's willingness to go to war to realize denuclearization if necessary. By demonstrating that resolve, not only would North Korea be deterred from retaliating; it would also be frightened into returning to denuclearization negotiations.

A bloody-nose attack could have been executed at a moment's notice. The United States had stealth-capable F-22 and F-35 aircraft in South Korea on an almost routine basis. US Navy surface ships, armed with cruise missiles and already programmed to strike specific, pre-selected North Korean targets, were now regularly patrolling the waters off North Korea's eastern coast. There was friction between

Mattis and McMaster about the issue of strikes, but strike authorization would only come from Trump. McMaster's influence would be limited to shaping that decision by whispering in Trump's ear and isolating interagency opinion against Mattis. But Mattis reportedly saw McMaster as his junior, and, in terms of formal military rank, he was, which made McMaster chafe. Frequent NSC requests for military strike options and planning work for strikes were thus often "slow-rolled" by the Pentagon or, according to some reports, altogether ignored.[44]

Experts almost universally thought the bloody-nose plan was mad. Nuclear scholars and Korea experts were among the most vocal, pointing out the fallacious logic of "bloody-nose theory," which, they argued, was likely to cause a war. Scholars began translating for the public academic insights that uniformly augured against preventive strikes:[45]

- You cannot reliably convince your enemy of your resolve to fight a war (and thereby achieve deterrence) by launching small attacks well short of war;
- The proactive use of violence, especially when decoupled from previously issued threats, does not measurably enhance one's ability to deter an adversary because it creates reputations for hostility rather than resolve;
- North Korea would have a difficult time distinguishing between a limited strike and an attempt at invasion, in part because of the backdrop of large shows of military force and bombastic threats. Not knowing whether an attack was limited or an attempt at regime change incentivizes North Korea to pursue a retaliatory hedge, launching nuclear weapons or conventional "counterforce" strikes against strategic bases and ports; and
- There was a high risk that preventive strikes would fail to achieve the very purposes at which they aimed (such as nuclear nonproliferation or regional stability). Even putting aside the expected costs, preventive attacks were a crude and unreliable way of seeking any hypothetical benefits.

But public opposition came from well beyond the community of scholars. Victor Cha, an influential Korea expert who served in the Bush administration, had been vetted for more than a year for the post of US ambassador to South Korea. In February, shortly after privately expressing his reservations about the "bloody nose" option to staff at the NSC, his nomination as ambassador was abruptly withdrawn. His became the highest-profile criticism of bloody-nose thinking, but he was joined by a number of other experts from government. Former Pentagon and CIA officials, Democrats and Republicans alike, took to television, newspapers, and social media to expose the folly of preventive attacks and explain why it was almost inevitable that North Korea would respond with violence in kind.[46] Given the circumstances, Kim Jong Un would have no choice but to respond to pressure with pressure; a preventive attack would beget retaliatory violence, and once that started, there was no telling how far it would escalate.

Even if the United States could avoid triggering a larger war, an attack would only further underscore the importance of North Korea having, and possibly using, nuclear weapons. And as happened with Trump's cruise missile strikes against Syria in April 2017, even if an isolated military action succeeded in deterring immediate retaliation, which was unlikely in the North Korea case, it would almost certainly not end up being an isolated act: to the contrary, the proactive use of force often presages greater military involvement and sets higher subsequent requirements for what it would take to convince an enemy of your willingness to fight. In other words, the use of force for the sake of deterrence creates "commitment traps." If, for instance, a strike with ten cruise missiles is intended to convey American seriousness of purpose, then later using fewer than ten cruise missiles to signal its enduring seriousness of purpose may well signal the opposite of what was intended—that America's seriousness of purpose was lessening. This rationale quickly leads to endlessly ratcheting up the requirements of deterrence.

The Trump administration never took public ownership of its advocacy for the bloody-nose option. The sheer intensity of public pushback and lack of intellectual justification made it a hard idea to own up to, and if they actually followed through with a bloody-nose strike after publicly promoting the idea, there would be no moral high ground for the United States in the aftermath. Even more problematic was that, to the extent that any US strike met the standard of premeditated aggression against another state, it would be illegal. Months of plotting and preparing would undermine any claim that North Korea's threat to the United States appeared "imminent."[47] A bloody nose would be an offensive, not defensive, attack under international law. Even in terms of domestic law, the unprovoked use of force would not have a clear legal basis—as with the still unsettled legal status of the Trump administration's strikes on Syria in April the year prior.

The bloody-nose issue dominated discussion and news headlines for nearly a month in what was arguably the peak of the crisis. Despite ultimately backing off the bloody-nose theory of preventive attack, the administration and its surrogates continued not only with maximum pressure, but making the case for general preventive war.

The atmosphere put the public sufficiently on edge that a botched alert exercise in Honolulu on January 13, 2018 led to tens of thousands of civilians in Hawaii believing that they were facing imminent attack. The Hawaii Emergency Management Agency texted a message to cell phones that read, "BALLISTIC MISSILE THREAT INBOUND TO HAWAII. SEEK IMMEDIATE SHELTER. THIS IS NOT A DRILL." It took 38 minutes for the agency to send out an updated text message that the original was a false alarm.

Stories from families and civilians poured out subsequently, describing in newspapers and on television their mind state and what they did during what they thought were the final moments of their lives.[48] Although the alert was the result of an operator error—specifically, the operator mistakenly believed a missile attack was happening—it generated immediate fears on a large scale. A ballistic missile attack struck everyone in Hawaii as plausible precisely because war talk about North Korea had become commonplace, because the Trump administration actively promoted a threat narrative about North Korea, and because Hawaii had begun intermittently testing nuclear alert sirens since the summer of 2017. The crisis had conditioned the Hawaiian public to expect the possibility of a future attack. For decades, nuclear scholars understood that "normal accidents" could lead to nuclear conflict.[49] The Hawaii missile alert incident made the theory feel real, undermining confidence in human control of nuclear weapons in the middle of a crisis.

9 HOW THE CRISIS ENDED

That nuclear war was averted at all during the first year and a half of the Trump administration had less to do with the United States, or even China, than to happenstance combined with the strategic opportunism of North and South Korea's leaders. Once Kim Jong Un demonstrated a viable ICBM capability, he sought a way to de-escalate the crisis and advance other aspects of North Korean strategy.

Kim treated the November 28, 2017 missile test as having achieved just that, following the ICBM test with a pivot to a more magnanimous approach involving restrained rhetoric and public diplomacy. Doing so allowed him to focus on the North Korean economy and alleviating international implementation of existing sanctions. The prospect of Trump ordering a preventive strike on North Korea may have given added incentive for Kim to extricate himself from a confrontational mode, but he would not have done so unless he had in hand a minimally viable nuclear deterrent. Kim sought nothing short of rejoining the international community, but with nuclear weapons and the ability to run North Korea without external interference.

From the time that Moon Jae-in, South Korea's president, came to office in May 2017, he openly telegraphed his desire to rekindle some kind of rapprochement with North Korea, to include a summit with Kim Jong Un. Moon's bet on diplomacy was crucial to alleviating the immediate pressures of war, but Moon sought more than just escaping the crisis: he wanted to remove the longer-term, structural pressures favoring war too, by trying to secure a peace regime in Korea to replace the 1953 Armistice Agreement and broker a meeting between Kim and Trump that aimed toward comprehensive denuclearization.

The Trump administration's escalating war of words and saber-rattling with the Kim regime through 2017 was inhospitable to dialogue, and had marginalized South Korea in the ongoing saga over North Korea's nuclear weapons. It was only when South Korea's hosting of the Winter Olympic Games neared—which Moon used to implore Trump to show some restraint and Kim used as part of his diplomatic pivot—that all sides were willing to press pause on something that was on the verge of being beyond anyone's control. After Kim demonstrated a level of nuclear capability sufficient to hold the United States at risk of a nuclear attack in November 2017, he immediately changed tactics and sought dialogue. This was the next phase in what had been Kim's strategy all along: pursuing diplomacy after demonstrating a minimally viable nuclear deterrent against the United States. The convergence of the Olympics with Moon's political priorities and Kim's strategy forestalled any serious near-term plans for a US attack, allowing both Koreas to change the narrative away from one of crisis to one of rapprochement.

A New Year's Pivot, or an Olympic Miracle?

Kim Jong Un gave a speech to ring in 2018 that signaled the beginning of the end of the nuclear crisis. It mimicked the themes of prior years, hailing advancements in its nuclear weapons, emphasizing economic progress, and, crucially, extending a rhetorical olive branch to South Korea. But the top-line issue in Kim's speech was his nuclear program, describing the various tests of the previous year as a "definite success."

> We attained our general orientation and strategic goal with success, and our Republic has at last come to possess a powerful and reliable war deterrent, which no force and nothing can reverse. Our country's nuclear forces are capable of thwarting and countering any nuclear threats from the United States, and they constitute a powerful deterrent that prevents it from starting an adventurous war. In no way would the United States dare to ignite a war against me and

our country. The whole of its mainland is within the range of our nuclear strike and the nuclear button is on my office desk all the time; the United States needs to be clearly aware that this is not merely a threat but a reality.[1]

Although perhaps sounding menacing on the surface, Kim went out of his way to stress he was not making a threat. Instead, his nuclear comments had two major purposes. First, they were a rhetorical pivot point, signaling to North Koreans that their nation's nuclear arsenal had reached such a level that it no longer needed to monopolize regime resources. Kim rationalized the past hardship of the North Korean people as necessary to achieve the country's nuclear deterrent, promising happier economic times in future. Second, his nuclear comments aimed to convey to all audiences (domestically and in Washington) that Kim exercised centralized command and control of nuclear launches. Centralized nuclear command and control allows for rapid launches with virtually no notice and executive control of nuclear decisions. Delegated nuclear command and control, by contrast, ensures the ability to retaliate with nuclear strikes even if the leader is taken out. The leader of a nuclear state, in other words, can optimize for speed and control or reliability, but not both at the same time. Kim Jong Un was telling the world North Korea's nuclear command and control system was centralized in him.

Outside North Korea, Kim's speech was read in two starkly different ways. Trump responded to Kim's boastful references to his nuclear arsenal by taunting him over Twitter: "North Korean Leader Kim Jong Un stated that the 'Nuclear button is on his desk at all times.' Will someone from his depleted and food starved regime please tell him that I too have a Nuclear Button, but it is a much bigger & more powerful one than his, and my Button works!" The personalized nature of the taunting, implied threat, and overt machismo made it a low moment for the US presidency in terms of public opinion. It was the most retweeted and commented-on tweet Trump had ever issued about North Korea. Whereas most comments in response to Trump tweets about North Korea usually expressed humor or fear of danger, the bulk of Twitter comments on this tweet expressed disappointment and ridicule of Trump; it was "unpresidential."[2]

Moon Jae-in, by contrast, saw an opportunity in the Kim speech, which appealed to the well-known preference of South

Korea's progressive government for dialogue over confrontation, especially ahead of the Olympic Games. The Kim speech proposed reconciliation, along with a list of demands:

> This year is significant both for the north and the south as in the north the people will greet the 70th founding anniversary of their Republic as a great, auspicious event and in the south the Winter Olympic Games will take place ... The north and the south should desist from doing anything that might aggravate the situation, and they should make concerted efforts to defuse military tension and create a peaceful environment. The south Korean authorities should respond positively to our sincere efforts for a détente ... They should discontinue all the nuclear war drills they stage with outside forces, as these drills will engulf this land in flames and lead to bloodshed on our sacred territory. They should also refrain from any acts of bringing in nuclear armaments and aggressive forces from the United States.

Kim's call for reconcilation paired with security concessions was not new, having appeared in previous speeches as well. Wasting no time, South Korea responded favorably to Kim's proposed reconciliation the following day. The diplomatic opening was Kim's initiative, but Moon had been laying the groundwork to take advantage of the moment when the time came. As early as November 2017, Moon had authorized talks with North Korea under the guise of an inter-Korean football competition, which gave positive signs to Kim that an Olympic olive branch was available.[3] During his meeting with Trump in Seoul two months earlier, Moon had quietly asked Trump to help make South Korea's hosting of the Winter Olympics a success, among other things, by delaying Key Resolve and Foal Eagle, the alliance's annual spring military exercises.[4] By December, and notwithstanding the administration's public posture of war preparations and talk of a bloody nose, the White House had agreed to Moon's request to delay exercises for the sake of the Olympics.

Even taking the most cynical view of Trump's White House (that it intended to launch a war), it would be in a more favorable international position to make its case if it was seen as an enabler of a successful Olympic Games rather than a spoiler of them. At any rate, the United States had little choice but to go along once Moon made his plea; the exercises were alliance exercises, and if it came down to it, South Korea could disrupt them by withholding its participation. Still, the Trump administration did not see agreeing to Moon's request as an exception to their continuing rejection of a "freeze for freeze." The United States was delaying exercises, not suspending them, and North Korea was not technically committing to a moratorium on its missile testing, even though it would be unlikely to carry out such testing during the Olympics period. But these may have been distinctions without difference. It was starting to look like America's ally and its enemy had maneuvered it into something the United States repeatedly refused to do: show restraint long enough to defuse the crisis, change the overall narrative, and jumpstart diplomacy.

The week after Moon proposed "high-level talks" in response to Kim's New Year's speech, North and South Korea engaged in a flurry of diplomatic activity with each other while the United States stood on the sidelines, consumed by debates about the "bloody nose" option. On January 9, both sides sent senior-level officials to meet at Panmunjom, the truce village straddling North and South Korea. Hours into the talks, North Korea agreed to send a "big delegation" to the Winter Olympics, signaling a willingness to allow the Games to proceed without incident.[5] Both sides came out of the January talks with positive, reconciliatory public statements, rekindling the tenor of North–South dialogue in the early days of the George W. Bush administration, which was the last time the United States and South Korea were in vehement *disagreement* about North Korea policy.

The following month, North Korea's high-level delegation arrived in Seoul, led by Kim Yo Jong, Kim Jong Un's sister. She was a trusted intimate of Jong Un even before being dispatched to lead the Olympics delegation, which included Kim Yong Nam (President of the Presidium of the Supreme People's Assembly, North Korea's administrative head of state). Kim Yo Jong was both a member of the Politburo and Vice Director of the Department for Propaganda and Agitation within the Korean Worker's Party—positions she occupied at Kim Jong Un's behest.

The North Korean delegation was planning to have side discussions with the United States during the latter's visit to the Olympic opening ceremonies, which took place on February 9 and 10. But Vice President Mike Pence, who was among the administration's strongest advocates for the preventive use of force against Pyongyang, led that delegation. On his way to South Korea, Pence stopped in Japan and indicated no bend whatsoever in the US posture toward Pyongyang, touting that "the toughest and most aggressive round of economic sanctions on North Korea ever" were imminent.[6] His remarks were fiery and unquestionably confrontational, which was consistent with the maximum pressure buildup toward military escalation that the administration had been following up to that point. Arriving in Seoul, Pence kept up what he saw as his mission to counter North Korean propaganda efforts, by inviting Otto Warmbier's father as his guest for the opening ceremonies, giving audience to North Korean defector stories, visiting the memorial for the South Korean ship *Cheonan* that North Korea torpedoed in 2010, and repeatedly and publicly denouncing North Korea in terms that aimed to deny North Korea the ability to change the narrative that made international pressure and isolation of the North possible.[7]

Hours before Kim Yo Jong and Pence were scheduled to meet, the North Korean delegation cancelled the meeting, specifically because Pence had taken such a confrontational line toward the North in the days leading up to it. Pence intended to use the meeting, which had been planned for weeks, to confront North Korea, not to launch negotiations. In that respect, and somewhat counterintuitively, the absence of US–North Korea interaction during the Olympics might have helped dissipate crisis pressures and keep North–South dialogue on track. Meme-inspiring images of the VIP box during the opening ceremonies went viral, showing a smug-looking Kim Yo Jong sitting only feet away from Pence, who sat stone-faced, refusing to acknowledge her presence. The two sides had to go awkwardly out of their way not to interact. Pence's Chief of Staff confirmed what transpired, but saw a tactical victory in how it played out for the Trump administration: "North Korea dangled a meeting in hopes of the vice president softening his message, which would have ceded the world stage for their propaganda during the Olympics ... This administration will stand in the way of Kim's desire to whitewash their murderous regime with nice photo ops at the Olympics."[8]

Nevertheless, the Olympics became a safety valve, giving North Korea a chance to withdraw from an escalating cycle of threats and insults, pausing missile testing, and momentarily putting the brakes on any possible White House plans to attack. Trump himself became more muted on North Korea, and took credit for the success of the Olympics, but the administration continued with its hawkish policy inertia. As the administration was forced to deny claims it was seeking to give Kim Jong Un a bloody nose, it nevertheless stayed faithful to maximum pressure. Even the symbolic backdrop of Olympics-induced rapprochement did not stop the Treasury Department from announcing new sanctions on North Korea amid reports that the United States was preparing a multinational naval blockade designed to enforce existing sanctions and prevent North Korea from trafficking in anything that might bolster the regime or its nuclear program.[9] North Korea's Foreign Ministry spokesman responded that "As we have stated on numerous occasions, we will consider any type of blockade an act of war against us."[10]

Washington's war talk also persisted through the Olympics. CIA Director Mike Pompeo was still publicly leaning into war, warning that while "the President is intent on delivering a solution through diplomatic means ... if we conclude that is not possible that we present the President with a range of options that can achieve his stated intention."[11] After speaking to Trump and his national security team, Republican Senator Jim Risch said, "If Kim Jong Un keeps doing what he's doing, he's gonna cause a war," and that war would be "very brief," but "of biblical proportions."[12] And Ambassador John Bolton, a Bush administration official who began advising Trump informally in 2017, published an op-ed in the *Wall Street Journal*, making the legal case for preventive strikes against North Korea—something he had advocated on television on at least six occasions in previous months.[13]

But these voices were drowned out by South Korean optimism about North–South dialogue. The Olympics helped make the dominant narrative on Korea a hopeful one, about diplomatic progress, with South Korea leading the way. Capitalizing on Olympics success and the symbolic portrait of Korean unity at the Games, Kim Yo Jong met with Moon Jae-in at the Blue House, presented him with a letter from her brother, and verbally conveyed an invitation for him to visit Pyongyang as soon as possible. After a series of lower-level meetings to arrange details, Moon quickly agreed to what would become the third North–South presidential summit ever held and the first in more than a decade.

Shortly after the Olympics, on March 6, Moon dispatched his National Security Adviser Chung Eui-yong and National

Intelligence Service Director Suh Hoon to Pyongyang as envoys, carrying a personal letter from Moon. The visit was partly aimed at continuing goodwill and coordination ahead of the Moon Jae-in summit with Kim Jong Un, but Chung and Suh also sought to probe North Korea on a number of issues: its willingness to suspend or eliminate its nuclear capabilities; its willingness to release three remaining American civilians it was holding prisoner; and its willingness to initiate dialogue with the United States. The South Koreans were trying to leverage their meeting with the North to broker diplomacy between the United States and North Korea. Kim Jong Un himself met with Moon's envoys, speaking for four hours, over what North and South Korean media portrayed as a jovial dinner. Kim even agreed to set up a direct phone line with Moon, saying, "Now if working-level talks are deadlocked and if our officials act like arrogant blockheads, President Moon can just call me directly and the problem will be solved."[14]

When Kim and Moon met at Panmunjom on April 27, they had more than a month of positive momentum at their backs. The world watched not just with hope, but with near sanguinity. It got to the point that when you typed "inter-Korean summit" in Twitter, an emoticon would automatically populate of two differently colored hands high-fiving together, meeting in a prayer gesture with little beams radiating out of it. For Kim, it was his best chance of getting sanctions relief and staving off a war with Trump. For Moon, his entire presidency was wagered on this one bet: he came to power partly on a promise of a different approach to North Korea. Both leaders had strong political incentives to ensure the inter-Korean summit was viewed as successful, and it was, in the near term. They shook hands, smiled, walked together, and talked together in front of media from around the world, including North Korean media. They met several times throughout the day, and at one point spent some 40 minutes speaking one on one, visible to cameras, but too distant for anyone to hear. Kim and Moon also issued what became known as the Panmunjom Declaration, a high-level statement of shared aspirations, reinforcing the goodwill on display throughout their meetings. The key points from the Panmunjom Declaration included:

- Aspiring to <u>peaceful unification</u> of the Peninsula "led by Koreans," through reconciliation and cooperation between North and South Korea.

- Fulfilling the various <u>economic projects</u> agreed to at the prior inter-Korean summit in 2007, including "practical steps towards the connection and modernization of the railways and roads" that would connect the two Koreas.
- Making "joint efforts to <u>alleviate the acute military tension</u> and practically eliminate the danger of war on the Korean Peninsula," through reciprocal measures of restraint along the DMZ and in the area of the Northern Limit Line dividing the Yellow Sea on Korea's western coast.
- Cooperating "to establish a permanent and solid <u>peace regime</u> on the Korean Peninsula. Bringing an end to the current unnatural state of armistice and establishing a robust peace regime on the Korean Peninsula is a historical mission that must not be delayed any further."
- Aspiring to the "common goal of realizing, through complete denuclearization, a nuclear-free Korean Peninsula ... South and North Korea agreed to actively seek the support and cooperation of the international community for the <u>denuclearization of the Korean Peninsula</u>."[15]

By design, these points of agreement skewed toward the general rather than the specific. They also involved the same themes, and even much of the same verbatim language, from the joint declarations issued after the inter-Korean summits in 2000 and 2007. Vague aspirational language about both unification and denuclearization, but a sense of urgency around tension reduction and replacing the Armistice Agreement with a "peace regime" repeated the rhythm of summits past. The striking similarities with past declarations were meaningful because past statements had no palpable effect on either North Korea's nuclear ambitions or inter-Korean relations.

But the Panmunjom Declaration generated genuine optimism in South Korea, accompanied by expectations that peace *and* denuclearization were at hand. And this was the inexplicable puzzle at the heart of all the ebullience surrounding a changed narrative about North Korea: South Korea, the United States, and the media were responding to North Korean overtures radically differently than in decades past, but the style and substance of North Korea's overtures were entirely consistent with what it had historically done. Collective amnesia disguised as a hubristic refusal to be bound by history; anything is possible. It would not be an exaggeration to say that the world and the political situation changed around the time of the inter-Korean summit, but North Korea did not. Kim did not introduce different commitments, language, or gestures than during past periods of diplomacy and negotiations.

Moon's ambitions and Kim's strategy converged perfectly. Their joint initiative abated the specific pressures, threats, and military posturing that made up the 2017 nuclear crisis. But both sides sought more than just crisis alleviation, and getting anything more required North Korea and the United States to end their rivalry too. That meant the Trump administration would have to entertain diplomacy with Kim.

Epilogue to a Crisis

The envoys Moon Jae-in dispatched to Pyongyang shortly after the Olympics, Chung Eui-yong and Suh Hoon, were scheduled to fly to Washington immediately following their trip to Pyongyang, which they did, arriving for meetings on March 8. En route to Washington, the Blue House (not North Korean media) issued a statement claiming:

> The North Korean side clearly stated its willingness to denuclearize ... It made it clear that it would have no reason to keep nuclear weapons if the military threat to the North was eliminated and its security guaranteed ... The North expressed its willingness to hold a heartfelt dialogue with the United States on the issues of denuclearization and normalizing relations with the United States ... while dialogue is continuing, it will not attempt any strategic provocations, such as nuclear and ballistic missile tests.[16]

Compared to the threats of imminent nuclear war only two months prior, it was a welcome sea change. For many who knew the history well, however, these positive yet noncommittal sentiments were shadows of the past; North Korea had long expressed nearly identical aspirations under Kim Jong Il and Kim Il Sung. That North Korean media and government organs made no mention of any of this, despite flatteringly covering the North–South dinner itself, allowed for skepticism about the Blue House statement and even raised the possibility that South Korea's envoys might have lost something in translation. North Korea had often used phrases like "denuclearization of the Korean

Peninsula" rather than its own denuclearization to imply that its disarmament would depend on dramatic concessions from the United States: at minimum, removing the US "nuclear umbrella" of protection from South Korea, and potentially also removing US troops from the Peninsula, though even those moves would be transactional and North Korea had in mind an even more total transformation of relations. With South Korea representing what North Korea said rather than hearing from North Korea directly, believing Kim was suddenly willing to denuclearize required a large leap of faith. Moon was willing to make that leap, and he wanted Trump to make that leap too.

Chung and Suh faced a mixed welcome when they arrived in Washington. On the one hand, Trump tweeted optimism: "Possible progress being made in talks with North Korea. For the first time in many years, a serious effort is being made by all parties concerned. The World is watching and waiting! May be false hope, but the U.S. is ready to go hard in either direction!" On the other hand, Chung and Suh were greeted by a contrarian press release from Vice President Mike Pence's office that reiterated hard-line tropes about North Korea: "All options are on the table and our posture on the regime will not change until we see credible, verifiable, and concrete steps toward denuclearization."[17] Tonally, Trump and Pence could not have been further apart.

Reports emerged about Chung and Suh carrying a letter signed by Kim to be delivered directly to Trump. Its contents were never publicly revealed. The most plausible message Kim would have delivered to Trump via letter would have involved a willingness to free the three remaining Americans it was detaining on humanitarian grounds, as a goodwill gesture. The United States and North Korea had a history of exchanging head-of-state letters in association with humanitarian gestures: General Jo Myong-rok brought a letter from Kim Jong Il to President Clinton in 1999; Secretary of State Madeline Albright brought a letter from Clinton to Kim Jong Il upon her visit to Pyongyang in 2000; Clinton brought a letter from Obama when he visited Pyongyang in 2009 to free two American journalists; and Director of National Intelligence James Clapper brought a letter from Obama when he visited Pyongyang for the same reason in 2014. It was also possible the letter included aspirational language about a peace treaty and denuclearization, in conjunction with an invitation to meet as heads of state.

Trump Makes the News

What transpired once Moon's envoys arrived at the White House—Trump's acceptance of a proposed meeting with Kim Jong Un—was so unexpected, counterintuitive, and controversial that it can only be understood in the larger context of Trump's presidential decision-making at the time. At this point in his presidency, Trump made a habit of trying to drive news media coverage in a way that was continuously favorable. That proclivity required a steady stream of fresh headlines, which meant no one story could be allowed to dominate for too long, especially if it was unflattering. Trump cultivated a number of dramatic storylines from the beginning of his term in office, one of which was North Korean nuclear weapons. From time to time, he would make sensational statements, tweets, or dramatic national decisions that would move that particular plot along, before quickly switching to a different plot. Every day of the Trump presidency was bringing new Trump-obsessed news headlines. And he was famously addicted to tracking how he was being portrayed in the media.

By early March 2018, this general habit of trying to steer the news in a favorable direction converged with two mounting scandals that threatened to bring down his presidency. No discussion of Trump's motivations for declaring a meeting with Kim can exclude these issues, about which he obsessed throughout his presidency. One was former FBI Director Robert Mueller's investigation into Russian interference in the 2016 presidential election (which expanded to include an investigation of the Trump family and Trump's business dealings) to determine if Trump or his inner circle had conspired with Russia to affect the outcome of the US election. A growing number of Trump aides and campaign advisers were being arrested, indicted, and even convicted in relation to the Mueller investigation at the time of the summit announcement in March. Trump's lawyer, Rudy Giuliani, would later cite the summit with North Korea as evidence of the high-stakes business of state that should preclude Trump from having to testify before or be subject to prosecution by Mueller's investigation team.[18]

The other, overlapping, scandal had just recently arisen. Stormy Daniels, a former porn star, alleged that she had an affair with Trump in 2006, shortly after his wife gave birth to their youngest son, and alluded to having first-hand knowledge of sexual fetishes that even Trump was likely to find embarrassing. The allegation of infidelity was only part of the scandal, however. On October 2016, one month before Trump was elected president, Daniels received a $130,000 payment for her silence and the signing of a non-disclosure agreement (NDA) that forbade her from speaking of her tryst with Trump. Trump's personal lawyer at the time, Michael Cohen, acknowledged the payoff, but continued to deny the affair and the NDA. Daniels claimed that her life was threatened in order to keep her from going public, and there was a possibility that the $130,000 "may have exceeded campaign contribution limits and violated U.S. law."[19] The story was salacious, embarrassing for Trump, and held out the possibility of two different felony charges against him. Most importantly, it dominated the headlines of every major American newspaper in early March, just as South Korea's envoys were arriving in Washington to brief Trump on their meeting with Kim Jong Un.

Chung and Suh arrived to brief CIA Director Mike Pompeo and National Security Adviser H. R. McMaster on Thursday March 8, planning to brief Trump himself the following day. US intelligence had already picked up the gist of Kim Jong Un's proposal, but Chung and Suh would be providing confirmation, as well as conveying impressionistic details.[20] On Thursday afternoon, Moon's envoys sat down for a meeting with key members of Trump's national security team, McMaster, Deputy Director of the CIA Gina Haspel, Pence, Mattis, Dan Coats, General Dunford, and Chief of Staff John Kelly. Trump received word that Moon's envoys were already at the White House and made the impromptu request to see them immediately. They told Trump that Kim seemed sincere in offering to denuclearize and release three Americans still detained in North Korea, and proposed meeting with Trump.

To everyone's surprise, Trump immediately agreed to meet with Kim, despite having no direct confirmation of such a request. Initially, Trump wanted to meet as soon as possible, but on the advice of his team and the South Koreans, he agreed to first allow the Kim–Moon summit to proceed. Trump then instructed Chung to brief the American press corps at the White House about the news. As Chung prepared to make his statement, Trump entered the White House press room—an act that itself was unprecedented—and grinningly told ABC News's Jonathan Karl to expect a "major announcement," saying, "hopefully, you [the media] will give me credit."[21] Chung's bombshell came hours later.

The weeks that followed were tumultuous and rife with mixed messages. After Moon's envoys made the announcement that Trump agreed to meet Kim, the White House seemed to backpedal, stating that "The President will not have the meeting without seeing concrete steps and concrete actions take place by North Korea."[22] Trump then took to Twitter to confirm his intent to meet Kim, stating, "Kim Jong Un talked about denuclearization with the South Korean Representatives, not just a freeze. Also, no missile testing by North Korea during this period of time. Great progress being made but sanctions will remain until an agreement is reached. Meeting being planned!" Rather than set low expectations for the meeting, Trump took the counterintuitive approach of building up expectations for the meeting by claiming that Kim agreed he would denuclearize. But North Korea gave no such indication publicly, and to the extent it later spoke of a desire to see the "denuclearization of the Korean Peninsula," it did so using an old rhetorical formulation that implied the United States first had to abandon its extended deterrence commitment to South Korea: it was *not* unilateral North Korean disarmament, as envisaged in the US demand for comprehensive denuclearization.[23]

Yet Trump himself betrayed a certain amount of ambivalence about the outcome of a meeting with Kim, the importance of implementation after agreement, and whether a meeting would happen at all. On March 10, at a Republican campaign rally in Pennsylvania, Trump gave a rambling speech during which he mentioned what some now called the "Hamburger summit," referring to Trump's quip during his 2016 campaign that he would be willing to have a hamburger with Kim Jong Un. Trump told the audience:

> Hey, who knows? It happens, if it doesn't happen. I may leave fast or we may sit down and make the greatest deal for the world and for all of these countries, including, frankly, North Korea and that's where I hope happens. But the press, for two hours, is going 'This is fantastic, this is amazing.' A certain anchor on CNN, fake as hell CNN, the worst.[24]

The comments indicated Trump's primary litmus of success was media favorability: the meeting with Kim could be a total failure (or not even happen) as long as the press gave him favorable coverage for a time. Trump was invested in steering news coverage more than he was diplomacy.

Layered on top of mixed signals about North Korea policy and a Trump–Kim meeting was personnel tumult. Tillerson was in Africa during the Korean envoy's trip to Washington, which itself was an odd decision, given the gravity of the Korea situation. Tillerson was unaware of Trump's decision to meet with Kim and woke up to it on the news. Days later, Tillerson was unceremoniously fired via Twitter. To be clear, while building toward what could be the biggest diplomatic moment in US foreign policy since Nixon went to China, the Trump administration had a hollowed-out diplomatic apparatus. It had no ambassador to South Korea, no Secretary of State, and Joe Yun (the special envoy for North Korea policy) had just announced his retirement.

Weeks later, Trump would also oust his National Security Adviser, H. R. McMaster. His replacement was John Bolton, a foreign policy uber-hawk who in the past had urged the bombing of Iran and had recently urged the same of North Korea. Bolton came out in support of the idea of a Trump–Kim summit, but for cynical reasons: he observed that North Korea was not a credible negotiating partner, argued that "Libya-style" rapid and comprehensive denuclearization was the only acceptable outcome of a summit, and predicted that the meeting would be a way to foreclose on future diplomacy if Kim Jong Un would not sign on to those stringent terms.[25] According to a friend of Trump, he "didn't want to pick Bolton, but he wanted to change headlines that weekend" (when Stormy Daniels did a tell-all interview on 60 Minutes).[26] Collectively, the administration's personnel problem, felt most acutely at the State Department, resulted in Trump relying primarily on the CIA to engage in direct talks with North Korea to coordinate the Trump–Kim meeting.[27] Pompeo himself, who replaced Tillerson as Secretary of State, but was still director of the CIA at the time, met with Kim Jong Un in Pyongyang as part of preparations for the Trump–Kim Summit.

The worst-kept secret in Washington was that Pompeo was positioning himself to eventually run for the presidency. And since Trump was by this point the kingmaker of the Republican Party, Pompeo had strong incentives to show unflinching loyalty to Trump's fluid policy positions and to give the North Korea summit (for which he was now Trump's point person) the appearance of success. Pompeo reportedly requested the release of three American detainees, which Kim granted a month before the June 12 summit, and floated the idea of Kim turning over five nuclear weapons to the French (the most "neutral" nuclear state) as a sign it was serious about denuclearization, which Kim refused.[28] Still, Pompeo came out of his meeting with Kim insisting that Kim was serious about at least talking denuclearization with Trump, and repeatedly promised that the administration would not be naive about Kim: "the Trump administration will not repeat the mistakes of the past. Our eyes are wide open and a bad deal is not an option."[29] Yet Bolton publicly took a noticeably harder line than Pompeo, and continued to insist on rapid and comprehensive denuclearization—a demand that caused North Korean state media to chafe and revert to belligerent statements that it had no intention of giving up nuclear weapons.

In the weeks following the inter-Korean summit, Trump began simultaneously speaking optimistically about the Korea situation and shifting the goalposts slightly. Officially, comprehensive denuclearization remained the formal goal. Rhetorically, Trump emphasized much more the thrill of achieving peace in Korea, though every past US president considered a peace treaty itself low-hanging fruit that would have been irresponsible to conclude as long as North Korea still pursued nuclear weapons. For the United States, denuclearization and peace had always been linked. But it was North Korea which, since the 1960s, most wanted a peace treaty. Kim Il Sung had always known that the easiest way to leverage US forces off the Peninsula (which had inevitable implications for the US–South Korea alliance) was to have a piece of paper saying there was no more war. Kim Jong Un now appeared to seek the same objective as his grandfather, but only he knew whether it was a cynical strategic move, a genuine effort to reset a half-century of entrenched rivalry with the United States, or some combination of both. Whatever the case, Trump was publicly smitten with the idea that he could be the man to bring about something meaningful in Korea. When asked by reporters in May whether he deserved the Nobel Peace Prize, Trump humble-bragged, "Everyone thinks so, but I would never say it."[30] At a rally of Trump supporters only days earlier (more than a month before the actual summit was scheduled to occur), the crowd chanted "Nobel" repeatedly, and for close to 30 seconds, Trump simply sat back with a large smile and absorbed the flattery, doing nothing to downplay it or caution the crowd against the high expectations that he had stoked himself over prior weeks. Trump believed that a peace treaty, and even the summit itself, would be a huge win in its own right, never mind that it was precisely what North Korea had long sought for largely strategic reasons. Regardless, the public speculation about a peace treaty as part of the summit moved the Peninsula further away from war and toward stability, as long as it appeared that peace might be at hand.

That changed briefly on May 24, 2018, when Trump called off the summit. Weeks prior, Bolton and Pence made public statements indicating that the United States had an all-in-one, comprehensive denuclearization model in mind ahead of the Trump–Kim summit, akin to what the United States negotiated with Libya during the Bush era. That deal ended badly for Libya's leader, Muammar Gaddafi, who was violently deposed in 2011. North Korea's foreign ministry bristled at the notion, warning of a "nuclear showdown," and dismissed the idea of denuclearization along such comprehensive lines. This was predictable, and may have been what Bolton and Pence intended; in the past, North Korea often invoked Libya's fate as one of the reasons it needed nuclear weapons. Gaddafi might still be in power if he had not negotiated away his nuclear program.

In addition to hostile statements rebuking Pence, Bolton, and the idea of rapid denuclearization, North Korean diplomats stood up a group of senior US officials in Singapore who were supposed to have a planning meeting with the North Koreans in preparation for the summit. Without explanation or excuse, the North Koreans simply failed to show up. Tony Schwartz, co-author of Trump's famed book, *The Art of the Deal*, claimed that "Trump has a morbid fear of being humiliated and shamed."[31] Might Kim Jong Un stand up Trump on the day of the summit as North Korea's diplomats did the US planning team, leaving Trump with the ultimate embarrassment rather than the ultimate deal? Too many data points now suggested the possibility not only of Kim refusing to denuclearize, but of leaving Trump in the lurch. At Bolton's urging, Trump concluded that Kim would not live up to the grandiose expectations of the Trump and Moon administrations. After consulting with his national security team, who overwhelmingly opposed the summit anyway, Trump dictated a public letter addressed to Kim, expressing regret at North Korea's newfound hostility and cancelling the planned summit before Kim could do the same.

The Show Must Go On

But both Trump and the North Korean foreign ministry expressed a will to continue dialogue, even though both sides remained miles apart on the most basic source of conflict. Trump still claimed he was seeking nothing short of comprehensive denuclearization, and North Korea offered only "comprehensive denuclearization of the Korean Peninsula," a watered-down version of the language it embraced in the past, even as it pursued nuclear weapons. The idea of the summit made too much sense for Trump and Kim personally, and planning for the summit resumed within 48 hours of its cancellation. Both leaders stood to benefit from a summit. Trump could project an image as a statesman and dealmaker despite worsening scandals at home, by doing something no president had done before. Kim could achieve an image as a powerful and peace-loving statesman seeking to build a better life for his countrymen. It did not matter the extent to which these images correlated with reality. It did not matter what a summit would or would not achieve for the United States or its allies. It did not matter that a summit risked normalizing North Korean nuclear weapons even as the ostensible US purpose of the summit was to eliminate them; Trump no longer seemed preoccupied with North Korean nuclear weapons by the time of the summit. So when North Korea's First Vice Foreign Minister Kim Gye-gwan and its Foreign Minister Ri Yong-ho issued statements with somewhat conciliatory tones immediately after Trump cancelled the summit, Trump agreed to resume planning for the big day.

Over the prior four months, the United States had shifted rhetorically from talking of "complete, verifiable, irreversible denuclearization of North Korea," as it had done for years, to adopting North Korea's way of referencing "denuclearization of the Korean Peninsula." Pompeo initiated the rhetorical shift in April, after meeting with Kim Jong Un in Pyongyang. Presumably, this was an attempt to bridge highly divergent negotiating positions between the two sides. But the US negotiating team led by Ambassador Sung Kim, a veteran of past nuclear negotiations with North Korea, struggled to make any substantive progress with its North Korean counterparts, regardless of the rhetorical accommodation.[32] Even so, the summit went ahead as scheduled. On June 12, 2018, Trump and Kim Jong Un met on Sentosa Island in Singapore for a summit whose ultimate outcome, the Trump administration insisted, would still be denuclearization. Trump became the first sitting American president to meet with the leader of North Korea. The two met one-on-one, with an interpreter, for 45 minutes, and then met again for several hours in meetings that included a small cadre of officials supporting each. During that time, Trump managed to show Kim a fictional movie trailer the US delegation had brought, which portrayed two contrasting paths for North Korea's future: a bleak one that promised war and poverty, or a prosperous one in which he gave up nuclear weapons and embraced economic reforms. It was a marketing tactic from his commercial real estate days, intended to entice Kim to invest in change. The images coming out of the summit were smiles and handshakes, but it was Trump who did most of the talking in public. Kim was pressed by reporters three times on whether he would give up his nuclear weapons, but declined to answer. When Kim addressed the media at all, it was with a gravelly Korean gravitas, speaking only in generalities: "The world is going to see a major change."[33] At the end of it, the two sides signed a joint communiqué, with the following key points:

- Both sides agreed to establish "new U.S.–North Korea relations" and pursue a "peace regime" for Korea.
- "President Trump committed to providing security guarantees" for North Korea.
- Kim Jong Un "reaffirmed his firm and unwavering commitment to the complete denuclearization of the Korean Peninsula."
- Both sides reaffirmed the Panmunjom Declaration from the April 27 inter-Korean Summit.
- Both sides agree to continue meetings at lower levels.

It was positive, but exceedingly thin. The communiqué was more of an outline than a deal, offering nothing in either substance or symbolism beyond the unprecedented meeting between heads of state and the promise of future dialogue. As such, the summit and the joint communiqué became something of a Rorschach test, both of Trump's presidency and of North Korean intentions. Nuclear experts and former US officials who had dealt with North Korea in the past overwhelmingly ridiculed the "deal" for failing to require anything specific of North Korea, and for failing to secure commitment language from Kim Jong Un that was at least commensurate with past agreements, such as the 2005 Joint Statement in which

North Korea "committed to abandoning all nuclear weapons and existing nuclear programs." Others, however, including an unlikely mix of optimistic Korea watchers and loyalist Trump supporters, saw the fact of the summit as positive in itself. Trump had consecrated the start of a diplomatic process that might still lead to denuclearization, and at the very least had kept the Peninsula further away from war.

As a bookend to his unprecedented meeting, while still in Singapore, Trump convened a press conference without Kim, reflecting on the summit extemporaneously for more than an hour. He repeatedly praised Kim, addressed him in his absence with the honorific of "Chairman," and, using North Korea's preferred language, said the United States would be stopping "war games" with South Korea because they were "very provocative" and expensive.[34] Trump also mused about his well-known desire to bring US troops in South Korea home at some point in the future. Days later, Trump confessed that suspending alliance military exercises was his proposal to Kim, implying he took advantage of the summit window to deal a blow to an alliance with South Korea that he long believed was a burdensome liability for the United States.

The day after the summit, Trump seemed to take an unearned victory lap on Twitter: "There is No Longer a Nuclear Threat from North Korea," he said, continuing, "President Obama said that North Korea was our biggest and most dangerous problem. No longer—sleep well tonight!" Yet the only thing that had changed in the situation was the valence of the rhetoric between the United States and North Korea. It was true that Trump promised to suspend military exercises that North Korea had long viewed as provocative, and that North Korea was not actively testing nuclear and missile devices. This was the de facto "freeze for freeze" deal that China had advocated for years as a stabilizing measure in Korea, but that the United States had always rebuffed. Yet North Korea had made no specific promises. It did not offer to rejoin the NPT or invite IAEA inspectors to verify anything related to a denuclearization process. Neither did it agree to suspend the production of highly enriched uranium or plutonium. And less than a month after the summit that Trump claimed eliminated the nuclear threat, North Korea was actually ramping up its reprocessing activity at key nuclear facilities. Worse, North Korea retained all of its nuclear facilities, all of its nuclear warheads, and all of its missile delivery vehicles, which were still dispersed to possibly dozens of locations across North Korea.

The month after the summit saw Trump and Pompeo insist that the North Korean nuclear threat was handled, while in reality it was more serious than it had ever been. If relations with North Korea soured for any reason at any point, it would be able to immediately and credibly threaten nuclear strikes against the United States and its allies, as it repeatedly did in 2017. The extent to which the situation with North Korea had *not* materially changed was on display when Pompeo, who was instrumental in making the summit happen, was visibly agitated the day after the summit while taking questions from reporters. During the presser, he was asked about how denucleariza-tion was going to be either verified or achieved and snapped, "I find that question insulting and ridiculous, and frankly ludicrous."[35] Earlier in the same event, he chastised a reporter for asking a similar question seeking details about what was agreed to, remarking, "Don't say silly things." Yet even Pompeo acknowledged the lack of material progress or even specific way forward in terms of a negotiating pro-cess: "We're prepared to execute this [joint communiqué] once we're in a position that we can actually get to a place where we can do it."[36] The entire summit was starting to look like theatre, not meaningful diplomacy in the name of the national interest. The progress made between leaders was in rhetorical valence, and possibly in symbolism, not in anything specific or material, and tremendous danger lingered in pretending otherwise.

What Did Kim Want?

Kim Jong Un's bid for twin summits, with Moon Jae-in and Trump respectively, were high-profile ways of getting well beyond the nuclear crisis, but they were only two in a series of North Korean diplomatic initiatives during 2018. As soon as Kim agreed to send a delegation to participate in the Olympics, North Korea's Track 2 dialogue with US and European officials resumed, as did formal diplo-matic communication with the United States through the New York Channel. At the end of March, Kim also made his first trip abroad as leader of North Korea, to Beijing, paying a visit to Xi Jinping. It was a successful attempt to repair its frosty strategic relationship with

China, ensuring closer coordination with its only formal ally ahead of major summits with the United States and South Korea. The trip was covered with much fanfare in Chinese and North Korean media, and Chinese (but not North Korean) state media Xinhua issued a statement that Kim was willing to denuclearize in a gradual, tit-for-tat fashion under certain conditions: "The issue of denuclearization of the Korean Peninsula can be resolved, if South Korea and the United States respond to our [North Korean] efforts with goodwill, create an atmosphere of peace and stability while taking progressive and synchronous measures for the realization of peace."[37] The aspirational yet highly conditional language, and the fact that it came from Chinese, but not North Korean media, replicated almost exactly how Kim Jong Il's October 2009 visit to Beijing played out. That meeting saw Chinese media making highly optimistic claims about what North Korea was willing to do, despite no such public confirmation from North Korea. That meeting also immediately preceded more than two years of US–North Korea negotiations that failed for a complex of reasons amounting to mutual bad faith.

While Kim's charm offensive focused heavily on China, South Korea, and occasionally the United States, it was global in scope. On March 29, immediately after Kim returned from Beijing, the International Olympic Committee Chairman, Thomas Bach, was invited to Pyongyang to meet with Kim. North Korea then dispatched its foreign minister, Ri Yong-ho, to a rare meeting with Russia's foreign minister in Moscow, also in an attempt to warm its bilateral relationship. That same month, Ri appeared at a ministerial meeting of the Non-Aligned Movement in Azerbaijan, hoping to further normalize its presence on the international stage. One of the North Korean diplomats present repeated Beijing's message coming out of the Kim meeting with Xi Jinping: "With regard to negotiations on the denuclearization of the Korean Peninsula, (the issue) can be resolved with phased, synchronized measures."[38] North Korea also invited a group of Southeast Asian former government officials and scholars to discuss how to improve relations with their countries, followed by the Executive Director of the World Food Programme. In short, North Korean diplomacy (after being frozen for a period of months during the crisis) was now working overtime to win over its Northeast Asian neighbors, Southeast Asian governments, Europe, and the United States.

Why the deliberate attitudinal pivot? The nuclear crisis was only a few months old, but already a rapidly fading memory. The diplomatic push was the strongest North Korea had made since Kim came to power in 2011. And the reconciliatory tone of North Korea's public diplomacy was a 180-degree contrast with its posture of defiance through much of 2016 and 2017.

For Kim Jong Un, the events that followed his January 2018 New Year's speech aligned with his strategy. After the twin summits with North Korea were publicly announced, Suzanne DiMaggio, who ran Track 2 dialogues with the North Koreans for years, told *Vanity Fair*:

> In my conversations with North Korean officials over the past two years, I have been struck with how clear they are about their strategy and the outcomes that they would like to see … It doesn't surprise me that after they have been able to declare that they have achieved a great deal of progress in their nuclear program, that they are now willing and eager to come to the table, because after all, they have strengthened their negotiating position … A meeting with the leader of the free world, the United States has been a long-standing goal of the North Korean leadership. In fact, this was raised to me when I visited Pyongyang last year [in 2017].[39]

DiMaggio's was the most detailed of many such accounts of North Korean intentions. North Korea told its strategy to anyone willing to listen in 2016 and 2017. When Kim and Trump were in the thick of their insulting exchanges in October the prior year, Choi Sun-hui, a longtime interlocutor in North Korea's foreign ministry, repeated publicly that North Korea had no interest in a nuclear dialogue with the United States until it had achieved an assured ability to strike the United States with nuclear weapons.

Kim's pivotal New Year's speech, moreover, was given only a month after North Korea demonstrated its longest ever ICBM test. North Korean propaganda commemorated the test in postage stamps celebrating "perfecting the national nuclear forces." The regime then sold the stamps as souvenirs to visiting foreign diplomatic delegations.[40] A nuclear status fait accompli.

The charm offensive followed its nuclear achievement chronologically, as planned. North Korea has never wanted to stand outside the international community in isolation, but neither has it been willing to conform to the expectations of the international community—on the nuclear issue, economic transparency, or human rights. North Korea had never internalized the norm of reciprocity in international cooperation, but that did not impede it from seeking international cooperation anyway when it suited the regime's interests. As we have seen, North Korea needed nuclear weapons as part of its theory of security. At the same time, the country has always sought economic prosperity, and economic development would eventually require sanctions relief. And in terms of geopolitics, the only way Kim could go about enlarging the already evident wedge between South Korea and the United States was to begin courting the former with appeals to *uri minjokkiri* (roughly translated as "between us folk/our people"). If he could have favorable relations with the United States, that, too, would be a boon, but not at the expense of having a nuclear arsenal.

Thus, Kim Jong Un's remedy for the situation he inherited in 2011 was to 1) demonstrate a reliable nuclear deterrent, 2) secure his rule against internal challengers, 3) improve his people's quality of life, and 4) elevate North Korea's international standing while retaining nuclear weapons. The long game that served as backdrop for all these moves was the meta-goal of Peninsula unification. That goal would be aided by diluting the US–South Korea alliance and ultimately removing US forces from South Korea—something numerous South Korean progressives had also long desired. But Kim was pursuing these goals in 2018 with far less of the military adventurism that his grandfather relied on, instead primarily leaning on small gestures and diplomacy (releasing the three remaining detained Americans, agreeing to freeze nuclear and missile testing, and publicly retiring a nuclear testing facility at Pungye-ri) from a position of strength and quieted defiance.

From 2011 through 2017, Kim prioritized the former two goals: demonstrating a reliable nuclear deterrent (through missile and nuclear testing at a rapid rate) and securing his rule against any whiff of internal dissent (through large-scale purges). His 2018 New Year's speech emphasized the latter two goals—prioritizing the economy and elevating North Korea's international standing—after having made significant progress on the former two. Whether or not Kim Jong Un intended economic reforms, going on the diplomatic offensive was a smart way of encouraging the international community, and especially

China, not to stringently implement the then-suffocating sanctions regime on North Korea.

Winning over Trump during the Singapore summit was a bonus. At the summit, Kim secured an agreement from Trump to suspend US military exercises with South Korea (which his 2018 New Year's speech explicitly called for), as well as a "peace regime" process designed to eventually realize the end of the Korean War and transform North Korea's geopolitical environment. The summit also seemed to make some difference in terms of status, domestically and internationally. Domestically, North Korean state propaganda released an extended video showing Kim in Singapore, surrounded by pomp and circumstance; a modern, affluent world leader. Internationally, CNN's Christiane Amanpour, among many others, made repeated reference to the summit as transforming Kim into a respected global leader: "Kim Jong Un has been now legitimated and legitimized on the international stage."[41] Trump embraced, rather than denied, that the summit normalized Kim as a world leader, commenting, "I went there, I gave him credibility ... I think it's great to give him credibility."[42] Also immediately following the summit, reports emerged that banks were preparing to finance a slate of inter-Korean business projects, providing Pyongyang with much needed foreign currency.[43] And as Pompeo admitted only two weeks after the summit, China's implementation of international sanctions on North Korea was already becoming less stringent, preventing the Trump administration's attempted strangulation of the North Korean economy from actually cutting off its breathing. Whatever it might ultimately mean for the United States and US–North Korea relations, the summit advanced Kim's agenda.

As ambitious as Kim's goals were, it is hard to imagine him having pursued anything else given the political, economic, and historical constraints he faced. Kim seemed to acknowledge as much in his comments at the summit: "It was not easy to get here. The past worked as fetters on our limbs, and the old prejudices and practices worked as obstacles on our way forward. But we overcame all of them, and we are here today."[44] His succinct statement, and his participation in the summit itself, could have been read in two ways. The optimistic one was that accumulated history shackled both leaders, guiding them toward a collision course until each took a gamble on a better path. The more skeptical interpretation was that Trump overcame a long history of America putting the nuclear issue first, and the North Koreans, consistent with Kim's January 2018 New Year's speech, overcame a nuclear imbalance of power that made bonhomie possible. In the moment, nobody knew which interpretation came closer to Kim's intent and the underlying reality, but the lack of progress toward nuclear dismantlement following the summit suggested the latter. In either case, encouraging a public narrative of rapprochement with the South, in particular, helped bring all of Kim's goals closer to reality. For North Korea, the key unknown was whether Kim's decision to prioritize the economy after demonstrating a minimally viable nuclear weapons capability meant he was willing to abandon his nuclear arsenal, circumscribe it, or persist with it unchanged. For the United States, the key unknown was whether it would abandon the demand of North Korean denuclearization, or insist upon it at any cost. The latter could be the seeds of a future crisis.

10 THE RISKS OF NUCLEAR WAR

The world was perilously close to nuclear conflict in 2017. Much closer, I fear, than future policymakers are likely to appreciate. The United States and North Korea threatened and taunted one another repeatedly, and in ways that were both unprecedentedly extreme and personalized. Both sides had large levels of military force postured toward one another. And each side had the ability to launch conventional and nuclear strikes against the other with little to no advance warning.

The situation had become a tinder box. Misperception, poor judgment, or a growing sense of desperation could have made any moment in 2017 the spark that set Northeast Asia ablaze. Events were headed that way when Kim Jong Un's nuclear and missile arsenal finally reached the point that it could plausibly strike the United States, allowing him to begin the next phase of his strategy: extending an olive branch to Moon and Trump while trying to win over world opinion.

Kim needed relief from both sanctions and the cloud of war. He feared the "bloody nose," not because of the destruction it would cause directly, but because he would have no choice but to retaliate with an even larger act of violence, and he surely knew that would result in war. Retaliation against what it saw as unprovoked aggression was baked into North Korea's strategic culture. A scared Kim Jong Un would be a defiant, not compliant, Kim Jong Un. The North Korean economy was also in shackles that were tightening over time because of the US-led international sanctions regime that increasingly cut off Pyongyang from foreign currency. Yet America's strategy did not deter Kim from pursuing his. Prior to Kim's diplomatic pivot and the fortuitously timed Olympics, war could have occurred at any time. Kim was willing to take that risk because nuclear weapons had become central to North Korea's theory of security and, counterintuitively, its economy. But with a minimally viable nuclear deterrent in hand, continuing to pursue ever-greater nuclear capabilities had diminishing returns and growing risks. The time had come for changing the valence of North Korea's posture toward the outside world, and Trump was keen to accommodate it.

This book has attempted to explain the historical origins of the Trump–Kim nuclear crisis by tracing what actually happened, and situating events in relation to prior US decisions, how North Korea thinks about its security, and the various rationales that might lead North Korea to use nuclear weapons generally. What follows is an attempt to explicitly draw out what made the nuclear crisis so dangerous. In most instances, the risks the United States took were gratuitous and therefore ill-advised. Contrary to the claims of the Trump administration and others, the policy of maximum pressure was the catalyst of the nuclear crisis, not the cause of its end.

Near-Misses

The Trump–Kim nuclear crisis could have produced war in at least three different ways: as a pathological choice; a conflict spiral resulting from deliberate escalation; or as a response to a "false-positive," based on one side misperceiving what the other side was doing. Crucially, these pathways were not substantially affected by whether Trump's tough talk at various points was genuine or a bluff. Paths to war depend on constituencies and the interactions of different actors' words and deeds; the sincerity of a single leader's rhetoric matters less than how others judge and respond to it.

A Pathological War of Choice

The year 2017 and early 2018 saw some constituencies within the US foreign policy community making the case not simply for preventive strikes against North Korea, but for preventive war. Senator Lindsey Graham estimated a 70 percent chance of using the "military option" if North Korea conducted another nuclear test, and claimed he was "literally willing to put hundreds of thousands of people at risk."[1] Senator James Risch commented, "If Kim Jong Un keeps doing what he's doing [testing nuclear weapons and missiles], he's gonna cause a war."[2] Retired Admiral Dennis Blair urged a large-scale military operation against North Korea's strategic assets, in the event that Kim conducted an atmospheric nuclear test.[3] And various Trump administration officials, including National Security Adviser H. R. McMaster, repeatedly argued that the United States faced a closing window of opportunity to resolve the nuclear crisis short of using military force.

This was not yet a majority view in Washington, but even some former Bush administration officials thought the logical case being made had echoes of the rhetorical buildup to the Bush-era decision to invade Iraq in 2003—America's other war of choice.[4] A majority of popular opinion was not needed to start a war. Before the nuclear crisis ended, the case for preventive war was gaining momentum.

What made the preventive war choice truly pathological was not merely that it would have been a choice with costs that vastly exceeded hoped-for benefits; it was that North Korea already had nuclear weapons that could range US territory. Nuclear war, the very thing preventive war advocates claimed to want to prevent, was almost inevitable if the United States launched a war of choice in Korea. The way war advocates coped with that contradiction was by drawing a false distinction between nuclear weapons used in the Asia-Pacific versus nuclear weapons used against the US homeland. But that distinction collapses under scrutiny because 1) the United States has significant territory in the Pacific, 2) the primary targets in Asia would inevitably be US bases, and 3) hundreds of thousands of American citizens already lived in range of North Korean missiles, to say nothing of the hundreds of thousands of non-US citizens who would become victims of nuclear conflict in the event of a preventive war. A premeditated decision for war would have been a pathological one.

An Escalation Spiral

Even before Trump came to office and settled on a strategy of maximum pressure, US Korea policy decisions increasingly began mirror-imaging North Korea's offensive, reputational theory of victory.

North Korea had long believed that deterring an American attack required offensive threats and occasional small-scale blows to the adversary; it was general deterrence through deliberate friction that accumulated over time.

The United States, too, began talking and acting as if generating deliberate friction with North Korea (through bomber deployments, military exercises, and rhetorical threats that became less veiled over time) would enhance deterrence. It was the essence of the spurious US formula for credible deterrence during most of the crisis— Capability × Interests × Signaling. That offensive attitudinal shift, making "Signaling" necessary to deterrence, predated Trump, but accelerated significantly on Trump's watch. By 2017, both the United States and North Korea claimed defensive motivations, yet both felt the need to militarily antagonize the other through various threatening signals.

The consideration of giving North Korea a "bloody nose," a limited strike intended to induce caution in North Korea, despite the high likelihood that it would induce the opposite, was a more potent extension of this same logic. Mimicking North Korea's already high-risk theory of victory was a recipe for inadvertent war. Given these clashing theories of victory, deliberate and incremental escalation was likely to produce escalation in kind from one's adversary rather than restraint. If the crisis continued, there was a growing risk that either the United States or North Korea would have taken a deliberate offensive kinetic action in the name of deterrence. Because both sides increasingly thought this way, what should have been inconceivable—the idea of "sleepwalking" into nuclear war—became eminently plausible.

A "False-Positive" War

A third way the Trump–Kim nuclear standoff could have led to war often seemed the most likely as events unfolded: either side misperceiving the other as having launched an imminent attack. Nowhere else on earth were opposing militaries more forward-deployed and ready to launch large-scale offensives or counter-offensives. Nowhere else on earth were opposing militaries held in stasis, equally prepared to strike on command (or in apparent self-defense) without the other side having any advance warning.

In such a tightly constrained decision-making environment, the ability to achieve the tactical advantage of striking first was so strategically valuable that it could be the difference between victory and defeat. This reasoning gave significant incentives to North Korea, and to a lesser extent the United States, to pay close attention to indicators that war was imminent. Launching a first strike made no strategic sense for either side *unless* they expected that an attack from the other side was inevitable or imminent, in which case they would suddenly have every incentive to try to launch a preemptive attack.

Early Warning Indicators and First-Use Instability

The trouble with the Korean Peninsula was that the leading indicators each side might look for to determine whether a war had been launched or an attack was imminent were continuously active. For the United States, key indicators of impending attack would include North Korean war rhetoric, the mass mobilization of North Korean forces, the forward deployment (near the DMZ) of North Korean forces, an elevated alert status or orders for "readiness" preparations given to North Korean forces, and large or unusual military exercise patterns. But most of these indicators were apparent for years, and, during the first year and a half of the Trump administration, all of them were. The constant potential for war at a moment's notice (which led to US Forces Korea adopting the slogan, "ready to fight tonight") made it virtually impossible to separate signal from noise when trying to tease out early warning.

But whereas the United States had some capacity to be caught off-guard in the sense that it could absorb the damage of being struck first and fight on, North Korea had no such margin. It was the militarily inferior adversary and its nuclear arsenal was exceedingly modest: at best, a few dozen bombs as of 2017. For North Korea to stand its best chance in any conflict, it had to strike first. And since at least the 1990s, North Korean diplomats had repeatedly warned that it would launch a preemptive war if it believed the United States was on the cusp of launching an invasion of the North. It had studied how the United States prepared for invasion in previous conflicts in the Middle East and was not willing to allow that to happen.

The exigencies of military strategy thus dictated a high degree of North Korean sensitivity to signs of impending US or South Korean attack; regime destruction could be the cost of being caught unawares. In short, and as detailed in Chapter 3, the structure of the situation was not favorable to nuclear first-strike stability. In determining whether the United States was launching a war in the heat of the moment, Kim Jong Un and his military were likely to ask a series of logical questions that were informed by North Korean hackers having stolen alliance war plans in 2016:[5]

- Are North Korean radars, communications, or computer networks being jammed or disrupted?
- Are North Korea's "strategic assets" (which includes its missiles and nuclear facilities) being targeted?
- Is a US aircraft carrier strike group in the vicinity of the Korean Peninsula?
- Are US nuclear-capable bombers or stealth aircraft present in Korea or Japan?
- Are US forces in or around Korea on heightened alert status or in heightened readiness posture?
- Has there been a US troop buildup in the region?
- Do US rhetorical statements accommodate the possibility of it launching war?
- Are American civilians being evacuated from South Korea?

In the midst of a crisis, answering only a fraction of these questions in the affirmative would have been sufficient for the North Korean military or its Strategic Rocket Forces (responsible for operational missiles) to urge launching what it would view as a preemptive attack. The danger from an early warning perspective was that most of these indicators were alight during Trump's first year in office. If the United States had conducted a "bloody nose" strike, all but the final indicator (non-combatant evacuation operations) would have been active. And at several points in 2017, rumors circulated that the final indicator was active too. Virtually all observable signs pointed to imminent attack.

A Series of Unfortunate Events

In the context of the nuclear crisis that emerged in 2017, any single event or military signal could have been misinterpreted in such a way that led either the United States or North Korea to launch what they thought were preemptive—but were in fact preventive—first strikes. There were dozens of specific opportunities for either side to misread the situation they were facing and order an attack, including:

- North Korea's placement of two ICBMs on mobile missile launchers, which some experts had previously argued was grounds for a US strike;
- Trump's surprise declaration he was sending an "armada" to Korea, rerouting the USS *Carl Vinson* aircraft carrier strike group in early April;
- Indications in April that Kim was planning a nuclear test, which Trump publicly noted might have forced him to launch a preventive strike against North Korea as punishment;
- The White House bussing in the full Senate for a briefing on North Korea in April, which had no precedent and was being covered in the media as an indicator of a pending US attack;
- Leaked reports that the United States was planning to shoot down North Korea's next ICBM test;
- The North Korean military's August threat to "envelope" Guam with missile fire to demonstrate its ability to strike at a US nuclear bomber base in the Pacific;
- Public reports of navy surface ships with "warning orders" to strike pre-programmed North Korean targets, patrolling in international waters outside North Korea's eastern coast;
- Reports that the United States was preparing a non-combatant evacuation operation in September;
- The Valiant Shield exercise involving the convergence of three aircraft carrier strike groups on the Pacific at the same time in November (which had not occurred in the decade prior), concurrent with a team of Navy SEALs making port in South Korea;
- The twice-monthly deployments of nuclear-capable assets near the DMZ throughout Trump's first year in office;
- The Vigilant Ace air force exercise in December 2017, which involved the deployment of more than 200 aircraft in Korea, including stealth aircraft and nuclear-capable assets; and
- The Hawaiian operator error leading to public panic about an imminent ballistic missile attack in January 2018.

Against a backdrop of crisis and mutual war threats, it would not have been irrational for Kim, Trump, or a lower-level military decision-maker on either side to launch a strike in response to any of these events. The forces were arrayed, authorities in place, and the rationale prebaked.

Did Maximum Pressure "Work?"

The US strategy of maximum pressure was as much a product of decision-making about North Korea from the Obama and Bush eras as it was of the Trump administration. By the time Trump took office, options for dealing with North Korea had narrowed considerably. North Korea had gone too far down the nuclear path to turn back, and existing US policy prioritized placating an assertive South Korean ally with more and better deployments of strategic military assets (at the expense of antagonizing North Korea), rather than trying to influence Kim Jong Un per se. As one US official admitted, "Nothing we were doing [in the final year of the Obama administration] was about fundamentally changing North Korea's calculations."[6] By 2017, the prevailing situation in Korea, and the accumulation of US decisions to that point, made a perhaps less bellicose version of maximum pressure almost inevitable, even if Hillary Clinton had won the 2016 presidential election.

Someone sympathetic to maximum pressure might point out that, yes, maximum pressure entailed significant risks, but risks of war were part of the plan. The nature of coercion, especially between nuclear powers, makes it a competition in risk-taking. But the definition of coercion does not tell us how to evaluate its efficacy. Put differently, risk-taking might be necessary for coercion, but the fact of taking risks tells us nothing about whether to expect the risks to pay off. Evaluating the merits of a strategy, especially a coercive strategy, requires weighing the risks involved, in the context of what is being pursued, against the likelihood of success. On Korea policy, it was the goal—comprehensive, verifiable, irreversible denuclearization of North Korea—that made the game of risking nuclear war not worth playing. A basic principle of sound strategy is to seek balance between means and ends, and unilateral disarmament of a nuclear-armed adversary was an increasingly and dangerously unrealistic pursuit. No measures short of war could have achieved it, and to most Americans, North Korean denuclearization was not worth fighting a war over. To then risk nuclear war was needlessly dangerous.

An alternative argument in favor of maximum pressure might be that it brought the nuclear crisis to an end by convincing North Korea to reconcile with South Korea and seek a meeting with Donald Trump. As a superficial narrative, this is not far-fetched, and indeed, the White House argued that Kim's pivot to diplomacy was "further evidence that our campaign of maximum pressure is creating the appropriate atmosphere for dialogue with North Korea."[7] Even the UN Secretary-General paid lip service to this logic, claiming in April 2018 that peaceful denuclearization was "on track" because of UN Security Council unity "that was able to come together and to have a very strong and meaningful set of sanctions."[8] But the facts available at the time of writing this do not entirely abide. The Trump administration succeeded in placing an unprecedented amount of pressure on the Kim regime, but strangulation of the North Korean economy and the continuous specter of preventive strikes had always been cause for North Korean defiance throughout the crisis, not capitulation. It had the effect of accelerating—not halting or slowing—the pace at which North Korea pursued the ability to launch nuclear ICBMs and MRBMs.

It was Kim's strategy from the outset to seek serious diplomacy *after* obtaining a plausible second-strike nuclear capability against the United States. Why? Because while security came first for Kim, diplomacy from a position of nuclear strength served many beneficial purposes at once. It encouraged decoupling the United States and South Korea from one another; it could help alleviate the biting pressure of sanctions implementation; it allowed Kim to divert some national security resources toward economic development; and it brought North Korea closer to de facto legitimation of its international standing as a nuclear power. Put another way, a single move (diplomacy) allowed Kim to simultaneously advance his position in many different games. It was North Korea's transparency about its strategy all along, coupled with the pattern of defiance and continuous missile testing, and followed by an immediate pivot after a successful ICBM demonstration, that together confirms the impetus for North Korea's diplomatic turn. Maximum pressure (a constant during the Trump administration) explains nothing about North Korea's behavior (a variable) on its own. At best, it was an important background condition, motivating Kim to expedite "completion" of his nuclear arsenal, which was the opposite of the policy's hoped-for outcome.

Future historians and policymakers may continue to litigate the extent to which maximum pressure might have helped facilitate the end of the nuclear crisis, but it must be remembered that maximum pressure also played a direct role in bringing about the greatest risks of nuclear war facing the United States since the 1962 Cuban Missile Crisis. Trump's aggressive missives on Twitter would have rung hollow if not for the United States continuing with Obama-era decisions that created a backdrop of maximum military and economic pressure and a situation of acute hair-trigger confrontation. All this for a goal—denuclearization—that was unachievable.

Strategist and historian Sir Lawrence Freedman once wrote that "So long as there is a measurable risk that a confrontation could end up with nuclear detonations there is every incentive to avoid confrontation."[9] By that measure, maximum pressure was about as large a failure as was possible without bombs dropping.

How to Manage the Risks of Nuclear War

Whatever other interests the United States might have, it is difficult to imagine there could have been a more important purpose for US policy toward the Korean Peninsula than preventing inadvertent nuclear war. Making that the foremost concern would not have eliminated the sanctions regime or concerns about North Korean nuclear proliferation to other countries or non-state actors, but it had direct implications for the mix of tools that should have been at the center of US policy and how they should have been employed: some combination of a continuously calibrated deterrence posture, arms control, and diplomacy aimed at a stable strategic situation.

Deterrence in the Second Nuclear Age

Out of both strategic necessity and political convenience, deterrence has always been the first principle of US policy toward North Korea. Regardless of whether the United States found itself in fleeting periods of rapprochement and productive negotiations with the North or outright mutual hostility, at no point has the United States compromised its deterrence posture toward Pyongyang, and for good reason: Even dovish scholars concede that the absence of a second Korean War over more than 60 years is primarily due to the credible threat that the United States would fight alongside the South to defeat the North should it launch another war.[10]

The primary strategic value of US forces in South Korea has been as a symbolic "trip wire" that ensures the United States will be committed to the fight if war breaks out anew, and in so doing it prevents that eventuality from occurring. For the United States, that commitment has been total. To convince both Koreas of that, it has engaged in recurring annual exercises involving large-scale troop mobilizations, the routine deployment of nuclear-capable bombers and submarines, and continuous consultations with South Korea about the US provision of its extended deterrence "nuclear umbrella."

But US force posture in and around Korea has been predicated on the assumption that North Korea did not have functional nuclear weapons. The look and feel of the American deterrence commitment was fashioned long before North Korea had the ability to place nuclear warheads on missiles capable of reaching the United States and its allies.

Over the past decade, however, North Korea *has* morphed into a second-tier nuclear-armed actor. Yet US deterrence policies between 2014 and 2018 showed no acknowledgement that North Korea had the ability to make any conflict go nuclear, that the strategic situation Kim Jong Un faced incentivized him to launch nuclear weapons early in a conflict, or that the presence of usable nuclear weapons in the North necessarily constrained how the United States ought to wield the threat of force against it. Deterrence against a militarily weaker state, with a small but capable nuclear arsenal, requires a different approach than deterrence against a larger adversary, or one with a large nuclear arsenal.

North Korea in 2017 was neither Saddam Hussein's Iraq nor the Soviet Union. Neither the threat of a conventional large-scale ground campaign nor the threat of mutually assured destruction was appropriate. Instead, as long as the United States maintained a commitment to South Korea, it needed (and still needs) to strike a delicate balance: minimize the role of US nuclear weapons in the deterrence mission for the Korean Peninsula, convey and follow through on a willingness to retaliate if attacked, but simultaneously abandon the threat of regime change or invasion.[11]

This is no easy set of tasks. They would require a different rhetorical posture toward the North than has historically been the case. They would require a different physical posture in and around South Korea as well. US Forces Korea would be better redesigned as a force capable of fighting and prevailing on its own in conflicts of limited scope and limited objectives; a rapid reaction force that could punish or deny the objectives of a North Korean attack without having to wait for large-scale reinforcements. More importantly, deterring a second-tier nuclear-armed adversary requires paying as much attention to the threat of inadvertency as to the threat that North Korea might launch a significant unprovoked attack. Because the United States enjoyed a large conventional military advantage over North Korea, its nuclear threats aimed at the North (in the form of deploying nuclear-capable assets to South Korea) were at best superfluous. Neither did the United States profit from pursuing regime change against someone armed with nuclear weapons. And if the United States had no intention to actually march northward, pursue regime change, unify the Peninsula by force, or use nuclear weapons of its own, then neither did it have any business threatening such actions, implicitly or explicitly.

If dramatic political change comes to Korea, deterrence may no longer be as necessary as it was in the past. There are even imaginable futures in which the United States and North Korea may find themselves in strategic alignment. But as long as deterrence was at the heart of US policy toward the North, the United States needed to be sensitive to the distinct risks of inadvertent nuclear war arising from North Korea's transformation from a small, conventional Cold War rival to one armed with a diverse array of nuclear weapons.

Arms Control

The most realistic but politically unpalatable strategy for preventing nuclear war was proposed years before the Trump–Kim nuclear crisis. What nuclear physicist and Stanford University Professor Siegfried Hecker dubbed the "Three Nos" addressed most aspects of the nuclear situation on the Korean Peninsula that generated risks of war. The "Three Nos" called for " 1) No new weapons; 2) No better weapons; and 3) No transfer of nuclear technology or weapons."[12]

The idea was to immediately minimize the threat of North Korea's nuclear weapons by locking it into its current level of nuclear capability. The assumption was that North Korea's ability to threaten nuclear destruction would only grow with time, so the earlier the United States moved to freeze its capabilities the better. The implication of the proposal, which was what had always made it a difficult sell politically, was that North Korea would be permitted to retain some functional nuclear arsenal. The United States and the international community would have had to make their peace with North Korea being a de facto nuclear weapons state, though if the initial "Three Nos" process was successful, it would become the starting point of a longer process aimed at rolling back North Korea's nuclear capability through more ambitious arms control negotiations, diplomatic normalization, and the gradual repeal of sanctions.

The "Three Nos" had drawbacks. Washington policymakers had been familiar with Hecker's formulation for years, but it was something that previous conservative South Korean governments staunchly opposed. It also required the United States to effectively abandon its goal of comprehensive denuclearization, which for reasons described in Chapter 4, was politically infeasible. The "Three Nos," moreover, was silent on what it might take to ensure stable deterrence on the Korean Peninsula, because the production of nuclear-armed missiles radically altered the military balance with North Korea. The requirements of deterrence against a nuclear-armed North Korea, which during the Obama administration had not been seriously thought through, needed to be harmonized with the requirements of arms control. But by 2017, experts started to acknowledge grudgingly that North Korean nuclear weapons were here to stay, making some version of Hecker's "Three Nos" more attractive in principle, especially as North Korean missiles began demonstrating a range capable of striking the United States. The remaining problem, of course, was that it was incompatible with the Trump administration's maximum pressure strategy of pursuing comprehensive denuclearization.

The "Three Nos" was the first realistic strategy to recognize implicitly that the foremost goal of the United States in Korea must be managing the risks of nuclear war. There were many other priorities: a durable alliance with South Korea, a nuclear-free South Korea, preventing a conventional war, North Korean human rights, horizontal nuclear proliferation, and more. To the extent possible, it made sense that the

United States would try to seek its many goals for Korea simultaneously. But sometimes priorities must be made, and there could have been no greater priority than averting nuclear war. In this respect, the "Three Nos" was ahead of its time.

Strategic Diplomacy

For three decades, the United States has intermittently engaged North Korea in negotiations over various issues: dismantlement of its nuclear program, its missile program, and occasionally seeking the release of US citizens detained in Pyongyang. But the United States government and surrogates in the Washington think-tank community have had exceedingly trivial interaction with North Korea outside of those negotiations or the preparations for them. Negotiations are important, but another form of diplomacy—one that builds toward strategic stability—has become even more essential now that nuclear weapons have taken up a central role in North Korea's own theory of security. To the extent that the United States only interacted with North Korea when it sought something tangible and specific, North Korea was likely to always treat such interactions as instrumental transactions. But another way was and still is possible, low-cost, and to the benefit of both sides. America's cultivation of its strategic relationship with China was a partial model.

When China first built nuclear weapons in the 1960s, it was in the throes of the murderous and dystopian Cultural Revolution. Mao Zedong's cult of personality still reigned. After a few years, however, a growing number of China hands and policymakers in the US government saw an interest in establishing a more stable, even cooperative co-existence with China, eventually making it possible for Nixon and Kissinger to make their rapprochement bid in 1971. While the motivations underpinning US policy on China have evolved over time, US policymakers have always ultimately judged that a stable strategic relationship was in both countries' interests. But mutual vulnerability to one another's nuclear weapons was just the starting point of stability. US policymakers have sought to gird mutual vulnerability with economic interdependence and institutionalized bilateral dialogues about every aspect of competition and cooperation, including, crucially, nuclear strategy and doctrine. Mutual vulnerability should be the last resort for ensuring stability, not the first.

Consequently, US nuclear experts, China hands, and former officials have spent years engaging in Track 1.5 (quasi-official) meetings with China's nuclear and strategy experts in a recurring dialogue about strategic and crisis stability. The purpose has not simply been confidence-building or developing habits of information-sharing between rivals. Rather, the aim of these discussions has been to give each side a chance to explain, preview, or warn about what each is doing with their respective nuclear postures, and how they view the actions and statements of the other. The entrenched nature of the dialogue, with the right blend of official and deniable information-sharing among experts, helps to minimize miscalculation and enhance understanding. Although susceptible to manipulation, at its best, the Sino-US strategic dialogue helps to prevent inadvertent nuclear war and informs the nuclear and deterrence policies the United States adopts toward China.

Of course, many aspects of the US approach to China simply did not apply to North Korea. The size, insularity, and opacity of North Korean markets, for instance, made economic interdependence as impossible as it would have been undesirable. But the strategic dialogue approach and the notion of building on a starting point of mutual vulnerability to one another's nuclear arsenals had some appeal for the North Korea case. It still does. In 2017, the United States knew frighteningly little about North Korean nuclear command and control, how it thought about the use of military force given the presence of nuclear weapons, and conditions that would have created pressures for it to launch nuclear strikes. And to the extent that US officials and experts have interacted with North Korean counterparts in the past, it has been with its professional diplomats from the Foreign Ministry, not the experts in the military and the party who dealt in strategic matters. Having multiple inroads into North Korea would have helped the United States round out the image of North Korea on which it based its decisions. Ultimately, an ongoing dialogue of relevant experts—at the Track 1 and Track 2 levels—communicating how each side thinks about deterrence and nuclear weapons could have helped close a dangerous knowledge gap in US policy toward North Korea and vice versa.

What the Future Holds

As with the outbreak of World War I, it takes only one short-sighted or highly biased leader taking one needless gamble, or misperceiving just one action of the other side, to put the gears of war in motion. The unique combination of North Korean strategy, South Korean opportunism, and the timing of the Olympics staved off a crisis that was heading toward war, but the world may not be so lucky to have that confluence of circumstances interceding again.

As this book goes to print, the future of the Korean Peninsula is very much in flux. The Trump–Kim summit was marketed as the beginning of a process toward both denuclearization and peace. Yet denuclearization remained as implausible following the Trump–Kim summit as it was during the 2017 nuclear crisis. Much hinges on whether the United States is willing to accept nuclear arms reductions or controls short of denuclearization, and whether Kim Jong Un is willing to meet the United States halfway. To insist on a nuclear-free Korean Peninsula at this point is to swim against the currents of history and North Korean strategic culture. Beyond the nuclear issue though, other post-crisis events have aligned in such a way that, however far off denuclearization might be, the extremes of nuclear war, peaceful Korean unification, or US troop withdrawal are all plausible in our lifetimes. This is partly because North Korea has achieved its long-sought nuclear strike capability, in part because Kim Jong Un eventually needs greater access to foreign capital if he is to deliver the economic prosperity he promises the North Korean people (and that means he needs to get along with the outside world), and in part because South Korean domestic politics have (as of this writing) shifted strongly in favor of reconciliation with the North. The year 2018 has given a peaceful path positive momentum. As such, the evolving political circumstances in Korea might naturally address the future risks of nuclear war as part of a larger decision: for war, reconciliation, or strategic realignment with (rather than against) North Korea.

But even in the most optimistic of projections about the future, policymakers and the public must remain attentive to the risks of nuclear war, if only so that the precarious and needlessly dangerous decisions of 2016 through 2018 do not replay. Washington and Seoul are full of foreign policy hawks distrustful of North Korea, much as Pyongyang is full of foreign policy hawks distrustful of the United States. All seem to believe that pressure was successful for their side in 2017, and they cannot all be right.

Processes of peaceful change have to survive prolonged periods of implementation, and therefore are vulnerable to disruption. Over a long enough time span, foreign policy hawks on either side of the Pacific will have their chance to amend or undermine such processes. The accumulated history of mistrust and the conflicting strategic interests of North Korea and the US–South Korea alliance have stacked the deck against long-term stability, even as the short term holds out the possibility of transforming relations for the better. As long as North Korean nuclear weapons exist, the risk of renewed crisis remains. It is therefore imperative to understand what it was that led the United States and the Korean Peninsula to the brink of nuclear disaster in the first place. The decisions, attitudes, and legacies that produced the Trump–Kim nuclear crisis may not end peacefully if repeated, in Korea or elsewhere.

NOTES

Introduction

1. Dan DeLuce, Jenna McLaughlin, and Elias Groll, "Armageddon by Accident," *Foreign Policy* (October 18, 2017), http://foreignpolicy.com/2017/10/18/armaged don-by-accident-north-korea-nuclear-war-missiles/.
2. As quoted in Bob Corker interview with Jonathan Martin and Mark Landler, "Bob Corker Says Trump's Recklessness Threatens 'World War III,'" *New York Times* (October 8, 2017).
3. White House official, September 29, 2017.
4. "N. Korea: Likelihood of War with U.S. 'Established Fact,'" *Chosun Ilbo* (December 8, 2017).
5. Charles F. Hermann, *Crises in Foreign Policy* (Indianapolis: Bobbs-Merrill, 1969).
6. Rick Gladstone, "Giuliani Says Kim 'Begged' on Hands and Knees to Revive Trump Summit," *New York Times* (June 6, 2018).
7. Hazel Smith, *Hungry for Peace: International Security, Humanitarian Assistance, and Social Change in North Korea* (Washington, DC: US Institute of Peace Press, 2005), p. 73.
8. Very little reliable information about Kim Jong Un is publicly available. Some of the best information comes from Jung Pak, *The Education of Kim Jong-Un* (Washington, DC: Brookings Institution, 2018), www.brookings.edu/essay/the-education-of-kim-jong-un/.
9. Hyonhee Shin and James Pearson, "The Thinking Behind Kim Jong Un's 'Madness,'" Reuters (November 30, 2017).
10. Thomas C. Schelling, *Arms and Influence* (New Haven, CT: Yale University Press, 1966), p. 1.
11. Uri Friedman, "Lindsey Graham: There's a 30% Chance Trump Attacks North Korea," *The Atlantic* (December 14, 2017), www.theatlantic.com/international/archive/2017/12/lindsey-graham-war-north-korea-trump/548381

Chapter 1

1. "The Cairo Declaration," November 26, 1943, History and Public Policy Program Digital Archive, Foreign Relations of the United States Diplomatic Papers,

The Conferences at Cairo and Tehran, 1943 (Washington, DC: USGPO, 1961), pp. 448–49, https://digitalarchive.wilsoncenter.org/document/122101.

2. The two military officers were Dean Rusk, who would later become Secretary of State, and Charles Bonesteel, who would later become commander of US forces in Korea during the 1960s.

3. Historians are not entirely settled on the question of Stalin's motivations for green-lighting Kim Il Sung's invasion of the South. See Donggil Kim and William Stueck, "Did Stalin Lure the United States into the Korean War?" *E-Dossier #1* (Washington, DC: NKIDP Woodrow Wilson International Center for Scholars, 2008).

4. Bradley K. Martin, *Under the Loving Care of the Fatherly Leader: North Korea and the Kim Dynasty* (New York: St. Martin's Press, 2004), pp. 66–67.

5. James Matray, "Dean Acheson's Press Club Speech Reexamined," *Journal of Conflict Studies* Vol. XXII, no. 1 (2002), https://journals.lib.unb.ca/index.php/jcs/article/view/366/578.

6. Harry S. Truman, "Statement by the President on the Situation in Korea" (June 27, 1950), as quoted in Gerhard Peters and John T. Woolley, The American Presidency Project, available online: www.presidency.ucsb.edu/ws/?pid=13538.

7. For histories of the Korean War itself, see especially William Stueck, *The Korean War: An International History* (Princeton University Press, 1997); David Halberstam, *The Coldest Winter: America and the Korean War* (New York: Hyperion Press, 2007); Bruce Cumings, *The Korean War: A History* (New York: Modern Library, 2010).

8. For the complicated history behind MacArthur's decision, its consequences for the war, and Truman's decision to fire MacArthur, see John W. Spanier, *The Truman-MacArthur Controversy and the Korean War* (New York: W.W. Norton & Company, 1965).

9. Limited war did not mean civilized war, if such a thing exists. The United States resorted to immoral and occasionally inhumane tactics in the name of winning the conflict, including razing entire North Korean cities with aerial bombing campaigns.

10. Cumings, *The Korean War*, p. 159.

11. As quoted in Richard H. Cohn and Joseph P. Harahan, *Strategic Air Warfare: An Interview with Generals Curtis E. LeMay, Leon W. Johnson, David A. Burchinal, and Jack J. Catton* (Washington, DC: Office of Air Force History, 1988), p. 88.

12. Balazs Szalontai, *Kim Il Sung in the Khrushchev Era: Soviet-DPRK Relations and the Roots of North Korean Despotism, 1953–1964* (Palo Alto, CA: Stanford University Press, 2005), ch. 4; Andrei Lankov, *Crisis in North Korea: The Failure of De-Stalinization, 1956* (Honolulu: University of Hawaii Press, 2007).

13. James Person, "'We Need Help from Outside': The North Korean Opposition Movement of 1956," CWIHP Working Paper #52 (Washington, DC: Woodrow Wilson International Center, 2006), p. 3.

14. Szalontai, *Kim Il Sung in the Khrushchev Era*, p. 85.

15. Brian R. Myers, *North Korea's Juche Myth* (Busan, Republic of Korea: Sthele Press, 2015).

16. Jae-Jung Suh, ed., *The Origins of North Korea's Juche: Colonialism, War, and Development* (Lexington, MA: Lexington Books, 2014).

17. Charles Armstrong, "Juche and North Korea's Global Aspirations," NKIDP Working Paper #1 (Washington, DC: Woodrow Wilson International Center, 2009).

18. Myers, *North Korea's Juche Myth*.

19. As Dae-Sook Suh notes, *juche* was intended as "counterweight to Soviet influence." Dae-Sook Suh, *Kim Il Sung: The North Korean Leader* (New York: Columbia University Press, 1988), p. 143.

20. Szalontai, *Kim Il Sung in the Khrushchev Era*, ch. 4.

21. Martin, *Under the Loving Care of the Fatherly Leader*, p. 60.

22. Van Jackson, *Rival Reputations: Coercion and Credibility in US–North Korea Relations* (Cambridge University Press, 2016), pp. 24–99.

23. Ibid.

24. For a history, see Trevor Armbrister, *A Matter of Accountability: The True Story of the Pueblo Affair* (Guilford, CT: Lyons Press, 1970).

25. Mitchell Lerner and Jong-Dae Shin, "New Romanian Evidence on the Blue House Raid and the USS *Pueblo* Incident," in NKIDP E-Dossier #5 (Washington, DC: Woodrow Wilson International Center, 2012), www.wilsoncenter.org/sites/default/files/NKIDP_eDossier_5_The_Blue_House_Raid_and_the_Pueblo_Incident.pdf.

26. CIA Directorate of Intelligence, "Kim Il Sung's New Military Adventurism," November 26, 1968, Freedom of Information Act request, released May 2007.

27. Van Jackson, "The EC-121 Shoot Down and North Korea's Coercive Theory of Victory," Sources & Methods (April 13, 2017), www.wilsoncenter.org/blog-post/the-ec-121-shoot-down-and-north-koreas-coercive-theory-victory.

28. Walter C. Clemens, "North Korea's Quest for Nuclear Weapons: New Historical Evidence," *Journal of East Asian Studies* Vol. 10, no. 1 (2010), pp. 127–54.

29. Don Oberdorfer, *The Two Koreas: A Contemporary History* (London: Warner, 1999), p. 250.

30. Michael J. Mazarr, *North Korea and the Bomb: A Case Study in Nonproliferation* (New York: St. Martin's Press, 1995), pp. 36–41.

31. Rosemary Foot, "Nuclear Coercion and the Ending of the Korean Conflict," *International Security* Vol. 13, no. 3 (1988/89), pp. 92–112; Peter Hayes, *Pacific Powderkeg: American Nuclear Dilemmas in Korea* (Lexington, MA: Lexington Books, 1991), pp. 60–62, 127–28.

32. As quoted in Thomas P. Bernstein and Andrew Nathan, "The Soviet Union, China, and Korea," in *The US-South Korean Alliance*, ed. Gerald L. Curtis and Sung-joo Han (Lexington, MA: Lexington Books, 1983), p. 119.

33. As quoted in Martin, *Under the Loving Care of the Fatherly Leader*, p. 437.

34. See, for example, Andrei Lankov, *The Real North Korea: Life and Politics in the Failed Stalinist Utopia* (Oxford University Press, 2014), pp. 179–90; Benjamin Habib, "North Korea's Nuclear Weapons Programme and the Maintenance of the Songun System," *Pacific Review* Vol. 24, no. 1 (2011), pp. 43–64.

35. Andrei Lankov, "Why Nothing Can Really Be Done about North Korea's Nuclear Program," *Asia Policy* Vol. 23, no. 1 (2017), p. 106.

36. Ibid.

37. As quoted in Dong-won Lim, *Peacemaker: Twenty Years of Inter-Korean Relations and the North Korean Nuclear Issue* (Stanford, CA: Shorenstein Asia-Pacific Research Center, 2012), p. 94.

38. Martin, *Under the Loving Care of the Fatherly Leader*, pp. 478–79.

39. Leon Sigal, *Disarming Strangers: Nuclear Diplomacy with North Korea* (Princeton University Press, 1999), p. 63.

40. Joel S. Wit, Daniel B. Poneman, and Robert L. Gallucci, *Going Critical: The First North Korean Nuclear Crisis* (Washington, DC: Brookings Institution Press, 2005).

41. As quoted in John Burton, "N. Korea 'Sea of Fire' Threat Shakes Seoul," *Financial Times* (March 22, 1994).

42. Wit, Poneman, and Gallucci, *Going Critical*, p. 181.
43. Oberdorfer, *The Two Koreas*, pp. 324–25.
44. Wit, Poneman, and Gallucci, *Going Critical*, pp. 34–39.
45. As quoted in Oberdorfer, *The Two Koreas*, p. 352.
46. US Government Printing Office, *Report of the Commission to Assess the Ballistic Missile Threat to the United States* (Washington, DC: US GPO, 1998).
47. Van Jackson, "Threat Consensus and Rapprochement Failure: Revisiting the Collapse of US–North Korea Relations, 1994–2002," *Foreign Policy Analysis* Vol. 14, no. 2 (2018), pp. 235–53.
48. US Department of State, "Principles and Opportunities for American Foreign Policy," statement by Warren Christopher, Secretary of State, *Dispatch* Vol. 6 (Boston, MA, 1995).
49. Victor D. Cha, *The Impossible State: North Korea, Past and Future* (New York: Ecco, 2012), p. 260.

Chapter 2

1. In what follows, I try to be transparent about issues where there are still serious debates among experts, but also present my best judgment based on logic and evidence.
2. Brad Roberts was the first person to use "theory of victory" in the North Korea context. Brad Roberts, *The Case for U.S. Nuclear Weapons in the 21st Century* (Palo Alto, CA: Stanford University Press, 2015).
3. As quoted in Martin, *Under the Loving Care of the Fatherly Leader*, p. 434.
4. As quoted in Evan Osnos, "The Risk of Nuclear War with North Korea," *The New Yorker* (September 18, 2017), www.newyorker.com/magazine/2017/09/18/the-risk-of-nuclear-war-with-north-korea.
5. "Record of Conversation between N.G. Sudarikov and Heo Dam, the Leader of the Ministry of Foreign Affairs of DPRK," April 16, 1969, History and Public Policy Program Digital Archive, RGANI: fond 5, opis 61, delo 462, listy 71–74, obtained by Sergey Radchenko and translated by Gary Goldberg, http://digitalarchive.wilsoncenter.org/document/134230.
6. "Record of Conversation between N.G. Sudarikov and Pak Seong-cheol, a Member of the Political Committee of the Workers' Party of Korea," April 16, 1969, History and Public Policy Program Digital Archive, RGANI: fond 5, opis 61, delo 466, listy 119–27, obtained by Sergey Radchenko and translated by Gary Goldberg, http://digitalarchive.wilsoncenter.org/document/134231.
7. "Minutes of Conversation on the Occasion of the Party and Government Delegation on Behalf of the Romanian Socialist Republic to the Democratic People's Republic of Korea," June 10, 1971, History and Public Policy Program Digital Archive, Archives of the Central Committee of the Romanian Communist Party, obtained and translated for the North Korea International Documentation Project (NKIDP) by Eliza Gheorghe.
8. Jackson, *Rival Reputations*, pp. 138–69.
9. See, for example, Van Jackson, "Does Nuclearization Impact Threat Credibility? Insights from the Korean Peninsula," in *North Korea and Nuclear Weapons: Entering the New Era of Deterrence*, ed. Sung-Chull Kim and Michael Cohen (Washington, DC: Georgetown University Press, 2017), pp. 89–112.
10. As quoted in Charles L. Pritchard, *Failed Diplomacy: The Tragic Story of How North Korea Got the Bomb* (Washington, DC: Brookings Institution Press, 2007), p. 38.

11. Mason Richey, "Turning It Up to Eleven: Belligerent Rhetoric in North Korea's Propaganda," *Parameters* Vol. 46, no. 4 (2016/2017), pp. 93–104.

12. As quoted in Osnos, "The Risk of Nuclear War with North Korea."

13. Memorandum of Conversation between President Clinton and Chairman Kim Jong Il (August 4, 2009).

14. As quoted in Soyoung Kim and Heekyong Yang, "North Korea Says U.S. Threats Make War Unavoidable, China Urges Calm," Reuters (December 7, 2017).

15. For all practical purposes, North Korea achieved a survivable capability during the Obama administration with the deployment of the KN-08, which was capable of firing from mobile platforms. But there is no consensus about what the threshold for survivability should be.

16. Jonathan Shieber, "North Korean Hackers Stole South Korean and U.S. War Plans," TechCrunch (October 10, 2017), https://techcrunch.com/2017/10/10/report-north-korean-hackers-stole-south-korean-and-u-s-war-plans/.

17. Wit, Poneman, and Gallucci, *Going Critical*, pp. 105, 126, 160.

18. Van Jackson, "Why Not Bomb North Korea? Theories, Risks and Preventive Strikes," *Korean Journal of Defense Analysis* Vol. 30, no. 1 (2018), pp. 1–19.

19. Vipin Narang, *Nuclear Strategy in the Modern Era: Regional Powers and International Conflict* (Princeton University Press, 2014).

20. Vipin Narang, "Why Kim Jong Un Wouldn't Be Irrational to Use a Nuclear Bomb First," *Washington Post* (September 8, 2017).

21. See, for example, Alexander George and Richard Smoke, *Deterrence in American Foreign Policy: Theory and Practice* (New York: Columbia University Press, 1974); Alexander L. George and William E. Simons, eds, *The Limits of Coercive Diplomacy*, 2nd edn (Boulder, CO: Westview Press, 1994); Wallace J. Thies, *When Governments Collide: Coercion and Diplomacy in the Vietnam Conflict, 1964–1968* (Berkeley: University of California Press, 1980).

22. The prevalence of misperception and its consequences was a major contribution of the "third wave" of deterrence theory. See Robert Jervis, *Perception and Misperception in International Politics* (Princeton University Press, 1976); Jeffrey Knopf, "The Fourth Wave in Deterrence Research," *Contemporary Security Policy* Vol. 31, no. 1 (2010), pp. 1–33.

23. Van Jackson, "Nukes They Can Use? The Danger of North Korea Going Tactical," 38 North (March 15, 2016), www.38north.org/2016/03/vjackson031516/.

24. Jackson, *Rival Reputations*.

25. Glenn H. Snyder, "The Balance of Power and the Balance of Terror," in *The Balance of Power*, ed. Paul Seabury (San Francisco, CA: Chandler, 1965), pp. 184–201.

26. See, for example, Patrick McEachern, *Inside the Red Box: Inside North Korea's Post-Totalitarian Politics* (New York: Columbia University Press, 2010); Young Whal Kihl and Hong Nack Kim, *North Korea: The Politics of Regime Survival* (New York: M.E. Sharpe, 2006); Daniel Byman and Jennifer Lind, "Pyongyang's Survival Strategy: Tools of Authoritarian Control in North Korea," *International Security* Vol. 35, no. 1 (2010), pp. 44–74.

27. Not everyone shares this view, but it is the most cogent and widely shared among policymakers. For the most persuasive statement of North Korea's unification goal, see B.R. Myers, "North Korea's Unification Drive," speech before the Royal Asiatic Society Korea Branch in Seoul (December 19, 2017), http://sthelepress.com/index.php/2017/12/21/north-koreas-unification-drive/. See also B.R. Myers, "A Note on Byungjin," SthelePress.com (August 30, 2017), http://sthelepress.com/index.php/2017/07/30/a-note-on-byungjin-b-r-myers/; Stephen Evans, "Is North Korea's Leader Kim Jong Un Rational?" BBC News (March 18, 2017), www.bbc.com

/news/world-asia-39269783; Sue Mi Terry, "North Korea's Strategic Goals and Policy towards the United States and South Korea," *International Journal of Korean Studies* Vol. 17, no. 2 (2013), pp. 63–91.

28. "Korean Youths in China Hail Successful Test-Fire of DPRK's Ballistic Missile," KCNA (February 20, 2017).
29. For a discussion, see Max Fisher, "North Korea's Nuclear Arms Sustain Drive for 'Final Victory,'" *New York Times* (July 29, 2017).
30. As quoted in Guy Taylor, "CIA Says North Korean Dictator Kim Jong Un is Not Crazy, But 'Very Rational,'" *Washington Times* (October 4, 2017).
31. "U.S. Military Gambling against DPRK May Lead to Its Total Destruction," Uriminzokkiri (undated), accessed October 27, 2017, www.uriminzokkiri.com/index.php?ptype=english&no=1037.
32. Ibid.
33. As quoted in Osnos, "The Risk of Nuclear War with North Korea."
34. Christine Kim and Michelle Nichols, "North Korea Says Seeking Military 'Equilibrium' with U.S.," Reuters (September 15, 2017).

Chapter 3

1. Barack H. Obama, "Barack Obama's Inaugural Address," *New York Times* (January 20, 2009).
2. US Department of Defense official, January 16, 2018.
3. See, for example, Hillary R. Clinton, Testimony before the Senate Foreign Relations Committee, "Nomination Hearing to be Secretary of State," Washington, DC (January 13, 2009), https://2009-2017.state.gov/secretary/20092013clinton/rm/2009a/01/115196.htm; Stephen W. Bosworth, "Remarks at the Korea Society Annual Dinner," Washington, DC (June 9, 2009), https://2009-2017.state.gov/p/eap/rls/rm/2009/06/124567.htm.
4. As quoted in "North Korea Withdraws from Six-Party Nuclear Talks," VOA News (November 2, 2009).
5. Ibid.
6. North Korea had sentenced the two journalists, Euna Lee and Lisa Ling, to 12 years' hard labor two months prior, on June 8. After the Clinton visit in 2009, North Korea arrested at least 14 other Americans on various charges through the rest of the Obama administration, raising the question of whether North Korea began to view them as bargaining chips.
7. Wendy R. Sherman, "Talking to the North Koreans," *New York Times* (March 7, 2001).
8. The memo was written by David Straub, a Korea expert and retired Foreign Service Officer. Straub accompanied Clinton during the trip in his private capacity as a researcher at Stanford University at the time.
9. Memorandum of Conversation between President Clinton and Chairman Kim Jong Il (August 4, 2009).
10. Ibid.
11. Ibid.
12. Ibid. See also Jesse Johnson, "Hacked Memo Reveals Details of Bill Clinton's 2009 Meeting with North Korea's Kim Jong Il," *Japan Times* (October 30, 2016).
13. Memorandum of Conversation between President Clinton and Chairman Kim Jong Il (August 4, 2009); Johnson, "Hacked Memo Reveals Details of Bill Clinton's 2009 Meeting with North Korea's Kim Jong Il."

14. "DPRK Foreign Ministry Vigorously Refutes UNSC's 'Presidential Statement,'" KCNA (April 14, 2009).

15. The Department of Defense played a marginal role in the making of North Korea policy during the first years of the Obama administration. Although they held similar views of North Korea as the rest of the interagency, there is some evidence of contrasting perspective. Secretary Gates's May 2009 speech, for example, conveys a much more hawkish and pessimistic tone than Ambassador Bosworth's speech the following month.

16. Although North Korea denied responsibility through external media, a North Korean military officer who defected the following year claimed that several of the sailors involved in the torpedo attack operation on the *Cheonan* received "Hero of the DPRK" awards. See "N. Korean Sailors Awarded Hero's Title for Attack on S. Korean Warship: Defector," Yonhap (December 7, 2012).

17. For a historical account of the events in this period, see Jackson, "Does Nuclearization Impact Threat Credibility?," pp. 89–112.

18. Jeffrey R. Bader, *Obama and China's Rise: An Insider's Account of America's Asia Strategy* (Washington, DC: Brookings Institution Press, 2011), pp. 88–90.

19. As quoted in Jack Kim, "North Korea Declares 'Sacred War' on U.S. and South," Reuters (July 24, 2010).

20. Jackson, "Does Nuclearization Impact Threat Credibility?," pp. 102–5.

21. Ibid.

22. Robert M. Gates, *Duty: Memoirs of a Secretary at War* (New York: Knopf, 2013), p. 416.

23. Ibid., p. 497. See also "After North Korean Strike, South Korean Leader Threatens 'Retaliation'," CNN.com (November 24, 2010), www.cnn.com/2010/WORLD/asiapcf/11/23/nkorea.skorea.military.fire/index.html?hpt=T1&iref=BN1.

24. President Lee's recollection of events was slightly different. He claimed in a later interview that a "high-ranking military officer" told him the existing rules of engagement did not allow for South Korean fighters to attack North Korea in that circumstance. "Lee Recalls Getting Tough with North Korea," *Chosun Ilbo* (February 5, 2013).

25. "S. Korea May Strike N. Korea's Missile Base: President Lee," *Korea Herald* (November 23, 2010); "NK Fires Shells onto S. Korean Island, Kills 2 Marines," *Dong-A Ilbo* (November 24, 2010).

26. As quoted in Kwon Hyuk-chul, "Defense Ministry Designates N. Korea 'Our Enemy' in White Paper," *Hankyoreh* (December 28, 2010).

27. Mark E. Manyin, Emma Chanlett Avery, Mary Beth Nikitin, Ian Rinehart, and Brock Williams, *U.S.–South Korea Relations* (Washington, DC: Congressional Research Service, October 28, 2015), p. 14.

28. For a detailed overview of DRP 307 and its implications, see Bruce W. Bennett, "The Korean Defense Reform 307 Plan," The Asan Forum Issue Brief (April 18, 2011), http://en.asaninst.org/contents/issue-brief-no-8-the-korean-defense-reform-307-plan-by-bruce-w-bennett-the-rand-corporation1/.

29. Rhee Sang-woo, *From Defense to Deterrence: The Core of Defense Reform Plan 307* (Washington, DC: Center for Strategic and International Studies, 2011).

30. Ibid.

31. See, for example, Kim Dae Joong, "Time for S. Korea to Develop Its Own Nuclear Arms," *Chosun Ilbo* (January 11, 2011).

32. "Chung Mong-joon: 67% of Citizens Support Stationing Nuclear Weapons as a Response to North Korean Nuclear Threat" [in Korean], Yonhap (February 24, 2011).

33. Terence Roehrig, *Japan, South Korea, and the United States Nuclear Umbrella: Deterrence After the Cold War* (New York: Columbia University Press, 2017), pp. 141–42.

34. This and other rationales are discussed in Jeffrey Lewis, "ROK Missile Rationale Roulette," Arms Control Wonk (October 9, 2012), www.armscontrolwonk.com /archive/205771/rok-missile-rationale-roulette/.

35. See, for example, "Senior Politician Calls for S. Korea to Have Nuclear Weapons," Yonhap (January 31, 2016); Rajaram Panda, "Should South Korea Go Nuclear?," *Asia-Pacific Review* Vol. 22, no. 1 (2015), pp. 148–76.

36. Kim, "North Korea Declares 'Sacred War' on U.S. and South."

37. For the most detailed, and candid, depiction of the Leap Day Deal process, see Jeffrey Lewis, "Rockets and the Leap Day Deal," Arms Control Wonk (March 23, 2012), www.armscontrolwonk.com/archive/205098/rockets-and-the-leap-day-deal/.

38. "DPRK Foreign Ministry Spokesman on Result of DPRK–U.S. Talks," KCNA (February 29, 2012).

39. Victoria Nuland, Press Statement, "U.S.–DPRK Bilateral Discussions" (February 29, 2012), https://2009-2017.state.gov/r/pa/prs/ps/2012/02/184869.htm.

40. See Lewis, "Rockets and the Leap Day Deal."

41. Several anonymous officials from the Obama administration told reporters after the Leap Day Deal was announced that the US delegation had confirmed North Korea understood that SLV tests would kill the deal. See ibid.

42. The United States publicly and privately stated that an SLV launch would nullify the deal. Following North Korea's announcement that it would conduct the test, the United States suspended its agreed-upon food aid. See Karen Parrish, "Officials Suspend North Korea Nutrition Aid over Planned Launch," Armed Forces Press Service (March 28, 2012).

43. On the contrasting preferences of the Foreign Ministry, the Workers' Party, and the military, see McEachern, *Inside the Red Box*.

44. Kurt Campbell, *The Pivot: The Future of American Statecraft in Asia* (New York and Boston, MA: Twelve, 2016), pp. 173–74.

45. Victor D. Cha, "Hawk Engagement and Preventive Defense on the Korean Peninsula," *International Security* Vol. 27, no. 1 (2002), pp. 40–78.

46. Mira Rapp-Hooper, "Decoupling is Back in Asia: A 1960s Playbook Won't Solve These Problems," War on the Rocks (September 7, 2017), https://warontherocks.com /2017/09/decoupling-is-back-in-asia-a-1960s-playbook-wont-solve-these-problems/.

47. "Transcript: Tom Donilon and Mike Morell on 'Face the Nation,' Jan. 7 2018," CBS News (January 7, 2018), www.cbsnews.com/news/transcript-tom-donilon-and-mike-morell-on-face-the-nation-jan-7-2018/.

48. John Barry, "Robert Gates Exit Interview: Concerns about U.S. Supremacy, Nuclear Proliferation, More," The Daily Beast (June 21, 2011), www.thedailybeast.com/robert-gates-exit-interview-concerns-about-us-supremacy-nuclear-proliferation-more.

49. Park Hyun, "US to Boost Missile Defense in Response to North Korean Threats," *Hankyoreh* (March 18, 2013).

50. News transcript, Department of Defense Press Briefing by Admiral Cecil Haney in the Pentagon Briefing Room (March 24, 2015).

51. Tony Capaccio, "North Korea Can Miniaturize Nuclear Weapon, U.S. Says," Bloomberg (April 8, 2015).

52. Antony J. Blinken, "Will Rex Tillerson Pass North Korea's Nuclear Test?," *New York Times* (March 15, 2017).

53. Peter Hayes and Scott Bruce, "Unprecedented Nuclear Strikes of the Invincible Army: A Realistic Assessment of North Korea's Operational Nuclear Capability," *North Korean Review* Vol. 8, no. 1 (2012), p. 85.

54. From a KCNA statement, as quoted in ibid.

55. "The DPRK's Nuclear Constitution," NAPSNet Policy Forum (June 13, 2012), https://nautilus.org/napsnet/napsnet-policy-forum/the-dprks-nuclear-constitution/.

56. Josh Rogin, "Obama's Asia Team Caught Off Guard, Partying When Rocket Launched," *Foreign Policy* (December 13, 2012), http://foreignpolicy.com/2012/12/13/obamas-asia-team-caught-off-guard-partying-when-rocket-launched/.

57. Ibid.

58. "Spokesman for DPRK Foreign Ministry Urges U.S. to Choose between Two Options," KCNA (February 12, 2013).

59. US Department of the Treasury, press release, "Treasury Sanctions North Korean Senior Officials and Entities Associated with Human Rights Abuses" (July 6, 2016), www.treasury.gov/press-center/press-releases/pages/jl0506.aspx.

60. "Kim Jong-un Placed on Sanctions Blacklist for the First Time by US," *The Guardian* (July 6, 2016).

61. "DPRK Foreign Ministry Hits US for Its Hideous Crime," KCNA (July 7, 2016).

62. For the history of the Sony hack as described here, see Travis Sharp, "Theorizing Cyber Coercion: The 2014 North Korean Operation against Sony," *Journal of Strategic Studies* Vol. 40, no. 7 (2017), pp. 898–926.

63. "U.S. Urged to Honestly Apologize to Mankind for Its Evildoing before Groundlessly Pulling up Others," KCNA (December 21, 2014).

64. White House Office of the Press Secretary, "Remarks by the President in Year-End Press Conference," Washington, DC (December 19, 2014), https://obamawhitehouse.archives.gov/the-press-office/2014/12/19/remarks-president-year-end-press-conference.

65. "Sony Hack: US Mulls Putting N Korea Back on Terror List," BBC News (December 21, 2014).

66. As quoted in Cecilia Kang, Drew Harwell, and Brian Fung, "North Korean Web Goes Dark Days after Obama Pledges Response to Sony Hack," *Washington Post* (December 22, 2014).

67. US Department of the Treasury, press release, "Treasury Imposes Sanctions Against the Government of the Democratic People's Republic of Korea" (January 2, 2015), www.treasury.gov/press-center/press-releases/pages/jl9733.aspx.

68. David E. Sanger and William J. Broad, "Trump Inherits a Secret Cyberwar Against North Korean Missiles," *New York Times* (March 4, 2017).

69. Ibid.

70. Suman Varandani, "North Korea Missile Test: Kim Jong Un Suspects Sabotage by US-South Korea, Orders Probe," *International Business Times* (October 29, 2016).

71. David E. Sanger and William J. Broad, "Hand of U.S. Leaves North Korea's Missile Program Shaken," *New York Times* (April 18, 2017).

72. Ibid. See also the database of North Korean missile tests at www.nti.org/analysis/articles/cns-north-korea-missile-test-database/.

73. Department of Defense official, January 16, 2018.

74. "U.S. Rejected North Korea Peace Talks Offer before Last Nuclear Test: State Department," Reuters (February 22, 2016).

75. Interviews with two different Obama administration officials conducted in 2018 confirmed that the State Department had effectively agreed to pursue peace treaty

talks in principle, but only in the context of denuclearization. One could not be a substitute for the other.

76. Ibid.

77. "U.S. Does Not Rule Out 'Parallel Process' of Peace Treaty, Nuclear Talks with N.K.: State Department," Yonhap (March 4, 2016).

78. Sarah Kim, "Kerry Says U.S. Is Open to a Peace Treaty with North," *JoongAng Ilbo* (April 13, 2016).

79. "U.S. Rejected North Korea Peace Talks Offer Before Last Nuclear Test."

80. As quoted in Kim, "Kerry Says U.S. Is Open to a Peace Treaty with North."

81. "U.S.–DPRK Negotiations and North Korean Provocations," Beyond Parallel (October 2, 2017), https://beyondparallel.csis.org/dprk-provocations-and-us-negotiations/.

Chapter 4

1. John Hudson, "Inside Hillary Clinton's Massive Foreign Policy Brain Trust," *Foreign Policy* (February 10, 2016).

2. "Democratic Presidential Candidates Debate," C-span.org (July 23, 2007), www.c-span.org/video/?200061-1/democratic-presidential-candidates-debate.

3. As quoted in Tom Raum, "Obama Debate Comments Set Off Firestorm," Associated Press (July 24, 2007).

4. Gates, *Duty*, pp. 289, 329, 511, 518–19.

5. "Transcript: Senate Confirmation Hearing: Hillary Clinton," *New York Times* (January 13, 2009).

6. Hillary for America, foreign policy adviser, December 26, 2015.

7. Ibid.

8. Hillary for America, foreign policy adviser, January 16, 2018.

9. Ibid.

10. Ibid.

11. "Clinton's Likely Defense Secretary Says U.S. Should Intensify Sanctions on N.K. Rather Than Negotiate," Yonhap (October 16, 2016).

12. Yi Yong-in, "Hillary's Campaign Team Signals Hardline Stance on North Korea," *Hankyoreh* (October 17, 2016).

13. Ibid.

14. Jiwon Song, "U.S. Official Encourages Plan for N. Korea Collapse," NK News (May 4, 2016), www.nknews.org/2016/05/u-s-official-encourages-plan-for-n-korea-collapse/.

15. David Brunnstrom, "Getting North Korea to Give Up Nuclear Weapons Probably 'Lost Cause': U.S. Spy Chief," Reuters (October 26, 2016).

16. Ibid.

17. As quoted in Tim Shorrock, "Hillary's Hawks Are Threatening Escalation Against North Korea," *The Nation* (October 28, 2016), www.thenation.com/article/hillarys-hawks-are-threatening-war-against-north-korea/.

18. US government official, January 2018.

19. Sanger and Broad, "Trump Inherits a Secret Cyberwar Against North Korean Missiles."

20. John Kerry, "Remarks at the US Naval Academy," Annapolis, MD (January 10, 2017).

21. Ibid.

Chapter 5

1. Philip Ewing, "FACT CHECK: Why Didn't Obama Stop Russia's Election Interference in 2016?," National Public Radio (February 21, 2018).
2. Michael Wolf, *Fire and Fury: Inside the Trump White House* (New York: Henry Holt and Co., 2018).
3. David Nakamura and Anne Gearan, "Obama Warned Trump on North Korea. But Trump's 'Fire and Fury' Strategy Wasn't What Obama Aides Expected," *Washington Post* (August 9, 2017).
4. As quoted in Osnos, "The Risk of Nuclear War with North Korea."
5. As quoted in Jenny Lee, "Aide Says Obama Urged Trump to Press China on North Korea," VOA News (February 22, 2017).
6. Ibid.
7. US Department of Defense official, February 9, 2018.
8. Steve Herman, "Little Contact Between Trump Team and State Department," VOA News (January 10, 2017), www.voanews.com/a/little-contact-between-trump-team -state-department/3670995.html.
9. Department of Defense official, January 10, 2018.
10. Richard Sisk, "Former US General Calls for Pre-emptive Strike on North Korea," Defense Tech (December 1, 2016).
11. Lee Yon-soo, "Ex-U.S. Military Chief Suggests Pre-emptive Strike on North Korea," *Chosun Ilbo* (September 19, 2016).
12. Kerry, "Remarks at the US Naval Academy."
13. Mike Pearl, "What Would Happen in the Minutes and Hours After North Korea Nuked the United States?," Vice News (December 21, 2016); Mark Fitzpatrick and Michael Elleman, "Pre-empting a North Korean ICBM Test," The Survival Editors' Blog (January 9, 2017); Stratfor, "What the U.S. Would Use to Strike North Korea," RealClearDefense (January 3, 2017); Daniel DePetris, "Should Washington Strike North Korea's Dangerous ICBMs Before It's Too Late?," *The National Interest* (January 7, 2017).
14. Joel Wit and Richard Sokolsky, "Washington's Dangerous Drums of War on North Korea," Defense One (December 12, 2016); Daniel Larison, "Attacking North Korea Would Be a Disaster," *The American Conservative* (January 9, 2017).
15. "What to Know about South Korean President Park Geun-hye's Influence-Peddling Scandal," *The Straits Times* (November 21, 2016).
16. Former Special Envoy for Six-Party Talks Joseph DeTrani in *The Nelson Report* newsletter (December 20, 2016).
17. "Memorandum of DPRK Foreign Ministry," KCNA (November 21, 2016).
18. Ibid.
19. Ibid.
20. "Kim Jong Un's 2017 New Year's Address," KCNA (January 2, 2017).
21. Ibid.
22. Maggie Haberman and David Sanger, "'It Won't Happen!' Donald Trump Says of North Korean Missile Test," *New York Times* (January 2, 2017).
23. "S. Korea to Create Special Unit to Strike at N.K. Wartime Leadership," Yonhap (January 4, 2017).
24. Joint Press Availability with Japanese Vice Foreign Minister Shinsuke Sugiyama and Republic of Korea Vice Foreign Minister Lim Sung-nam, Washington, DC (January 5, 2017).
25. "N. Korea Has Likely Built Two ICBMs, Placed Them on Mobile Launchers: Sources," Yonhap (January 19, 2017).

26. Choe Sang-hun, "Trump Tells South Korea That Alliance with U.S. Is 'Ironclad,'" *New York Times* (January 30, 2017).
27. As quoted in Phil Stewart, "U.S. Warns North Korea of 'Overwhelming' Response if Nuclear Arms Used," Reuters (February 3, 2017).
28. "National Peace Committee Urges U.S. and South Korean Puppet Forces to Repent of Their Act of Spawning Nuclear Issue," KCNA (February 3, 2017).
29. Jeffrey Lewis, "North Korea Is Practicing for Nuclear War," *Foreign Policy* (March 9, 2017).
30. As quoted in Ariel Zilber, "It Was All Part of a Master Plan," *Daily Mail* (September 26, 2017).
31. Doug Bock Clark, "The Untold Story of Kim Jong Nam's Assassination," *GQ Magazine* (September 25, 2017).
32. As quoted in Bill Powell, "Kim Jong Un, Donald Trump and the Looming Nuclear Crisis in North Korea," *Newsweek* (March 7, 2017), www.newsweek.com/2017/03/17/kim-jong-un-north-korea-nuclear-crisis-ballistic-missiles-564433.html.
33. Trump administration official, January 10, 2018.
34. Joint Statement for the Inaugural Meeting of the Extended Deterrence Strategy and Consultation Group, Washington, DC (December 20, 2016).
35. The content of the background briefing to reporters—which the State Department did not make public—was documented in *The Nelson Report* newsletter (March 14, 2017).
36. Rex W. Tillerson, "Remarks with Foreign Minister Yun Byung-Se Before Their Meeting," Seoul, Republic of Korea (March 17, 2017).
37. Song Jung-a, "US 'Strategic Patience' with N Korea Has Run Out, Says Tillerson," *Financial Times* (March 18, 2017).
38. Mike Mullen, Sam Nunn, and Adam Mount, "A Sharper Choice on North Korea: Engaging China for a Stable Northeast Asia," Independent Task Force Report No. 74 (New York: Council on Foreign Relations, 2016).
39. White House official, February 1, 2018.
40. Jackson, "Threat Consensus and Rapprochement Failure."
41. House Committee on Foreign Affairs, Subcommittee Hearing, Asia and the Pacific, "Pressuring North Korea: Evaluating Options," March 21, 2017, https://foreignaffairs.house.gov/hearing/subcommittee-hearing-pressuring-north-korea-evaluating-options/.
42. Matt Spetalnick, "Trump National Security Aides Complete North Korea Policy Review: Official," Reuters (April 3, 2017).
43. As quoted in "Donald Trump Warns China the US Is Ready to Tackle North Korea," *Financial Times* (April 3, 2017).
44. Background Briefing by Senior Administration Officials on the Visit of President Xi Jinping of the People's Republic of China, Washington, DC (April 4, 2017).
45. As quoted in "North Korea Focus of Donald Trump, Xi Jinping Talks at Mar-a-Lago," *The Australian* (April 7, 2017).
46. Adam Entous and Evan Osnos, "Jared Kushner Is China's Trump Card," *The New Yorker* (January 29, 2018).
47. Ibid.
48. As quoted in Gerard Baker, Carol Lee, and Michael Bender, "Trump Says He Offered China Better Trade Terms in Exchange for Help on North Korea," *Wall Street Journal* (April 12, 2017).
49. "Transcript: National Security Adviser General H.R. McMaster on MSNBC with Hugh," *Hugh Hewitt Show* (August 5, 2017), www.hughhewitt.com/national-security-advisor-general-h-r-mcmaster-msnbc-hugh/.

50. Harriet Alexander, Danny Boyle, and Barney Henderson, "US Launches Strike on Syria—How It Unfolded," *The Telegraph* (April 7, 2017).

51. Ibid.

52. Shannon Pettypiece, Justin Sink, Jennifer Jacobs, and Toluse Olorunnipa, "From Steak Dinner to Situation Room: Inside Trump's Syria Strike," Bloomberg Politics (April 8, 2017).

53. Entous and Osnos, "Jared Kushner Is China's Trump Card."

Chapter 6

1. David B. Larter, "Carried Away: The Inside Story of How the *Carl Vinson*'s Canceled Port Visit Sparked a Global Crisis," *Navy Times* (April 23, 2017).

2. Harris's beliefs about deterrence are discussed further below, but for US Pacific Command's justification, see Anna Fifield, "U.S. Navy Sends Strike Group Toward Korean Peninsula," *Washington Post* (April 9, 2017).

3. Van Jackson, "Why Mattis Versus Kim Jong Un Will End Badly for Us All," War on the Rocks (April 20, 2017), https://warontherocks.com/2017/04/why-mattis-versus-kim-jong-un-will-end-badly-for-us-all/.

4. The literature on signaling and deterrence is too large to do justice to here. The most useful findings come from Robert Jervis, *The Logic of Images in International Relations* (New York: Columbia University Press, 1970).

5. US 3rd Fleet Public Affairs, "*Carl Vinson* Strike Group Departs Singapore for Western Pacific" (April 9, 2017), www.navy.mil/submit/display.asp?story_id=99815.

6. Department of Defense official, January 10, 2018.

7. Ibid.

8. For a chronology of this incident, see Aaron Blake, "The White House's Misleading Statements about Trump's 'Armada' Heading to North Korea," *Washington Post* (April 18, 2017).

9. Press Briefing by Press Secretary Sean Spicer, Washington, DC (April 11, 2017), www.whitehouse.gov/briefings-statements/press-briefing-press-secretary-sean-spicer-041117/.

10. Katie Reilly, "President Trump on His Plan for North Korea: 'You Never Know, Do You? You Never Know,'" *Time* (April 12, 2017).

11. Bill Neely, "North Korea Warns It Would Use Nuclear Weapons First If Threatened," NBC News (October 17, 2016), www.nbcnews.com/news/world/north-korea-warns-it-would-use-nuclear-weapons-first-if-n665791.

12. Matthew Yglesias interview with Barack Obama, "Obama: The Vox Conversation, Part Two: Foreign Policy," Vox (January 2015), www.vox.com/a/barack-obama-interview-vox-conversation/obama-foreign-policy-transcript.

13. William Arkin, Cynthia McFadden, and Kenzi Abou-Sabe, "U.S. May Launch Strike If North Korea Reaches for Nuclear Trigger," NBC News (April 13, 2017), www.nbcnews.com/news/world/u-s-may-launch-strike-if-north-korea-reaches-nuclear-n746366.

14. Ibid.

15. Ibid.

16. Josh Rogin, "Trump's North Korea Policy Is Maximum Pressure, Not Regime Change," *Washington Post* (April 14, 2017).

17. Anna Fifield, "White House Warns North Korea Not to Test US Resolve, Offering Syria and Afghanistan Strikes as Examples," *Washington Post* (April 17, 2017).

18. "Remarks by the Vice President to US-Japanese Business Community," Tokyo, Japan (April 19, 2017), www.whitehouse.gov/briefings-statements/remarks-vice-president-us-japanese-business-community/.

19. As quoted in Jeff Daniels, "North Korea's Hidden Submarine Threat Is Another Worry as Regime Warns It's 'Ready' for War," CNBC (April 12, 2017), www.cnbc.com/2017/04/12/north-korea-submarine-threat-is-another-worry.html.

20. "The Latest: Japan Taking Steps to Respond to Korea Crisis," Associated Press (April 14, 2017).

21. Although widely reported as an anti-ship ballistic missile test, some analysts argue it was actually an intermediate-range ballistic missile.

22. "'This Week' Transcript: High Alert, North Korea," ABC News (April 16, 2017), http://abcnews.go.com/Politics/week-transcript-high-alert-north-korea/story?id=46819310.

23. Christopher P. Cavas, "Nothing to See Here: US Carrier Still Thousands of Miles from Korea," *Defense News* (April 17, 2017), www.defensenews.com/naval/2017/04/17/nothing-to-see-here-us-carrier-still-thousands-of-miles-from-korea/.

24. "President Trump Promises New Approach to North Korea," Fox News (April 17, 2017), http://video.foxnews.com/v/5401315513001/?#sp=show-clips.

25. Stephen J. Adler, Steve Holland, and Jeff Mason, "Exclusive: Trump Says 'Major, Major' Conflict with North Korea Possible, But Seeks Diplomacy," Reuters (April 28, 2017).

26. Margaret Talev and Jennifer Jacobs, "Trump Says He'd Meet with Kim Jong Un under Right Circumstances," Bloomberg Politics (May 1, 2017), www.bloomberg.com/news/articles/2017-05-01/trump-says-he-d-meet-with-north-korea-s-kim-if-situation-s-right.

27. Ibid.

28. As quoted in Jeremy Diamond and Zachary Cohen, "Trump: I'd be 'Honored' to Meet Kim Jong Un, under 'Right Circumstances,'" CNN.com (May 2, 2017), https://edition.cnn.com/2017/05/01/politics/donald-trump-meet-north-korea-kim-jong-un/index.html.

29. Adler, Holland, and Mason, "Exclusive: Trump Says 'Major, Major' Conflict with North Korea Possible, but Seeks Diplomacy."

30. "Trump on North Korea: I Don't Want to Telegraph What I'm Doing," Fox News (April 18, 2017), http://insider.foxnews.com/2017/04/18/trump-north-korea-i-just-dont-telegraph-my-moves.

31. Ankit Panda and Dave Schmerler, "When a North Korean Missile Accidentally Hit a North Korean City," *The Diplomat* (January 3, 2018), https://thediplomat.com/2018/01/when-a-north-korean-missile-accidentally-hit-a-north-korean-city/.

32. "Trump: I Will Not be Happy If North Korea Conducts Another Nuclear Test," CBS, *Face the Nation* (April 29, 2017), www.cbsnews.com/news/trump-i-will-not-be-happy-if-north-korea-conducts-another-nuclear-test/.

33. Ibid.

34. Eric Li, "Trump's Tough Talk about North Korea Might Actually End the Crisis," *Washington Post* (May 5, 2017).

35. Spencer Ackerman and Justin McCurry, "US Military Considers Shooting Down North Korean Missile Tests, Sources Say," *The Guardian* (April 18, 2017).

36. Ibid.

37. Alexander Mallin and Meghan Keneally, "Senators Describe 'Long and Detailed' White House Briefing on North Korea," ABC News (April 26, 2017), http://abcnews.go.com/Politics/president-trump-invites-full-senate-white-house-special/story?id=47026601.

38. "Tillerson: US Strategy on North Korea Relies on China's Participation," Fox News (April 27, 2017), www.foxnews.com/politics/2017/04/27/tillerson-us-strategy-on-north-korea-relies-on-chinas-participation.html.

39. Ibid.

40. Ibid.

41. Department of State official, February 27, 2018.

42. "Tillerson: US Strategy on North Korea Relies on China's Participation."

43. Oki Nagai and Tsuyoshi Nagasawa, "US Could Leave Kim in Place if Pyongyang Scraps Nukes," *Nikkei Asian Review* (May 9, 2018), https://asia.nikkei.com /Politics-Economy/International-Relations/US-could-leave-Kim-in-place-if-Pyongyang-scraps-nukes.

44. Van Jackson, "Don't Believe the Hype: China's North Korea Policy is All Smoke and Mirrors," War on the Rocks (February 20, 2017), https://warontherocks.com/2017/02/dont-believe-the-hype-chinas-north-korea-policy-is-all-smoke-and-mirrors/.

45. "N. Korea's Grain Imports from China Surge in March," Yonhap (May 3, 2017).

46. As quoted in Uri Friedman, "Why China Isn't Doing More to Stop North Korea," *The Atlantic* (August 9, 2017), www.theatlantic.com/international/archive/2017/08/north-korea-the-china-options/535440/.

47. Statement by Foreign Minister Wang Yi at the UN Security Council Ministerial Session on the Nuclear Issue on the Korean Peninsula, New York (April 28, 2017), www.fmprc.gov.cn/mfa_eng/zxxx_662805/t1458508.shtml.

48. Somini Sengupta and Choe Sang-hun, "'You Either Support North Korea, or You Support Us,' U.S. Envoy Says," *New York Times* (May 18, 2017).

49. Ju-min Park, "North Korea Sends Rare Letter of Protest over New U.S. Sanctions," Reuters (May 12, 2017).

50. "N.K. Urges S. Korea to End 'Confrontational' Policies as Moon Takes Office," Yonhap (May 11, 2017).

51. As quoted in Choe Sang-hun, "North Korea Says Missile It Tested Can Carry Nuclear Warhead," *New York Times* (May 14, 2017).

52. Gaby Galvin, "North Korea Denies Mistreatment of Otto Warmbier," *U.S. News & World Report* (June 23, 2017), www.usnews.com/news/world/articles/2017-06-23/north-korea-we-are-the-biggest-victim-in-otto-warmbiers-death.

53. Bruce Klingner and Sue Mi Terry, "We Participated in Talks with North Korean Representatives. This Is What We Learned," *Washington Post* (June 22, 2017).

54. Jay Solomon, "Top North Korean Nuclear Negotiator Secretly Met with U.S. Diplomats," *Wall Street Journal* (June 18, 2017).

55. "Remarks by President Trump during Roundtable of the American Technology Council," Washington, DC (June 19, 2017), www.whitehouse.gov/briefings-statements/remarks-president-trump-roundtable-american-technology-council/.

56. "Secretary of State Rex Tillerson and Secretary of Defense Jim Mattis at a Joint Press Availability," Washington, DC (June 21, 2017), https://kr.usembassy.gov/062117-secretary-state-rex-tillerson-secretary-defense-jim-mattis-joint-press-availability/.

57. Ibid.

Chapter 7

1. White House official, September 29, 2017. Tillerson was also reportedly opposed to attacking North Korea, but Tillerson's unfriendly relationship with McMaster and the friction between the NSC and the State Department marginalized him.

2. James Clapper, "Korea Chair Platform Keynote Remarks," Center for Strategic and International Studies, Washington, DC (June 27, 2017).

3. Ibid.
4. John Schilling, "What Is True and Not True about North Korea's Hwasong-14 ICBM: A Technical Evaluation," 38 North (July 10, 2017), www.38north.org /2017/07/jschilling071017/.
5. "Statement by Secretary Tillerson," Washington, DC (July 4, 2017), https://paei .state.gov/secretary/20172018tillerson/remarks/2017/07/272340.htm.
6. Ibid.
7. "Kim Jong Un Supervises Test-Launch of Inter-continental Ballistic Missile," KCNA (July 5, 2017).
8. Kim Gamel, "US, S. Korea Respond to North's ICBM Test with Missiles of Their Own," *Stars and Stripes* (July 4, 2017).
9. Ibid.
10. Chairman Joseph Dunford, "Tank Talk," Aspen Security Forum 2017, Aspen, Colorado (July 22, 2017), http://aspensecurityforum.org/wp-content/uploads/ 2017/07/Tank-Talk.pdf.
11. Director Mike Pompeo, "The View from Langley," Aspen Security Forum 2017, Aspen, Colorado (July 20, 2017), http://aspensecurityforum.org/wp-content /uploads/2017/07/The-View-from-Langley.pdf.
12. Ibid.
13. Ibid.
14. As quoted in Heesu Lee and Kanga Kong, "Kim Jong Un Says Entire U.S. in Range of North Korea's ICBM," Bloomberg Politics (July 29, 2017), www.bloomberg.com /news/articles/2017-07-29/kim-jong-un-says-entire-u-s-within-range-of-north-korea- icbm.
15. Erik Ortiz and Arata Yamamoto, "Senator Lindsey Graham: Trump Says War with North Korea an Option," NBC News (August 2, 2017), www.nbcnews.com/news/ north-korea/sen-lindsey-graham-trump-says-war-north-korea-option-n788396? icid=today_hp_NBCtopheadlines.
16. Ibid.
17. Joby Warrick, Ellen Nakashima, and Anna Fifield, "North Korea Now Making Missile-Ready Nuclear Weapons, U.S. Analysts Say," *Washington Post* (August 8, 2017).
18. Peter Baker and Choe Sang-Hun, "Trump Threatens 'Fire and Fury' Against North Korea If It Endangers U.S.," *New York Times* (August 8, 2017).
19. As quoted in John Walcott, "Trump's 'Fire and Fury' North Korea Remark Surprised Aides: Officials," Reuters (August 10, 2017).
20. Ellen Mitchell, "Mattis Warns North Korea of 'Destruction of Its People'," *The Hill* (August 9, 2017), http://thehill.com/policy/defense/345908-mattis-warns-north- korea-of-destruction-of-its-people.
21. As quoted in Katrina Manson and Bryan Harris, "North Korea Threatens Guam after Trump 'Fire and Fury' Vow," *Financial Times* (August 10, 2017).
22. Ibid.
23. Yasmeen Serhan and Kathy Gilsinian, "North Korea Answers Trump's Vague Threats with Specific Ones," *The Atlantic* (August 10, 2017), www.theatlantic.com/interna tional/archive/2017/08/north-korea-answers-trumps-vague-threats-with-specific-ones /536433/.
24. Baker and Choe, "Trump Threatens 'Fire and Fury' Against North Korea If It Endangers the U.S."
25. "President Trump Remarks on North Korea and Opioid Crisis," Bedminster, New Jersey, C-Span (August 10, 2017), www.c-span.org/video/?432426-1/president- trump-warning-north-korea-tough.

26. As quoted in Nolan D. McCaskill, "Trump Says 'Fire and Fury' Warning to North Korea Maybe Not 'Tough Enough,'" POLITICO (August 10, 2017), www.politico.com/story/2017/08/10/trump-says-fire-and-fury-warning-to-north-korea-could-have-been-even-stronger-241492.

27. "Kim Jong Un Inspects KPA Strategic Force Command Element," North Korea Leadership Watch (August 15, 2017), www.nkleadershipwatch.org/2017/08/15/kim-jong-un-inspects-kpa-strategic-force-command-element/.

28. Ibid.

29. Nick Wadhams and Jennifer Epstein, "Trump Says North Korea's Kim Is 'Starting to Respect' America," Bloomberg Politics (August 23, 2017), www.bloomberg.com/news/articles/2017-08-23/trump-says-north-korea-s-kim-is-starting-to-respect-america.

30. US Department of the Treasury, Press Center, "Treasury Targets Chinese and Russian Entities and Individuals Supporting the North Korean Regime," Washington, DC (August 22, 2017), www.treasury.gov/press-center/press-releases/Pages/sm0148.aspx.

31. Sengupta and Choe, "'You Either Support North Korea, or You Support Us,' U.S. Envoy Says."

32. John Wagner and Anna Fifield, "Trump: 'All Options Are on the Table' After North Korea Launched Missile Over Japan," Washington Post (August 29, 2017).

33. Joshua Berlinger and Taehoon Lee, "Seoul Steps Up Military Response to North Korea Nuclear Test," CNN (September 4, 2017), https://edition.cnn.com/2017/09/04/asia/north-korea-nuclear-test/index.html.

34. "North Korea Slapped with UN Sanctions After Nuclear Test," BBC News (September 12, 2017).

35. As quoted in Christine Kim and Michelle Nichols, "North Korea Says Seeking Military 'Equilibrium' with the U.S.," Reuters (September 15, 2017).

36. Cindy Saine, "White House Says Now Is Not the Time to Talk to North Korea," VOA News (October 2, 2017).

37. "Remarks by President Trump to the 72nd Session of the United Nations General Assembly," New York (September 19, 2017), www.whitehouse.gov/briefings-statements/remarks-president-trump-72nd-session-united-nations-general-assembly/.

38. "Statement of Chairman of State Affairs Commission of DPRK," KCNA (September 22, 2017).

39. Margaret Besheer, "North Korean Foreign Minister Lashes Out at Trump," VOA News (September 24, 2017), www.voanews.com/a/north-korea-foreign-minister-lashes-out-at-trump-at-united-nations/4041596.html.

40. Ibid.

Chapter 8

1. Lee Yong-soo, "Top U.S. Official in Charge of Evacuations Visited S. Korea," Chosun Ilbo (September 20, 2017).

2. As quoted in Olivia Beavers, "North Korea Warns US of 'Unimaginable' Nuclear Strike," The Hill (October 19, 2017), http://thehill.com/policy/defense/356166-north-korea-warns-us-of-unimaginable-nuclear-strike.

3. Zachary Cohen, "North Korean Hackers Stole US–South Korea War Plans, Official Says," CNN (October 11, 2017), https://edition.cnn.com/2017/10/10/politics/north-korea-hackers-us-south-korea-war-plan/index.html.

4. Sophie Tatum, "Corker: Tillerson, Mattis and Kelly 'Separate Our Country from Chaos,'" CNN (October 6, 2017), https://edition.cnn.com/2017/10/04/politics/bob-corker-mattis-tillerson-kelly/index.html.

5. Leigh Ann Caldwell and Vivian Salama, "Breakdown in North Korea Talks Sounds Alarms on Capitol Hill," NBC News (October 25, 2017), www.nbcnews.com/news/north-korea/lack-talks-north-korea-sounds-alarms-capitol-hill-n813951.

6. As quoted in ibid.

7. Jonathan Martin and Mark Landler, "Bob Corker Says Trump's Recklessness Threatens World War III," *New York Times* (October 8, 2017).

8. Stephanie Perry and Hannah Hartig, "Poll: America's Fear of North Korea is on the Rise," NBC News (October 19, 2017), www.nbcnews.com/politics/white-house/poll-americans-fear-north-korea-rise-n811986.

9. Marcus Weisgerber, "EXCLUSIVE: US Preparing to Put Nuclear Bombers Back on 24-Hour Alert," Defense One (October 22, 2017), www.defenseone.com/threats/2017/10/exclusive-us-preparing-put-nuclear-bombers-back-24-hour-alert/141957/.

10. "Having Nuclear Weapons 'Matter of Life and Death' for North Korea: Agency," Reuters (October 21, 2017).

11. Alex Ward, "The US Military Tweeted Out Bad Information About Its Nukes. North Korea Will Notice," Vox (November 15, 2017), www.vox.com/world/2017/11/15/16657752/north-korea-twitter-trump-silo-b1.

12. Dennis Blair, "Chairman's Message: Trump's Trip to Asia and Fundamentals to Consider in a High-Stakes Environment," Sasakawa USA (November 6, 2017).

13. "Trump's Reckless Remarks Bringing Calamity," *Rodong Sinmun* (November 4, 2017).

14. "Remarks by President Trump to the National Assembly of the Republic of Korea," Seoul, Republic of Korea (November 7, 2017), www.whitehouse.gov/briefings-statements/remarks-president-trump-national-assembly-republic-korea-seoul-republic-korea/.

15. Richard Engel, "Advisers Pulled Back Trump from Harder Line on N. Korea," NBC News (November 11, 2017), www.nbcnews.com/politics/white-house/advisers-pulled-back-trump-harder-line-n-korea-n819621.

16. "U.S. Envoy Says No Communication, No Signal from North Korea Amid Nuclear Crisis," Reuters (November 17, 2017).

17. Osnos, "The Risk of Nuclear War with North Korea."

18. Anna Fifield, "North Korea Taps GOP Analysts to Better Understand Trump and His Messages," *Washington Post* (September 26, 2017).

19. Mark Mazetti and Mark Landler, "North Korea's Overture to Jared Kushner," *New York Times* (June 17, 2018).

20. Susan Glasser, "They Want to Know if Trump's Crazy," *POLITICO Magazine* (November 13, 2017), www.politico.com/magazine/story/2017/11/13/north-korea-trump-secret-talks-global-politico-215822.

21. Osnos, "The Risk of Nuclear War with North Korea."

22. Christine Kim, "North Korea Says 'Breakthrough' Puts U.S. Mainland within Range of Nuclear Weapons," Reuters (November 29, 2017).

23. "DPRK Gov't Statement on Successful Test-Fire of New-Type ICBM," KCNA (November 29, 2017).

24. Ibid.

25. Zachary Cohen, Ryan Browne, and Nicole Gaouette, "New Missile Test Shows North Korea Capable of Hitting All of US Mainland," CNN (November 30, 2017), https://edition.cnn.com/2017/11/28/politics/north-korea-missile-launch/index.html.

26. "Remarks by President Trump in Meeting with Congressional Leadership," Washington, DC (November 28, 2017), www.whitehouse.gov/briefings-statements/remarks-president-trump-meeting-congressional-leadership/.

27. Ibid.

28. Cohen, Browne, and Gaouette, "New Missile Test Shows North Korea Capable of Hitting All of US Mainland."

29. Jeff Daniels, "Pentagon Scenario of a New Korean War Estimates 20,000 Deaths Daily in South Korea, Retired US General Says," CNBC (September 25, 2017), www.cnbc.com/2017/09/25/korean-war-simulation-by-dod-estimates-20000-deaths-daily-in-south.html.

30. Nicholas Kristof, "Slouching Toward War with North Korea," New York Times (November 4, 2017).

31. Ibid.

32. Friedman, "Lindsey Graham."

33. Ibid.

34. "South Korea, U.S., Kick Off Large-Scale Exercise Amid North Korean Warnings," Reuters (December 4, 2017).

35. Ibid.

36. "N. Korea: Likelihood of War with U.S. 'Established Fact,'" Chosun Ilbo (December 8, 2017).

37. "World Faces 'Last Best Chance' to Avoid War with North Korea, US General Warns," Sky News (December 13, 2017), https://news.sky.com/story/world-faces-last-best-chance-to-avoid-war-with-north-korea-us-general-warns-11168427.

38. Rachel Ansley, "Tillerson's Take on US Foreign Policy: A Year in Review," New Atlanticist (December 13, 2017), www.atlanticcouncil.org/blogs/new-atlanticist/tillerson-s-takes-on-us-foreign-policy-a-year-in-review.

39. "White House Contradicts Tillerson on North Korea," BBC News (December 14, 2017).

40. Ibid.

41. Ben Riley-Smith, "Exclusive: US Making Plans for 'Bloody Nose' Military Attack on North Korea," The Telegraph (December 20, 2017).

42. Gerald F. Seib, "Amid Signs of Thaw in North Korea, Tensions Bubble Up," Wall Street Journal (January 9, 2018).

43. Based on interviews for this book, Mattis, Tillerson, and Dunford were said to be opposed to preventive strikes on North Korea, while Pence, Pompeo, Harry Harris, McMaster, and much of the NSC favored them.

44. Eric Levitz, "Report: H.R. McMaster to be Fired—at Kelly and Mattis's Behest," New York Magazine (March 1, 2018), http://nymag.com/daily/intelligencer/2018/03/report-mcmaster-to-be-fired-at-kelly-and-mattiss-behest.html.

45. Scott D. Sagan, "The Korean Missile Crisis," Foreign Affairs (November/December 2017), pp. 72–82; Jackson, "Why Not Bomb North Korea?"

46. Van Jackson, "Want to Strike North Korea? It's Not Going to Go the Way You Think," POLITICO Magazine (January 12, 2018), www.politico.com/magazine/story/2018/01/12/north-korea-strike-nuclear-strategist-216306; Abraham Denmark, "The Myth of the Limited Strike on North Korea," Foreign Affairs (January 9, 2018), www.foreignaffairs.com/articles/north-korea/2018-01-09/myth-limited-strike-north-korea; Jung Pak, Sue Mi Terry, and Bruce Klingner, "Bloody Nose Policy on North Korea Would Backfire: Ex-CIA Analysts," USA Today (February 9, 2018).

47. Scott Sagan and Allen Weiner, "Bolton's Illegal War Plan for North Korea," New York Times (April 6, 2018).

48. Alex Wellerstein, "The Hawaii Alert Was an Accident. The Dread It Inspired Wasn't," Washington Post (January 16, 2018).

49. Scott D. Sagan, The Limits of Safety: Organizations, Accidents, and Nuclear Weapons (Princeton University Press, 1993).

Chapter 9

1. "Kim Jong Un's 2018 New Year's Address," The National Committee on North Korea (January 1, 2018), www.ncnk.org/node/1427.
2. Hans Schattle and Youngwuk Kim, "Global Public Perceptions of Online Brinkmanship: Evaluating President Trump and His Twitter Rhetoric on North Korea," draft paper presentation for the 59th Annual International Studies Association, San Francisco, CA (April, 2018).
3. "Several Meetings Led to Olympics Breakthrough: Sources," *JoongAng Ilbo* (January 3, 2018).
4. Josh Rogin, "Trump Asks South Korea's President: 'Do You Have to Reunify?'," *Washington Post* (November 15, 2017).
5. Elise Hu, "North and South Korea Reach Breakthroughs in First High-Level Talks in 2 Years," National Public Radio (January 9, 2018).
6. As quoted in Christine Kim and Hyonhee Shin, "North Korea Says No U.S. Talks Planned at Olympics, Pence Vows Continued Pressure," Reuters (February 8, 2017).
7. Ashley Parker and Anna Fifield, "Pence's Olympic Mission: Countering North Korean Propaganda," *Washington Post* (February 9, 2018).
8. Ashley Parker, "Pence Was Set to Meet North Korean Officials During the Olympics Before Last-Minute Cancellation," *Washington Post* (February 20, 2018).
9. Matt Spetalnick, Phil Stewart, and David Brunnstrom, "Exclusive: U.S. Prepares High-Seas Crackdown on North Korea Sanctions Evaders—Sources," Reuters (February 24, 2018).
10. "U.S. Hit for Bringing Clouds of War to Hang over Korean Peninsula," KCNA (February 24, 2018).
11. Jim Sciutto and Dana Bash, "Nuclear Missile Threat a 'Red Line' for Trump on North Korea," CNN (March 1, 2018), https://edition.cnn.com/2018/03/01/politics/north-korea-trump-nuclear-missile-threat-red-line/index.html.
12. Uri Friedman, "Senator James Risch Explains His Warning about 'Biblical' Conflict with North Korea," *The Atlantic* (March 4, 2018), www.theatlantic.com/international/archive/2018/03/senator-risch-north-korea/554714/.
13. John Bolton, "The Legal Case for Striking North Korea First," *Wall Street Journal* (February 28, 2018).
14. Peter Baker and Choe Sang-hun, "With Snap 'Yes' in Oval Office, Trump Gambles on North Korea," *New York Times* (March 10, 2018).
15. "Panmunjom Declaration for Peace, Prosperity and Unification of the Korean Peninsula," Panmunjom, Korea, April 27, 2018.
16. As quoted in Choe Sang-hun and Mark Landler, "North Korea Signals Willingness to 'Denuclearize,' South Says," *New York Times* (March 6, 2018).
17. "Statement from Vice President Mike Pence on North Korea," Washington, DC (March 6, 2018), www.whitehouse.gov/briefings-statements/statement-vice-president-mike-pence-north-korea/.
18. Giuliani made public references to North Korea as a deliberate distraction from Trump's legal or publicity troubles on at least four occasions between March and June 2018. See, for example, Amber Phillips and Callum Borcher, "Rudy Giuliani's Revealing Interview with Sean Hannity Annotated," *Washington Post* (May 3, 2018).
19. "Trump Says He Did Not Know about $130,000 Payment to Stormy Daniels," Reuters (April 6, 2018).
20. This rendition of events comes from Baker and Choe, "With Snap 'Yes' in Oval Office, Trump Gambles on North Korea."

21. Live report from Michael DelMoro, @MikeDelMoro Twitter account (March 8, 2018), https://twitter.com/MikeDelMoro/status/971873149414445056.

22. Jonathan Karl, Jordyn Phelps, and Katherin Faulders, "Trump Agrees to Meeting with North Korean Leader Kim Jong Un on Denuclearization," ABC News (March 9, 2018), http://abcnews.go.com/Politics/major-announcement-coming-south-korea-north-korea-trump/story?id=53621671.

23. For an analysis of the historical context of North Korean references to denuclearization, see Jeffrey Lewis, "The Word That Could Help the World Avoid Nuclear War," New York Times (April 4, 2018).

24. "Donald Trump Speaks at a Make America Great Again Rally in Pennsylvania," Factba.se (March 10 2018), https://factba.se/transcript/donald-trump-speech-rally-saccone-pennsylvania-march-10-2018.

25. "Interview: Trump–Kim Talks to Be 'A Very Short Meeting' If Pyongyang Won't Discuss Denuclearization," Radio Free Asia (March 23, 2018), www.rfa.org/eng lish/news/korea/interview-bolton-03232018130326.html.

26. As quoted in Gabriel Sherman, "He's Sitting There Bitching and Moaning: Inside Trumpworld, Allies Fear the Boss Could Go Postal and Fire Mueller," Vanity Fair (April 10, 2018), www.vanityfair.com/news/2018/04/inside-trumpworld-allies-fear-the-boss-could-go-postal-and-fire-mueller.

27. Mark Landler, "Spies, Not Diplomats, Take Lead Role in Planning Trump's North Korea Meeting," New York Times (March 16, 2018).

28. "US Requests 5 North Korean Nuclear Weapons be Transferred to France This Month" [in Korean], Naver.com (May 11, 2018), http://m.news.naver.com/read .nhn?mode=LSD&sid1=001&oid=022&aid=0003272755.

29. Secretary Pompeo, @SecPompeo Twitter account (May 4, 2018).

30. John Wagner, "'Everyone Thinks So, But I Would Never Say It': Trump Weighs In on Whether He's Deserving of a Nobel Peace Prize," Washington Post (May 9, 2018).

31. Philip Rucker, Ashley Parker, and Josh Dawsey, "'The North Koreans Simply Stood Us Up': The Inside Story of How Trump and Kim's Summit Fell Apart," The Independent (May 25, 2018).

32. "Trump–Kim Summit: US-North Korean Officials Meet for Working-Level Talks," The Straits Times (June 11, 2018).

33. As quoted in Charlie Campbell, "Kim Jong Un Promises 'Major Change' After First Ever Summit Between Leaders of U.S. and North Korea," Time (June 12, 2018).

34. "Press Conference by President Trump," Capella Hotel, Singapore (June 12, 2018), www.whitehouse.gov/briefings-statements/press-conference-president-trump/.

35. Michael Crowley and Louis Nelson, "'Ludicrous': Pompeo Snaps at Reporters Seeking Clarity on North Korea Deal," POLITICO (June 13, 2018), www.politico .com/story/2018/06/13/trump-north-korea-no-nuclear-threat-643532.

36. Ibid.

37. An analysis of the Xinhua transcript provided in Rick Noack, "China's Official Release on Kim Jong Un's Visit, Annotated," Washington Post (March 28, 2018).

38. "N. Korean Diplomat Reaffirms Commitment to 'Phase, Synchronized' Denuclearization," Yonhap (April 10, 2018).

39. Abigail Tracy, "Not Exactly the 'A-Team': Is Trump Getting Played By Kim Jong Un?," Vanity Fair (March 9, 2018), www.vanityfair.com/news/2018/03/donald-trump-kim-jong-un-north-korea-negotiations.

40. Portions of this section originally appeared in Van Jackson, "What Kim Jong Un Wants from Trump," POLITICO Magazine (April 30, 2018), www.politico.com /magazine/story/2018/04/30/what-kim-jong-un-wants-from-trump-218115.

41. "U.S.–North Korea Summit Coverage," *Cuomo Prime Time*, transcript, CNN.com (June 12, 2018), http://edition.cnn.com/TRANSCRIPTS/1806/12/CPT.02.html.
42. As quoted in Helene Cooper and Mark Landler, "Trump's Promises to Kim Jong Un Leave U.S. and Allies Scrambling," *New York Times* (June 15, 2018).
43. "Banks Preparing for Possible Resumption of Inter-Korean Projects," Yonhap (June 14, 2018).
44. "Remarks by President Trump and Chairman Kim Jong Un of the State Affairs Commission of the Democratic People's Republic of Korea Before Bilateral Meeting," Capella Hotel, Singapore (June 11, 2018), www.whitehouse.gov/briefings-statements/remarks-president-trump-chairman-kim-jong-un-state-affairs-commission-democratic-peoples-republic-korea-bilateral-meeting/.

Chapter 10

1. Friedman, "Lindsey Graham."
2. Friedman, "Senator James Risch Explains His Warning About 'Biblical' Conflict with North Korea."
3. Blair, "Chairman's Message."
4. Kori Schake, "The North Korea Debate Sounds Eerily Familiar," *The Atlantic* (December 8, 2017), www.theatlantic.com/international/archive/2017/12/north-korea-iraq-war-george-w-bush-trump/547796/.
5. These indicators originally appeared in Jackson, "Want to Strike North Korea?"
6. US Department of Defense official, February 9, 2018.
7. As quoted in Luis Sanchez, "White House: 'Maximum Pressure' Campaign on North Korea is Working," *The Hill* (March 27, 2018), http://thehill.com/home news/administration/380585-white-house-maximum-pressure-campaign-on-north-korea-is-working.
8. "Transcript of the Press Conference by the Secretary-General with the Prime Minister of Sweden," Stockholm, Sweden (April 23, 2018), www.un.org/sg/en/content/sg/press-encounter/2018-04-23/transcript-press-conference-secretary-general-prime-minister.
9. Lawrence Freedman, "General Deterrence and the Balance of Power," *Review of International Studies* Vol. 15, no. 2 (1989), p. 205.
10. David Kang, "International Relations Theory and the Second Korean War," *International Studies Quarterly* Vol. 47, no. 3 (2003), pp. 301–24.
11. These requirements were initially proposed in Van Jackson, "Preventing Nuclear War with North Korea," *Foreign Affairs* (September 11, 2016), www.foreignaffairs.com/articles/north-korea/2016-09-11/preventing-nuclear-war-north-korea.
12. William J. Perry, "How to Contain North Korea," *POLITICO Magazine* (January 10, 2016), www.politico.com/magazine/story/2016/01/north-korea-nuclear-weapons-contain-213516.

INDEX